PAT BROWN, MBA

# Financial Literacy For Pilots

*"Navigate Your Money Like You Navigate the Skies – Confidently, Strategically, and With Purpose"*

ABRAM 47 BROWN

*First published by AbramBrown47 2025*



*First edition*

*ISBN: 978-1-967737-30-7*

*This book was professionally typeset on Reedsy.*
*Find out more at reedsy.com*

# Contents

# Preface

**Why I Wrote This Book—and Why You're Holding It Now**

There's a moment in every pilot's life that doesn't get talked about. It's not a mechanical failure. It's not a diverted route. It's not even that surprise schedule change that messes with your entire month.

It's that quiet moment, alone in a hotel room, or halfway through a four-day trip, when you check your bank account—or open your retirement app—and think:

> "How am I flying 90 hours a month and still not financially free?"

If that sounds familiar, you're not alone. And you're not broken.

You're just like thousands of other pilots who've spent years mastering the cockpit but never got a real education in how to fly their financial lives.

I wrote *Financial Literacy For Pilots* because I've sat across from pilots at every stage of their career—regional first officers barely covering their bills, major airline captains making $300,000 a year and still feeling broke, and retired legends realizing they're not sure if they can afford to stay retired.

And every single one of them has said some version of the same thing:

> "I wish someone had taught me this stuff sooner."

Well, this book is that "someone." And that "sooner" is now.

## This Book Is for You If…

- You're 27 and just graduated from flight school, carrying six figures in student loan debt and wondering how you'll ever get ahead.
- You're 38 and finally making good money, but unsure where it's all going—or how to make it work smarter for your future.
- You're 45 and juggling kids, mortgage payments, fatigue, and crash pad costs, all while trying to figure out how to invest, save, and not screw it up.
- You're 60 and thinking about retirement, but unsure whether you've built a glidepath or a cliff.
- You're a spouse or partner, watching your favorite pilot provide so much for everyone else—while quietly sacrificing their own peace of mind.

Wherever you are—this book is for you.

And not just because you need a Roth IRA or insurance policy or budgeting system.

Because you deserve to feel *in control.* You deserve to feel *calm.* You deserve to feel *clear-headed* about your future—and proud of the legacy you're building for your family, your crew, and yourself.

## What Makes Pilots Different?

Pilots aren't like most professionals.

You don't punch a clock. You bid lines. You don't have a normal 9-to-5 income. You have base pay, per diem, profit sharing, and a bonus check that shows up out of nowhere when the airline beats projections.

You can't just call in sick for two weeks to fix your finances. You have to plan midair.

Your schedule is irregular. Your time is spoken for. And your career has a *hard stop* at age 65—by federal law. There's no "just keep working part-time" for a few years like in other careers. When your last flight is logged, you're done.

That's a very specific challenge. But it's also a powerful opportunity.

Because with the right plan, the right system, and the right mindset, pilots can build extraordinary wealth. Not because you get rich overnight—but because you have the discipline, structure, and long-term thinking that financial success *requires.*

This book meets you there.

## What This Book Covers

We're going far beyond "save money and spend less."

You'll learn how to:

- Automate your finances around your bid schedule
- Max out your retirement accounts—without guesswork
- Protect your income from disability or grounding
- Create a budget that actually fits your aviation lifestyle
- Avoid the scams and hype that target high-income professionals
- Plan for retirement with clarity—including what happens after the FAA Age 65 rule kicks in
- Coordinate Social Security, Medicare, pensions, and your 401(k)
- Teach your kids (or grandkids) the financial literacy you never got
- Build a legacy that lasts—whether that's for your family, your community, or the next generation of aviators

Each chapter is a conversation. Not a lecture.

No fluff. No judgment. No fancy financial jargon.

Just real talk. Real strategies. And real stories from pilots just like you.

## What I Hope You'll Feel

By the time you finish this book, I don't want you to feel smarter about money—I want you to feel stronger in your own skin.

I want you to feel like your paycheck isn't something you *chase* anymore—it's something you *command.*

I want you to look at your retirement savings and feel calm, not confused.

I want you to walk through your front door after a long trip, kiss your kids or your partner or your dog, and think, *"This is the life I built—with intention, not accident."*

You deserve that. You've earned that.

## A Final Word Before We Take Off

This book isn't about being perfect. It's about being *prepared.*

You don't have to be a CPA or financial advisor to build wealth.

You just need to do what you already do every time you take off:

Follow the checklist. Trust the system. Make small corrections early.

You've already mastered the skies.

Now it's time to master your money—with the same precision, discipline, and confidence that made you a pilot in the first place.

Strap in.

This is your financial flight plan.

Let's take control of it—together.

—Pat Brown, MBA

Financial Advisor | Former Athlete | Advocate for Financial Literacy in Aviation

# How to Use This Book

**Your Personal Flight Manual for Financial Confidence**

This book is not meant to be read cover to cover in one sitting like a novel.

It's designed to be flown like a checklist. A briefing packet. A toolkit. A resource.

Something you can return to again and again—at every altitude of your career.

Whether you're 28 and still in a crash pad, 45 and balancing family and finances, or 64 and wondering how to land your last year right—this book meets you there.

Here's how to get the most out of it.

## 1. Start With the Chapters That Speak to You Most

This isn't school. There's no quiz. You don't need to read Chapter 1 to understand Chapter 12.

Flip through the table of contents and ask yourself:

- "What's my biggest financial question right now?"
- "What do I feel the least confident about?"
- "Where do I keep telling myself, 'I'll figure that out later'?"

Start there. Bookmark it. Highlight it. Dog-ear it. Make it yours.

## 2. Read With a Pen—Not Just Your Eyes

You're not a passive reader. You're a captain.

You're here to take control.

Underline the phrases that hit home. Circle the action steps. Write notes in the margins. Ask questions to bring to your financial advisor, spouse, or fellow pilot.

This book isn't just about information—it's about transformation.

And transformation starts when you *engage* with it.

## 3. Use the "Financial Preflight Checklist" at the End of Each Chapter

At the end of every chapter, you'll find clear, bold calls to action.

Not vague advice—actual steps:

- "Download your last three months of spending."
- "Schedule a 15-minute 'money preflight check' every Sunday."
- "Automate $500/month into your Roth IRA before your next bid cycle."

Take one step. Just one.

Then take another next week. That's how you build momentum—and money confidence.

## 4. Don't Try to Do Everything at Once

Pilots know: too much information, too fast = mental overload.

This isn't about doing *everything.* It's about doing *the right next thing.*

If you just read one chapter a week and apply the advice, in one year your financial life will look completely different.

Give yourself grace. But don't let yourself off the hook. Small consistent action > big overwhelming plans.

## 5. Read With Your Crew in Mind

If you have a spouse or partner—read it together.

If you have kids—start a conversation.

If you're part of a union or pilot group—bring a copy to the table.

This book isn't just for you. It's for the people who count on you.

And it's for the version of you who doesn't want to feel confused, scattered, or guilty about money anymore.

## 6. Return to It at Every Career Milestone

This isn't a one-and-done read. It's your flight manual for a lifetime.

Come back to it when:

- You get your first upgrade or bonus
- You hit 10,000 flight hours and start wondering about exit planning
- You're considering buying a second home or relocating after retirement
- You're helping your kids fill out FAFSA or open a bank account
- You've had a hard month and need to reconnect with your "why"

Just like you wouldn't fly without reviewing your preflight, you shouldn't navigate life transitions without revisiting your financial plan.

This book helps you do both.

## 7. Make It Part of Your Life—Not Just Your Library

You can leave this book on a shelf. Or you can let it change how you think, plan, talk, and act around money.

Read it slowly. Reread it often. Talk about it with others.

Write your own notes in the margins.

Track your progress in a notebook, spreadsheet, or app.

Let it be more than just a book. Let it be a turning point.

**Final Thought:**

You didn't earn your wings to live stressed about spreadsheets.

You didn't train thousands of hours to wonder if you can retire with dignity.

You didn't spend your career lifting others to feel grounded by financial confusion.

This book is your permission slip to chart a new course.

So… grab your pen. Flip to the chapter that hits home.

And take that first step toward confidence, clarity, and calm.

You've got this.

Let's fly.

# About the Author

**Pat Brown, MBA**, is a financial educator, advisor, former professional athlete, and lifelong advocate for clarity in money matters. After playing Division I football at the University of Kansas and briefly competing in the Canadian Football League, Pat transitioned from the field to the financial world—bringing with him the discipline of a playbook, the vision of a coach, and the empathy of someone who knows what it feels like to start from scratch.

Over the past two decades, Pat has guided hundreds of professionals—athletes, doctors, pilots, coaches, and business owners—through the intimidating terrain of budgeting, investing, insurance, and legacy planning. His work has helped families build wealth, avoid financial mistakes, and gain confidence in their financial lives without guilt, shame, or jargon.

What makes Pat different is his ability to teach finance like a teammate—not a salesman. He breaks down complex topics using locker room language, relatable stories, and real-world tools. He believes financial literacy should feel like empowerment, not punishment.

He's the founder of multiple financial literacy platforms, including:

- **FinancialLiteracyForNIL.com**
- **FinancialLiteracyForDoctors.com**
- **FinancialLiteracyForCollegeCoaches.com**
- **FinancialLiteracyForAttorneys.com**
- **FinancialLiteracyForDentists.com**

...and now, *Financial Literacy For Pilots*—his tribute to the hard-working, high-performing, high-stress world of aviation professionals who have spent a lifetime lifting others but may still feel financially grounded themselves.

Pat is a husband, father of two daughters, and a passionate speaker who's presented to hospital boards, student-athlete groups, university teams, and retirement associations. He currently serves as a wealth manager and sits on several community and hospital boards.

Whether you're cruising at 35,000 feet or grounded by questions about what's next, Pat's mission is clear:

**To help you fly your financial life with intention, confidence, and control—on every leg of your journey.**

# Pilots Are Trained to Handle Emergencies—But What About Their Finances?

You're trained to handle the unexpected. Engine failures. Weather systems. Medical emergencies. You troubleshoot complex systems at 35,000 feet, stay calm under pressure, and guide hundreds of lives safely through the skies.

But when it comes to managing your own financial life—budgeting, investing, retirement planning, taxes, or insurance—you may feel like you're flying blind.

This isn't a judgment. It's a systemic gap.

Most highly trained professionals—especially pilots—were never taught how money really works.

There's no *Financial Navigation 101* in flight school.

There's no financial module in recurrent training.

There's no standard checklist for building wealth between now and age 65.

So it's no surprise that even seasoned captains often admit:

- "I make six figures but feel like I have nothing to show for it."
- "I don't know if I'm saving enough—or too much."
- "I've never really understood how taxes, investing, or pensions fit together."
- "I don't trust financial advisors, so I just do nothing."
- "I'm not sure what life looks like after I hang up the wings."

And yet—pilots are uniquely equipped to succeed financially.

You understand systems. You follow procedures. You manage risk. You review data. You think long-term. You don't panic under pressure. All of those traits—when applied to money—can make you a powerful financial operator.

## When You Apply Pilot Logic to Your Finances

- **Budgeting** becomes a fuel calculation—how far can I go with what I've got?
- **Investing** becomes altitude control—what's the best way to climb over time without stalling out?
- **Retirement planning** becomes a flight plan—what's my route, what are the waypoints, and where are the alternate airports?
- **Taxes** become headwinds—sometimes unavoidable, but you can plan for them and still stay on course.
- **Insurance** becomes redundancy—systems that don't just reduce risk but give you the confidence to keep flying through the unknown.

You don't need to become a financial expert. But you do need to think about money like you would any flight: with awareness, preparation, and checklists.

## What's At Risk If You Don't

Without financial literacy—even brilliant pilots can end up:

- Trapped in flying schedules or bases they've outgrown—because of financial obligations
- Living well below their income potential—due to disorganized finances or fear
- Paying excessive interest, fees, or penalties—just from lack of planning
- Missing early investment windows that could have compounded into

generational wealth
- Failing to maximize their airline benefits or union plans
- Reaching age 65 unsure if they can truly afford to retire—or if they even want to

And that's not just a personal problem—it's an industry-wide issue when seasoned aviators can't retire comfortably or mentor the next generation because they're still chasing financial stability.

## What's Possible If You Do

With strong financial literacy, pilots can:

- Build wealth on autopilot with confidence and structure
- Design a career path that supports their family, health, and long-term vision
- Take breaks or early retirement on their own terms
- Start aviation businesses, charities, or passion projects after retirement
- Sleep better on overnights knowing their money is working for them—not the other way around
- Model smart financial habits to their crew, kids, and community

You don't need hype. You don't need to become a day trader. You don't need another online "hot tip."

You need clear, honest, checklisted financial guidance—designed for the lifestyle, pressures, and challenges that only pilots understand.

## Why This Book Exists

This book isn't just about numbers. It's about *altitude*.

Financial literacy gives you freedom to navigate career turbulence, clarity to make high-stakes decisions, and control over the next 10, 20, or 30 years of your life.

It gives you permission to plan boldly, spend wisely, invest early, and land smoothly—on your terms.

Because when pilots master their money, they don't just retire well.

They fly smarter. They mentor better. They live freer. They become the kind of captain others aspire to follow—not just in the cockpit, but in life.

And that's a legacy worth building.

# Why I Wrote This Book

I didn't start my career as a pilot. But I've spent more than two decades working closely with them—as a financial advisor, educator, and advocate for financial literacy. And over the years, I've seen a pattern that's too consistent to ignore:

**Pilots—some of the most capable, disciplined, and focused professionals I've ever known—are often underprepared when it comes to money.**

That disconnect has stayed with me.

It's not because pilots are careless. Far from it.

It's because the financial world often speaks a language that doesn't align with how pilots think. It's filled with vague suggestions, emotion-driven headlines, product pitches, and generic advice that's hard to trust—and harder to apply.

Meanwhile, pilots are looking for logic. For checklists. For systems. For strategy. You don't need fluff or fear. You need a clear route and a safe approach.

That's why I made it my mission to help bridge the gap between the cockpit and the balance sheet.

## I Believe This:

**Pilots deserve financial education that matches their mindset.**

You've trained for decades to think clearly under pressure. You live by procedure. You operate at the highest standards. Your financial education should do the same.

**You shouldn't have to figure this out alone.**

No one hands you a money manual when you earn your ATP license. And most financial content—whether online or on TV—either talks down to you or tries to sell you something. This book is different. It's built to support, not sell.

**When pilots thrive financially, everyone benefits.**

I've seen too many aviators held back by money stress—unable to retire on time, say no to burnout, or leave something meaningful behind. But I've also seen the opposite: pilots who took control of their financial life, and used that freedom to launch businesses, mentor others, support causes they care about, or simply spend more time with the people they love.

That's the goal.

This book isn't about perfection. It's about power—the kind that comes from knowing how to manage your income, plan for the future, and weather financial turbulence without panic.

This isn't just a job for me. It's personal. I believe financial literacy is the runway to freedom, legacy, and peace of mind. I believe every pilot has earned the right to understand money on their own terms—not as a source of stress, but as a tool for purpose.

If this book helps even one pilot fly smarter with their finances and land retirement with clarity and confidence, every page will have been worth it.

I'm honored to walk this journey with you.

Let's build financial altitude—on purpose, with precision, and for the long haul.

**— Pat Brown, MBA**

*Financial Literacy Advocate*

info@financialliteracyforpilots.com

www.financialliteracyforpilots.com

# Pilots Don't Wing It—And Neither Should Your Finances

Pilots don't fly by instinct alone. You're trained to plan precisely, follow checklists, respond to turbulence with calm, and execute complex procedures under pressure. You don't guess. You verify. You adjust. You rely on systems.

That same mindset—the one that gets you from takeoff to landing safely—can be your greatest advantage in building long-term financial success.

This book isn't about hype, hope, or hot stock tips. It's about **structure, systems, and sustainability**. It's about approaching your financial life like you'd approach a flight plan or pre-check procedure—with clarity, discipline, and a mission to arrive safely at your destination.

Here's how to apply a pilot's mindset to money—and how this book is built to help.

## 1. Start With a Clear Flight Plan

Before you ever step into the cockpit, you know your destination. You plan your route, fuel needs, alternates, and airspace transitions.

**Your financial life needs the same clarity.**

- Are you flying toward early retirement?
- A future free from debt?
- Buying your dream home or supporting your kids through college?
- Building generational wealth?
- Leaving a meaningful legacy?

Start by identifying your financial destination. What does success look like for you—on your terms?

When your goals are clear, every financial move becomes more purposeful. You're not just saving or investing "because you should"—you're doing it to stay on course.

## 2. Think in Systems, Not Silos

An airplane is a finely tuned system. The engines, avionics, hydraulics, fuel, and navigation don't operate in isolation. Every part impacts the rest.

**Your money is the same.**

- Budgeting affects how much you can invest.
- Taxes affect your retirement decisions.
- Insurance protects the assets you've built.
- Your career path impacts your income trajectory.

In this book, we approach your finances as a **system**—interconnected, responsive, and needing regular coordination. You'll see how every part of your money ecosystem touches the others.

When you think in systems, you build smarter. And stronger.

## 3. Don't Wait for Perfect—Iterate

As a pilot, you know: the weather isn't always ideal. The data isn't always complete. The route changes midair.

You adapt. You improvise. You keep flying.

Yet when it comes to money, many pilots get stuck in what we call **financial paralysis**—waiting for the perfect time to invest, the perfect advisor, the perfect job, the perfect plan.

Here's the truth: perfection isn't coming.

**Instead, treat your finances like a flight plan.**

- File the plan.
- Adjust along the way.
- Stay flexible but intentional.

Start with a simple budget. Begin investing even if you're not 100% sure. Revisit and revise. Think "version 1.0" now, and "version 2.0" next quarter. Iterate your way to excellence.

## 4. Automate Like a Flight System

Pilots trust systems. Auto-throttles. VNAV. Automation isn't laziness—it's efficiency. It frees up cognitive space for the unexpected.

Your finances should work the same way.

**Automate what you can:**

- Retirement contributions
- Investment allocations
- Loan payments
- Emergency fund savings
- Credit card payments

The more you automate, the more consistent your progress will be—even during high workload months or surprise expenses. Think of automation as your personal copilot—it won't fly the whole plane, but it'll keep you steady on the route.

## 5. Run Your Numbers—But Fly With Purpose

Aviation is a numbers game—fuel flow, crosswind components, weights and balances—but the mission behind every flight matters just as much.

Same with money.

Yes, you need to know your net worth. Your tax bracket. Your retirement savings rate. But your **why** is what really matters.

- Is it more time with family?
- Freedom to say no to burnout?
- The ability to give back?
- Peace of mind that your spouse and kids are taken care of?

Let your values define your financial destination. Then let the math guide you there.

## 6. Monitor and Maintain

Just like an aircraft needs routine maintenance, your finances do too. Ignore the small stuff, and the system fails later.

**Do your monthly preflight:**

- Review spending
- Track investment performance
- Update your goals
- Revisit your insurance
- Check your credit

Your financial life isn't a one-and-done checklist. It's a flight plan you review regularly and adjust based on changing conditions.

A well-maintained aircraft doesn't just stay airworthy—it performs better, lasts longer, and gives you peace of mind.

## 7. Call in the Right Crew

You don't fly solo on every mission. Some require a full flight crew. Same with money.

**Knowing when to call in help is a sign of strength, not weakness.**

- A **financial advisor** helps coordinate your overall strategy, investments, retirement planning, and long-term vision.

- A **CPA** ensures tax efficiency and helps you stay out of IRS turbulence.
- An **estate attorney** protects your legacy and ensures your will, trust, and documents are in order.
- An **insurance specialist** can fine-tune your coverage—disability, life, liability, and long-term care.

You don't have to know everything. You just need to know where to turn.

## In Short:

- Define your **financial destination**
- See money as a **system**, not a list of one-off choices
- **Iterate** instead of chasing perfection
- **Automate** your progress wherever possible
- Balance **logic and math** with **purpose and values**
- Commit to **routine maintenance**
- Build your **team**—and fly with confidence

**Approach your financial life like the biggest, most meaningful flight you'll ever take—because it is.**

You're the pilot. You're the flight planner. You're the crew. You're the one who will feel the turbulence—and enjoy the view at cruising altitude.

So let's make sure you arrive where you want to be—with fuel to spare, systems in check, and a clear runway ahead.

# Let's Get Real for a Second

Pilots are some of the most disciplined, capable, and detail-driven professionals in the world. You spend years mastering aircraft systems, aerodynamics, emergency protocols, and crew resource management. You train harder and longer than most people realize—and then you spend your career responsible for lives in motion, high above the earth, under constant scrutiny and ever-evolving regulations.

But let's be honest about something that doesn't get talked about in flight briefings or simulator check rides:

**Too many pilots are financially underprepared.**

Not because you're reckless or uninterested.

But because no one ever taught you how this stuff works.

You didn't learn financial planning at flight school. You didn't get a course on investing during your airline ground school. There's no "Money Management 101" between your ATP and your type rating. Yet the decisions you make about your finances will determine whether you can retire on time, take care of your family, buy that vacation home, or walk away from the cockpit with peace of mind.

This book—and this chapter—is about calling out that gap. Not to shame anyone. Not to point fingers. But to help you stop flying blind when it comes to your money.

## What Do We Mean by Financial Literacy?

Financial literacy doesn't mean you need to become a stock trader, CPA, or real estate expert. It doesn't mean following every market update or knowing every tax code by heart.

It means being able to answer questions like:

- Am I building net worth, or just collecting paychecks?
- What happens if I can't pass my medical tomorrow?
- Do I know the difference between my 401(k), Roth IRA, and deferred comp plan?
- Am I prepared for retirement—or just hoping things work out?
- Do I have the right insurance, or am I wasting money on the wrong kind?
- Am I letting lifestyle creep drain the financial runway I'm working so hard to build?

Financial literacy is about understanding how **money flows through your life**—so you can direct it instead of being directed by it.

It's knowing how to:

- Read your own net worth statement
- Build a spending plan that reflects your priorities
- Evaluate the true cost of debt, taxes, and investment fees
- Protect your family, your income, and your legacy
- Make money decisions with confidence—not guesswork

And above all: it's about using your hard-earned income to create freedom—not just fancier stuff.

## Why Pilots Are Uniquely Vulnerable

There are specific reasons why pilots—especially commercial and corporate aviators—are particularly at risk when it comes to financial stress or missed opportunities.

*1. High Income, High Pressure*

Pilots often earn strong incomes—but it comes with demanding schedules, fatigue, relocation stress, and mental load. That income might be irregular (charter or contract work), vary by seniority (union-based pay), or be affected by medical status. When you earn a lot but don't plan a lot, it's easy to fall into the "I'll figure it out later" trap.

*2. The FAA Age 65 Rule*

Unlike many professionals who can ease into retirement, commercial pilots hit a hard stop. Once you turn 65, you're done in the cockpit—whether you're ready or not. That's a huge pressure point. Without careful planning, it creates financial turbulence at the exact moment you should be gliding into your golden years.

*3. Identity = Pilot*

Flying isn't just a job—it's an identity. And when your identity is tied up in your career, it's easy to delay planning for life outside the flight deck. You tell yourself you'll deal with finances "after upgrade," "after this bid," "after we move hubs." But someday comes fast—and you don't want to find yourself financially unprepared when it does.

*4. Complex Compensation*

Pilots often have access to multiple types of retirement and benefit plans: 401(k), profit sharing, deferred comp, stock purchase plans, per diem structures, HSA, life insurance, and more. But if you don't understand how they work, you may leave thousands (or hundreds of thousands) on the table over your career.

### *5. Trust Issues—and Time Constraints*

You work in an industry built on precision and accountability. So when financial advisors start throwing buzzwords and product pitches your way, it's easy to tune out or distrust the whole process. Add in a rotating schedule and family demands, and financial planning becomes just another thing to "get around to later."

## What the Gap Looks Like in Real Life

This isn't theory. These are real stories from real pilots:

- The 59-year-old senior captain who never saved outside his 401(k)—and now realizes he'll need to fly until the last legal day just to cover basic retirement needs.
- The 38-year-old first officer who keeps getting promoted but can't figure out where the money goes every month.
- The charter pilot who got a $200,000 tax bill because he didn't set aside money from his 1099 income.
- The couple (both pilots) with strong household income—but zero estate planning, mismatched insurance, and no idea how to talk about money without arguing.
- The newly retired pilot who was forced to sell his rental property at a loss because he didn't plan for income replacement after losing his medical.

This book exists so that *your* story doesn't end up on that list.

## Why This Isn't Taught (And Why It Should Be)

We don't expect pilots to figure out takeoff procedures on their own. We train. We brief. We rehearse emergencies.

But when it comes to finances? We're told:

"Just contribute to your 401(k) and hope it works out."

"Buy a house as soon as you can."

"Use a Roth IRA if you can."

"Get insurance—but don't overpay."

That's like saying, "Just keep the shiny side up and the greasy side down." It sounds good. But it doesn't help in real life.

**Financial literacy should be part of every pilot's career training.** Until it is, this book is here to close that gap.

## What Happens When Pilots Gain Financial Clarity

When you know how money works—and how it works for *you*—everything shifts.

- You make better career decisions (because you're not just chasing pay)
- You create options for your family
- You invest with confidence
- You stop reacting to money—and start directing it
- You stop "hoping things work out" and start designing a life that works on purpose

Pilots don't fly without a plan. You shouldn't retire without one either.

## What This Book Will Help You Do

This isn't about turning you into a financial guru. It's about giving you:

- Plain-language breakdowns of your 401(k), IRA, HSA, insurance, and benefits
- Strategies for managing variable income, bonuses, and stock options
- A toolkit for budgeting, saving, and investing—even if you're just starting
- Guidance for preparing for retirement, healthcare costs, and Social

Security
- Red flags to avoid—scams, overpriced products, lifestyle inflation
- Questions to ask any financial advisor, CPA, or insurance agent
- A way to align your financial decisions with your values, goals, and legacy

## Closing the Gap—One Pilot at a Time

I've spent over two decades helping professionals across industries, including many pilots, navigate their financial lives. I've seen the pressure, the stress, the missed opportunities—and the breakthroughs.

When a pilot takes control of their finances, it's not just about dollars.

It's about confidence.

It's about freedom.

It's about the ability to say "no" to burnout and "yes" to what matters.

**That's why this book exists.**

To close the gap.

To replace guesswork with guidance.

To help you fly your financial life with the same confidence and control you bring to every flight.

Let's chart your course—together. You've got the tools. You've got the discipline.

Now let's give you the clarity.

**Welcome aboard. Let's build a plan that flies.**

# Part I: Pre-Flight Checks – Starting Out Strong

This section lays the foundation for a financially successful career in aviation. Just like every flight begins with a careful inspection and checklist, your financial journey as a pilot must begin with awareness, preparation, and intentionality. This section is designed for aspiring aviators, student pilots, and early-career professionals navigating the high costs of flight school, low initial pay, and the realities of building hours.

You'll learn how to evaluate the true cost of becoming a pilot—including licensing, ratings, housing, and relocation—and how to fund your journey with smart strategies that won't leave you financially grounded for years. We explore everything from student loans and side hustles to crash pads and budgeting during flight training.

Credit-building, income planning, and tax basics are covered in real-world language, helping you set strong habits before your first airline paycheck hits. You'll discover how to make every dollar of early income count—even if it's coming from instructing, regional flying, or ferry work.

Whether you're flying props or simulators right now, **Part I** helps you build a financial checklist that will serve you from day one to retirement. It's not just about surviving your training years—it's about taking control early so you can soar later.

# Chapter 1: The True Cost of Becoming a Pilot

Let's start with a truth most aviation brochures won't print in bold: Becoming a pilot is expensive. Not kind-of expensive. Not manageable-with-a-couple-scholarships expensive. We're talking six figures, upfront, long before you ever touch the throttle in a commercial jet. And yet, thousands of pilots push through anyway—not because it's cheap or easy, but because the skies call to them. If you're one of them, you deserve to go in with your eyes wide open and your finances tight.

This chapter is about mapping the full financial runway before takeoff. We're not just talking about tuition or fuel. We're talking opportunity cost, insurance, debt structure, time, and everything you give up along the way. And most importantly, how to manage it like a pro.

**Flight School: Sticker Price vs. Real Price**

You see the ads: "Become a pilot for $80,000!" But once you add check rides, testing fees, ground school, simulator hours, examiner fees, medical exams, headset, iPad, and travel? You're easily looking at $100,000–$120,000, minimum. More if you're at an aviation university or paying out-of-pocket rather than using a bundled program.

Break it down:

- Private Pilot License (PPL): $10,000–$15,000
- Instrument Rating: $8,000–$10,000
- Commercial License: $20,000–$30,000

- Multi-Engine Rating: $5,000–$10,000
- Certified Flight Instructor (CFI): $5,000–$8,000
- Time-building to 1,500 hours: Variable, often unpaid or break-even

Each step isn't just a credential. It's a cost center.

**Financing Your Training: Loans, Grants, and Pay-As-You-Go**

Most pilots don't have $100K lying around. So you finance. But aviation-specific loans can come with high interest rates, limited deferment options, and a lot less flexibility than federal student loans. There's often no income-driven repayment, no forgiveness, and minimal grace periods.

Compare options:

- Sallie Mae Career Training Loans: High interest, 5–20 years
- LendingTree or pilot-specific lenders: Sometimes flexible, but usually private
- VA Benefits: Incredible if you're eligible
- Part 141 schools with job pipelines: Some have tuition reimbursement or financing with partner airlines

But remember—if you're financing $100,000 at 9% over 15 years, you're paying over $180,000 total. Interest is not a footnote. It's half your journey.

**The Time Cost of Building Hours**

You need 1,500 hours to get your ATP. Most instructors earn $20–$30/hour—only when flying. Time between students isn't paid. And many pilots log hours flying jumpers, towing banners, ferrying planes, or flight instructing in rural towns far from family or support.

In real terms: you may earn $20K–$30K/year during this time. You'll also be covering rent, food, transportation, and loan payments. The math is tight. You'll likely live lean. It's normal. It's temporary. But it needs to be planned for.

**Opportunity Cost: What You Give Up to Fly**

Let's be honest: pursuing aviation means delaying other careers. A college grad in tech or finance may earn $70K–$90K out of school. You might make $22K while instructing. That difference compounds fast.

Even a two-year delay on investing can mean hundreds of thousands less by retirement. But if you treat flying like a career and your finances like a business, you can catch up. The key? Awareness and intention.

**Pros and Cons: Aviation Schools vs. Universities vs. Self-Structured Paths**

**Aviation University Pros**

- Structured pipeline
- Networking
- College degree

**Cons**

- Most expensive
- Slow path to 1,500 hours
- Degree may not apply outside aviation

**Part 141/141+ Airline Pathway Schools Pros**

- Faster to hours
- Job placement pipelines
- Airline tuition reimbursement programs

**Cons**

- May lack college degree
- High pressure, fast pace
- Contract obligations

**Self-Structured/Modular Paths Pros**

- Cheapest overall

- Flexibility
- Can work while training

**Cons**

- Takes longer
- Harder to build network
- No job guarantees

**Action Steps for Early-Career Pilots**

- Create a full cost breakdown of your training path
- Research all financing options—grants, VA, sponsorship, employer programs
- Estimate monthly loan repayment and compare to projected instructor pay
- Set up a basic budget BEFORE you start training
- Start building credit early with a secured card or travel card

**Plain-Language Money Lessons Nobody Taught You**

- **Loan interest compounds DAILY.** Even small deferments or missed payments snowball.
- **Per diem isn't free money.** It helps with expenses, but don't treat it like a raise.
- **Crash pads and roommates can save thousands.** Don't rush into long-term leases.
- **Just because it's a "dream job" doesn't mean you can skip the math.** Financial pressure kills passion.
- **Make money decisions based on data, not desire.** The cockpit is emotional. Your finances shouldn't be.

**Real-Life Scenario: Jason, Age 26**

Jason finished a university aviation program with $135K in student loans. He got his CFI and moved to Arizona to instruct. He makes about $25/hour, but only logs 18 flight hours/week. His gross pay is under $2,000/month. Rent and living expenses are $1,400/month. Loan payments? $1,200/month.

He called it a "dream job." Three months in, he calls it "barely surviving."

With a little coaching, Jason moved into a crash pad ($400/month), picked up extra hours on the weekend, and switched to income-based repayment on his federal loans. He started tracking spending and realized he was spending $300/month on fast food. Not anymore. Within six months, he created breathing room.

**You Don't Have to Be Broke to Build Hours**

Flying lean doesn't have to mean living in chaos. With structure, clarity, and strategy, you can keep your eyes on the prize and your finances steady. The trick is getting honest about the full cost early.

You don't need to fear the price of flying. You just need to plan for it.

**Call to Action:**

Make one financial move before wheels-up tomorrow:

- Price out your full training cost
- Build a simple budget in Excel or an app
- List your current debts, interest rates, and payment status
- Pick one thing to cut or one thing to automate

**Just one.** Then do another next week. Small moves. Big momentum.

**Final Word:**

This chapter wasn't written to scare you. It was written to equip you. If you know the cost, you can plan the course.

You didn't earn your wings to live paycheck to paycheck.

You didn't pour your soul into this career to be stressed about groceries.

Own your financial cockpit. Take the controls.

You can be broke today and still be building wealth tomorrow.

Your future self will thank you.

So will your bank account.

So will your sanity.

# Chapter 2: Funding Your Flight Training – Loans, Scholarships, and Alternatives

Let's not sugarcoat this: flight training is one of the most expensive career onramps in existence. Unlike many professional paths that offer subsidized education, tuition waivers, or federal support, becoming a pilot often feels like financing your dreams on a credit card with turbulence ahead. But it doesn't have to be that way. This chapter is here to talk plainly, honestly, and strategically about how to fund your flight training without crashing your financial future.

If you're reading this, you might already be tens of thousands into the journey. Maybe you're looking at that mountain of flight hours still to come and wondering how you'll afford it. Or maybe you're at the very beginning, comparing loans and scholarships and asking yourself: is this even possible?

Yes. It is. But not without a plan.

**Understanding the Full Scope of Flight Training Costs**

Before we talk money sources, let's define the mission. Here's a simplified version of what most pilots need to reach 1,500 hours:

- Private Pilot License (PPL): $10,000 - $15,000
- Instrument Rating: $8,000 - $10,000
- Commercial License: $20,000 - $30,000
- Multi-Engine Add-on: $5,000 - $10,000
- Certified Flight Instructor (CFI): $5,000 - $8,000

- CFI-I + MEI: $3,000 - $8,000
- Time-building to 1,500 hours: Variable (often done instructing, which may pay just enough to get by)

Total: Easily $80,000 - $120,000+

And that doesn't include living expenses, travel, examiner fees, headset, charts, apps, uniforms, or insurance. Knowing the real number is your first step in taking ownership.

**Financing Options: A Real-World Breakdown**

Let's talk about what pilots actually use to fund training:

1. **Personal Savings**
2. If you've got it, great. But most don't. If you do, still be strategic. Don't blow your entire safety net in six months. Spread it, budget it, and supplement it with other options.
3. **Federal Student Loans (if you attend a degree-granting university)**
4. Available only at accredited schools. Better terms than private loans, with options like:

- Income-Driven Repayment (IDR)
- Public Service Loan Forgiveness (for some VA-eligible or public service roles)
- Deferment and forbearance flexibility

Cons:

- Slower timeline
- More expensive schools
- May still need private loans to cover full costs

1. **Private Loans**
2. These are the go-to for non-university Part 141 and 61 schools.

Options include:

- Sallie Mae Career Training Loans
- Wells Fargo (less common now)
- Discover and Citizens Bank
- Credit unions or niche aviation lenders

Key tips:

- Shop around and compare APRs
- Know the repayment terms: deferment, interest-only, or full repayment during school?
- Watch origination fees and variable interest rates

1. **Flight School-Sponsored Financing**
2. Some schools partner with lenders. Be cautious:

- Are they marking up interest?
- Are there restrictions if you drop out or pause training?
- Is there any forgiveness or deferment flexibility?

1. **Airline Cadet Programs**
2. More carriers are investing in talent pipelines. Some offer partial reimbursement, tuition deferral, or conditional job offers.

Examples:

- American Airlines Cadet Academy
- United Aviate
- SkyWest Pilot Pathway Program
- Republic Airways LIFT Academy

Pros:

- Structured path
- Some financing help
- Possible job placement

Cons:

- Competitive
- May come with training contract obligations

1. **Military or ROTC Programs**
2. If you qualify, this is one of the best options. Full training coverage, salary, benefits, and experience that translates.

Cons:

- Requires service commitment
- Different career path (not for everyone)

1. **Scholarships**
2. Often overlooked, but real money is out there.

Top sources:

- Aircraft Owners and Pilots Association (AOPA)
- Women in Aviation International (WAI)
- Organization of Black Aerospace Professionals (OBAP)
- EAA, NGPA, The Ninety-Nines

Pro tips:

- Apply early and often
- Tailor your applications
- Treat it like a job—every dollar saved is a dollar you won't owe later

1. **Employer Education Benefits**
2. Are you working full-time while training? Some employers (especially government, healthcare, or union-based) offer tuition reimbursement for professional development.

Even Amazon has a career choice program that can fund flight school.

**Pros and Cons: Choosing Your Financing Mix**

**Pay-As-You-Go Pros:**

- No debt
- Flexible
- No lender strings attached

**Cons:**

- Slower timeline
- May delay career progress
- Stress from juggling work and training

**Private Loan Pros:**

- Fast access to funds
- Complete training without work interruption

**Cons:**

- Higher interest
- Fewer protections
- Repayment often starts immediately

**Cadet Program Pros:**

- Job prospects

- Mentorship
- Some cost coverage

**Cons:**

- Less flexibility
- Job guarantee isn't absolute
- Contracts can be binding

**Action Steps**

- Build a spreadsheet of projected total training cost
- Research at least 5 loan options and compare interest, terms, and deferment
- Make a scholarship application tracker
- Talk to 3 pilots who chose different funding paths and ask what they wish they knew
- Map out your time-to-1,500-hours timeline, with cost per phase

**Plain-Language Lessons No One Told You**

- Interest doesn't sleep. Deferment still means the clock is ticking. The sooner you pay down interest, the more you save.
- Scholarships aren't just for top students. They're for motivated ones.
- Not all cadet programs are equal. Read every contract. Know your out.
- Your financial runway is as important as your flight time. Don't stall halfway to your goal.
- Mixing funding types isn't failure. It's strategy.

**Real-Life Scenario: Danielle, Age 24**

Danielle started training at a Part 61 school while working full-time at a restaurant. She took out $50K in loans but applied for 8 scholarships, winning 3. She structured her payments to cover interest while in school, so her loan balance didn't grow.

When she hit 1,500 hours, she owed less than $40K and had never once missed a payment.

Her secret? "I treated it like an investment, not a dream."

**Call to Action:**

Before wheels-up tomorrow:

- Choose one scholarship and apply for it
- List your top 3 financing options side-by-side
- Make a 90-day plan to cover your next training milestone
- Open a separate account for flight training savings

One move. One decision. One less burden.

**Final Word:**

You can love flying and be smart about money. The cockpit doesn't demand financial sacrifice. It demands financial strategy.

You're not stuck.

You're not behind.

You're just building altitude.

Don't fund your future on fumes.

Chart your plan.

Secure your runway.

And keep climbing.

Your future self will thank you.

So will your crew.

So will your sanity.

# Chapter 3: Comparing the Civilian, Military, and International Paths

Let's get something straight right away: there is no single "right" path to becoming a pilot. Whether you take off from a civilian flight school, wear a military uniform, or cross international borders to chase your wings, each route comes with its own altitude, headwinds, and fuel burn. But what most pilots never get is a transparent, financial breakdown of each of these paths.

That's what this chapter is here to give you. Not a recruiter pitch. Not a glossy brochure version. But the real-world trade-offs, timeframes, dollar signs, and long-term consequences of each major route into aviation—civilian, military, and international.

If you're early in your journey, this chapter is your roadmap. If you're already deep into one of these paths, it's your chance to optimize your route and understand how your financial profile is shaped by the path you took to the cockpit.

**Civilian Path: The Self-Investor's Journey**

This is the path most pilots reading this book are either on or have taken. You find a flight school. You pay out-of-pocket or borrow to fund it. You build hours. You hustle.

**Financial Pros:**

- No military commitment or service obligation
- Total control over pace and timeline

- Eligible for regional airline bonuses, tuition reimbursement, or airline cadet programs

**Financial Cons:**

- $80,000 - $120,000+ in up-front training costs
- Loan payments start quickly, often before you're earning much
- No salary during training
- Delayed income curve; most civilians won't make six figures until year 5+

**Other Trade-offs:**

- Limited benefits early on (no housing, no insurance, no retirement plans during training)
- Early years can be financially and emotionally stressful
- You carry the risk—and the reward

**Real Scenario:**

Brandon, age 25, is instructing 20 hours/week after finishing his ratings. His student loan payments are $950/month. He's sharing a crash pad with four other instructors. He eats peanut butter sandwiches three days a week. But he's got control of his schedule, he's logging hours, and he'll upgrade to a regional airline in less than a year.

The path is tight. But he owns every mile of it.

**Military Path: Serve to Fly, Fly to Serve**

Many of the highest-performing airline pilots today came through the military. The U.S. Air Force, Navy, Marines, Coast Guard, and Army all offer training routes to fly jets, helicopters, and transport aircraft.

**Financial Pros:**

- No up-front training costs; the government pays for everything
- Competitive pay during training (and while building hours)

- Full housing, healthcare, retirement contributions, and tax-advantaged benefits
- GI Bill and post-service education benefits

**Financial Cons:**

- Commitment: Often 10 years of service after earning wings
- Difficult to hold civilian jobs or pursue private investing during service
- Longer path to civilian airline career if staying full-term
- Limited control over location, missions, or life path during active duty

**Other Trade-offs:**

- Highest quality flight training in the world
- Valuable leadership, technical, and operational experience
- Risk of deployments, danger, and family separation
- Transition out of military life can be financially and emotionally complex

**Real Scenario:**

Maria, 33, is leaving the Air Force after a 12-year career flying C-130s. She's debt-free. She has a government pension. Her resume shines. But she's also adjusting to civilian airline life, where scheduling, culture, and pay are very different.

She enters the majors with built-in financial strength. But she had to serve first.

**International Path: Across Borders and Oceans**

Some pilots train overseas and come to the U.S. to convert licenses. Others begin in the U.S. and return to their home country. Either way, flying internationally adds complexity and cost.

**Financial Pros:**

- Some countries subsidize training or offer airline-sponsored programs

- Certain international airlines fast-track pilots into First Officer roles
- Currency differences may create financial opportunity (but also volatility)

**Financial Cons:**

- Licensing conversions can be expensive and time-consuming
- Visa restrictions limit earning opportunities in the U.S.
- Student visa holders cannot work off-campus, reducing income options
- Higher costs due to relocation, housing, and compliance with multiple regulatory bodies

**Other Trade-offs:**

- May face discrimination, language barriers, or cultural adjustments
- Navigating foreign tax systems and currency exchange risks
- Opportunities depend heavily on political and market conditions

**Real Scenario:**

Ravi, 28, trained in India but came to the U.S. to convert his ratings. He's now a CFI working toward 1,500 hours. He can't legally take on a second job. He's sharing a bedroom and budgeting every dollar. But once he hits his target, he plans to return home, where he can command a captain's salary immediately.

High risk. High reward. High complexity.

**Comparing Career Timelines and Earning Potential**

**Path:** Civilian

**Age Starting Pay:** 22–25

**Age Six-Figure Potential:** 27–32

**Total Cost to Train:** $100K+

**Risk:** High

**Control:** High

**Path:** Military
**Age Starting Pay:** 24–26
**Age Six-Figure Potential:** 35–40 (post-service)
**Total Cost to Train:** $0 (Govt. paid)
**Risk:** Medium
**Control:** Low
**Path:** International
**Age Starting Pay:** 22–28
**Age Six-Figure Potential:** Varies
**Total Cost to Train:** Varies
**Risk:** High
**Control:** Low–Medium

These numbers are not gospel. They are generalizations. But they help you spot the pattern:

- **Civilian** = early struggle, mid-career gains
- **Military** = delayed entry, long-term stability
- **International** = huge variation, lots of complexity

These numbers are not gospel. They are generalizations. But they help you spot the pattern:

- Civilian = early struggle, mid-career gains
- Military = delayed entry, long-term stability
- International = huge variation, lots of complexity

**Pros and Cons: Real Talk, No Spin**

**Civilian Pros:**

- Freedom to pivot
- Fast path to airlines
- Full ownership of finances

**Civilian Cons:**

- High debt load
- No benefits early
- Must hustle for hours and connections

**Military Pros:**

- Full financial coverage
- World-class experience
- Retirement and benefits

**Military Cons:**

- Less flexibility
- Risk of injury or burnout
- Delayed civilian earning

**International Pros:**

- Global perspective
- Possible fast track
- Diverse resume

**International Cons:**

- Regulatory friction
- Limited U.S. work options
- Currency risk and travel expenses

**Action Steps**

- Interview one pilot from each path. Ask what they would change.

- Create a cost-benefit breakdown for your path—training, income, risk, benefits
- If military, calculate the net worth difference with your pension
- If civilian, calculate the interest on loans over 10 years
- If international, map conversion and visa timelines alongside cash flow

**Plain-Language Breakdowns**

- Military pilots earn salary + benefits from day one. Civilians earn when they start flying students.
- International pilots often spend double converting ratings and face immigration barriers.
- Airline recruiters may favor military experience for leadership and discipline, but time-to-hire matters.
- Civilian pilots must build financial habits early, because income starts lower.
- Military and international pilots often get a late start on personal investing.

**Real-Life Trade-Offs in the Jumpseat**

- You're a 40-year-old regional pilot with $100K in debt. The military wouldn't have allowed that, but would you have signed a 10-year contract at age 20?
- You're an international student with 1,500 hours but no work visa. You trained in the U.S., but you can't fly here yet. Now what?
- You're a military retiree with a pension and 3,000 jet hours, but no civilian type rating. You're applying next to a 30-year-old regional captain who flies a similar aircraft. Who has the edge?

**Call to Action:**

Before you sleep tonight:

- Pick one thing you wish you knew when you started. Write it down.
- Choose one financial mistake your path tends to create. Make a plan to avoid it.
- Reach out to a pilot from a different path and ask them to tell you one truth you won't hear on a brochure.

**Final Word:**

This isn't about which path is best. It's about knowing the true costs, the long game, and the mindset required to succeed regardless of how you started.

Every flight has its own weather. Every career its own headwind.

But with clarity, courage, and a plan, you can fly through it.

Choose your path. Own your choices. Build your freedom.

Your future self will thank you.

So will your crew.

So will your sanity.

# Chapter 4: Budgeting as a Student Pilot or Flight Instructor

Let's get one thing straight right from the start: You don't have to be making six figures to be financially powerful. You just have to know how to fly your money the way you fly your aircraft—with control, discipline, and a plan for turbulence. This chapter is for every pilot who's ever eaten Ramen in the back of a hangar, who's picked up extra sim time just to cover rent, or who's wondered how to balance a headset, a side hustle, and $80K in student loans all at once.

Whether you're in flight school or just started instructing, you're probably not flush with cash. But you do have something even more important: time. Time to build habits, lay the groundwork, and avoid the financial stalls that can derail a promising aviation career.

This chapter will show you how to budget like a pro from day one—not in theory, but in cockpit-ready steps that respect your lifestyle, your goals, and your hustle.

**The First Thing: Admit That Budgeting Isn't About Deprivation**

You're not here to cut out every joy in your life. You're here to create options. Budgeting isn't about never eating out. It's about knowing when you can without wondering if the debit card will decline. It's not about sacrifice. It's about strategy.

A budget is your pre-flight checklist for your financial life. You wouldn't take off without checking your fuel, flaps, and forecast. Don't fly financially blind either.

**Step One: Know Your Numbers Cold**

Most student pilots and CFIs can rattle off V-speeds but couldn't tell you what they spent on food last month. That stops here.

Track every dollar for 30 days. Not forever. Just one month. Use a notebook. Use an app. Use your bank statement. Doesn't matter. Just start.

You're looking for:

- Income (even if inconsistent)
- Fixed expenses (rent, car, phone)
- Variable expenses (food, fuel, hangouts, gear)
- Debt payments (loans, credit cards)

You need the numbers. Not vibes. Not guesses. Real numbers.

**Step Two: Build a Barebones Budget That Keeps You Airborne**

This is your minimum viable lifestyle. You might not like it. But it's your safety altitude.

Let's say:

- Rent: $600 (shared housing)
- Utilities: $100
- Car insurance: $80
- Gas: $150
- Groceries: $250
- Student loan interest: $200
- Miscellaneous: $150

Total: $1,530/month

If you're flight instructing part-time and bringing in $1,800/month, you're surviving. Not thriving. But surviving is step one.

Anything above this number goes to:

- Emergency fund
- Extra debt payments

- Flight training (if still in progress)
- Health insurance or professional development

**Step Three: Create a 3-Tier System**

You don't need 14 budget categories. Try this:

1. **Essentials (Must-Haves):** Rent, utilities, groceries, insurance, debt minimums
2. **Future (Smart Moves):** Emergency fund, extra debt payments, IRA contributions
3. **Flex (Nice-to-Haves):** Eating out, subscriptions, random gear upgrades

Every time money comes in, divide it. Even if it's small. Even if it's just $300 from an intro flight. Split it up and fly with intention.

**Income Hacks for Student Pilots and CFIs**

Let's be real—your paycheck might not cover everything. So let's talk supplemental income.

- **Freelance work:** Editing, writing, remote gigs
- **Airport jobs:** Line service, front desk, fueling
- **Delivery apps:** Flexible but wear and tear on your car
- **Online tutoring or teaching English**
- **Flight simulator instruction**

Anything that doesn't jeopardize your rest, safety, or hours is fair game. But don't trade every waking moment for dollars. Your energy is fuel too.

**Big Leaks to Watch Out For**

You're not broke because of Starbucks. You're broke because of disorganization. The leaks aren't always big. But they add up.

Watch for:

- Overdraft fees

- Eating out every day between flights
- Buying gear without comparing prices
- Fueling up at the most expensive gas station near the airport
- Not meal prepping
- Impulse spending after a long day flying

Create a habit of reviewing your spending weekly. Just like reviewing your logbook or METARs. It's not emotional. It's operational.

**Emergency Funds Even for the Lean Years**

You need a cash buffer. Even if it's $500. Then $1,000. Then $2,000. You'll need it when:

- Your car needs brakes
- Your headset breaks
- You get weathered out for a week and lose income

Emergency funds are oxygen. Not optional.

**Debt Strategy While Making Peanuts**

You might not be able to pay off your loans fast. That's okay. But you must avoid falling behind.

Tips:

- Call lenders before you miss a payment
- Pay interest even during deferment to stop balance growth
- Use income-driven repayment plans if federal
- Track your total balance every month. Don't avoid it. Own it.

**Student Discounts and Pilot Perks**

Use them.

- Flight school discounts for simulator time
- Pilot rates at hotels and travel sites
- Student pricing on software and apps

- Ask local businesses for aviation discounts—you'd be surprised

You're not begging. You're being resourceful.

**Meal Prep, Not Meal Guilt**

You're on the go. But food waste is cash waste. Pick 3-4 easy meals you can rotate. Rice, beans, eggs, pasta, protein powder. Make it boring. Make it consistent.

You don't need a diet plan. You need a repeatable routine.

**Real Life Scenario: Luis, Age 23**

Luis is instructing 15 hours/week and Ubering 10 hours/week. He built a $1,000 emergency fund in six months by cutting takeout to once a week, switching to a cheaper phone plan, and automating $50/month into savings.

He logs every dollar in a Google Sheet. He's not rich. But he's in control. And that's wealth.

**Action Steps**

- Track every dollar for 30 days
- Build your barebones budget
- Set a $500 emergency fund goal
- Pick one income boost strategy and test it this month
- Automate a $20 savings transfer every payday

**Plain-Language Money Lessons Nobody Taught You**

- Budgeting isn't about restriction. It's about clarity.
- Being broke doesn't mean you're bad with money. It means you're early in your journey.
- $10 decisions matter. But only if they're happening every day.
- Automation beats motivation every time.
- Cash flow is king. Net worth comes later.

**Call to Action:**

Make one financial move before wheels-up tomorrow:

- Cancel a subscription
- Cook instead of grabbing fast food
- Transfer $10 into savings
- Check your bank balance and write down the number

Just one move. Then another next week.

**Final Word:**

You don't have to be making a captain's salary to feel financially powerful. You just have to fly your money with purpose.

You're already handling engines, weather, navigation, radio calls, and human lives. You can absolutely handle your rent, food, and loan balance.

This isn't about shame. It's about showing up with swagger.

You didn't come this far to feel broke and defeated.

Budget like a pro.

Fly like a leader.

Build your altitude with every decision.

Your future self will thank you.

So will your crew.

So will your sanity.

# Chapter 5: Managing Student Loans While Building Flight Hours

Student loan debt isn't just a number on a spreadsheet—it's a weight you carry in your flight bag. When you're a pilot logging hours, every dollar matters. Your margins are tight, your schedule is inconsistent, and your goals are sky-high. And yet, you're staring down five or six figures of student loan debt that doesn't care how many check rides you've passed.

But here's the good news: you don't have to be overwhelmed. You just need a system.

This chapter is for the pilot flying sunrise-to-sunset instruction blocks while trying to afford brake pads for their car. It's for the pilot who made it through flight school but now feels like they're losing altitude financially. It's for the pilot who wants to make smart money moves now—not five years from now, when the interest has ballooned and options have narrowed.

Let's talk about how to manage your student loan debt while building flight hours. Real talk. Real tactics. Real relief.

**Start Here: Know Exactly What You Owe**

You can't manage what you won't measure. So the first step is clarity.

Pull every loan:

- Federal: Use studentaid.gov to view your full federal loan summary
- Private: Log into each individual lender's site or pull a credit report

for a full list

Track:

- Total balance
- Interest rate
- Loan type (subsidized, unsubsidized, private, PLUS)
- Minimum monthly payment
- Current repayment status (grace, deferment, forbearance, active)

Make a spreadsheet. No excuses. This is your financial pre-flight briefing.

**Federal Loans: Your Safety Net (If You Use It Well)**

If you have federal student loans, you have options.

**Income-Driven Repayment (IDR)** plans adjust your monthly payment based on your income. As a flight instructor or low-earning first officer, this could be your best short-term move.

Main IDR Plans:

- **SAVE (Saving on a Valuable Education)** – Replaces REPAYE. Most favorable terms for low-income borrowers
- **PAYE / IBR** – Older plans, still useful for some with higher debt relative to income

What to Know:

- Payments could be $0-$200/month depending on income
- Interest may be subsidized under certain plans
- Enrolling early prevents missed payments and default
- Must recertify income annually

**Deferment/Forbearance:**

- Temporary pause on payments

- Interest still accrues (except for subsidized loans in deferment)
- Not a long-term strategy

**Action:** If you're not earning much, apply for IDR immediately. It protects your credit, keeps your loans in good standing, and can limit interest accrual.

**Private Loans: Less Flexible, Still Manageable**

Private lenders don't offer IDR, forgiveness, or the same level of options. But you can still manage them.

**Tactics:**

- Call and ask about income-based plans or interest-only payments
- Ask for a temporary interest rate reduction
- Automate payments to qualify for interest rate discounts
- Avoid forbearance unless absolutely necessary

**Consider Refinancing—But Only When You're Stable**

- Don't refinance federal loans into private early on—you lose protections
- Once you're earning stable income (regional airline or better), you may refinance to lower rates

**The Rule of Thumb: Make Minimums, Then Stack**

While building hours, your job is to stay current, not pay everything off tomorrow. But interest doesn't stop. So:

- Always make minimum payments
- If income allows, pay interest monthly (especially on unsubsidized or private loans)
- When possible, stack payments to highest-interest loans first (avalanche method)

**Loan Forgiveness: Understand the Landscape**

Public Service Loan Forgiveness (PSLF) may not apply to most pilots, but it's worth knowing.

To qualify:

- Work full-time for a qualifying nonprofit or government agency
- Make 120 qualifying payments under an IDR plan

Some CFIs or aviation instructors at public colleges may qualify. If you work for a Part 141 school affiliated with a university, ask HR.

Otherwise, forgiveness after 20-25 years of IDR may still be an option.

**Flying While Broke: How to Stay in the Sky Financially**

It's not glamorous. But it's doable. Key habits:

- **Crash pads** over apartments
- **Meal prep** over takeout
- **Flight school perks** (free sim time, fuel discounts, pro deals)
- **Pick up intro flights and ferry flights** for extra cash
- **Uber or delivery** during off days (watch tax implications)

Every dollar counts. Every saved dollar goes toward freedom.

**Real Talk: When to Pay More, When to Wait**

- Pay **extra on high-interest private loans** as soon as you can
- Stay current on federal loans with IDR while your income is low
- Build a **$1,000 emergency fund** before sending extra to loans
- Once earning $60K+, start paying aggressively

Don't rush into big payments if it means draining your cash buffer.

**Compound Interest: Why Time Is Your Co-Pilot and Your Enemy**

Every month you don't pay, interest adds more. But every extra payment you make early? It saves you hundreds or thousands later.

Example:

- $50,000 loan at 6.8%
- Pay $100/month extra from day one = $11,000+ saved in interest

Tiny moves now = huge results later.

**Real-Life Story: Jake, 26, Instructor in Texas**

Jake owes $92K in loans. He's instructing 25 hours/week, delivering groceries on weekends, and living in a shared three-bedroom house. He pays $300/month toward loans and throws $50/month at his highest-interest private lender.

In 18 months, he hasn't missed a payment, and he's knocked $4,200 off his balance. It's not flashy. But it's forward.

**Credit Score and Your Loan Behavior**

Never miss payments. Ever.

Late payments hurt your:

- Credit score
- Refinance eligibility
- Security clearance (for some jobs)

Use auto-pay. Set calendar reminders. Your credit is your financial reputation.

**Mental Health and Money Shame**

Debt can feel crushing. It can make you feel behind, embarrassed, or hopeless. Don't let it.

You're not behind. You're on a different path. You're flying a longer leg.

Talk to other pilots. Share numbers. Share wins. Money shame thrives in silence. Break it.

**Action Steps**

- Log into every loan account and record balances, interest, and terms
- Apply for IDR or request modified payment plans today
- Automate payments, even if minimum
- Open a spreadsheet or budgeting app to track every loan

- Transfer $10 toward your highest-interest loan tomorrow

**Plain-Language Lessons Nobody Taught You**

- A $0 IDR payment still counts as an on-time payment
- Every month you avoid default protects your future options
- You don't have to pay everything off right now—you just have to stay in the game
- Refinancing is a tool, not a miracle
- Momentum matters more than perfection

**Call to Action:**

Make one financial move before you sleep tonight:

- Check your student loan balance
- Set a reminder to apply for IDR
- Send $20 to your smallest or highest-interest loan
- Email your lender and ask about hardship options

Just one move. Then do another next week.

**Final Word:**

Debt doesn't make you a bad pilot. Ignoring it is the only mistake you can't recover from.

You didn't come this far to be grounded by interest.

You're a professional. Start flying your finances like you fly your aircraft:

- With discipline
- With awareness
- With long-range vision

You have the power to take control.

Your future self will thank you.

So will your crew.

So will your sanity.

# Chapter 6: Renting, Crash Pads, and Creative Housing Solutions

Let's talk about one of the most frustrating parts of a pilot's early financial life: where you sleep.

When you're building hours, commuting to a base, or hopping from sim training to reserve duty, your housing situation becomes a unique type of puzzle. You're not a 9-to-5 office worker with a predictable daily routine. You're a traveling professional, constantly packing and unpacking, often away more than you're home. So why should you pay full rent for a place you barely live in? And how do you strike a balance between saving money and maintaining your sanity?

This chapter is all about helping you rethink housing through the lens of flexibility, cost efficiency, and personal sustainability. Because if you're not strategic, housing can become one of the biggest budget busters in your flying career.

**Start Here: Define What Housing Actually Means in Your Life Phase**

There's a difference between housing and home.

Early-career? Housing might be nothing more than a crash pad and a few Tupperware containers in a shared fridge.

Mid-career with a family? It might be a stable residence for your spouse and kids, with you gone half the month.

Late-career? Maybe you're downsizing or relocating for lifestyle reasons, while balancing a second home or vacation property.

Wherever you are, define your **needs**, not your assumptions. The world told you that you're supposed to have your own apartment. Or buy a house by 30. Or settle near your airline hub. But aviation doesn't play by those rules. And neither should you.

**Option 1: Crash Pads**

The OG pilot housing hack. Crash pads are typically shared apartments or homes—often near airline hubs—rented out by the bed or room to pilots commuting in and out.

**Pros:**

- Dirt cheap (as low as $250–$400/month)
- No long-term lease
- Surrounded by other pilots (which means networking and shared rides)
- Often walking distance or a short shuttle ride from the airport

**Cons:**

- Shared space (can be 4–8 pilots per room in some setups)
- Limited privacy
- First-come-first-served sleeping arrangements
- Often older properties with minimal upkeep

Crash pads are ideal for:

- Commuters who don't want to get a second apartment
- Instructors or low-hour pilots who need to stay near training facilities
- Short-term assignments, reserve duty, or new base transitions

**Financial Insight:**

If you're commuting from your home in Phoenix to a base in Dallas, your crash pad cost may be less than 10% of what a second apartment would cost. Multiply that savings across 12–24 months, and you're pocketing thousands.

**Option 2: Renting Smart**

Maybe you need more stability than a crash pad. That doesn't mean you need to blow half your paycheck on a one-bedroom downtown.

**What to look for:**

- Flexible lease terms (month-to-month, sublets, roommate arrangements)
- Furnished short-term rentals (great for contract flying or sim training stints)
- Rentals near public transit or airport shuttles

**Roommates:**

- Split costs, share resources, and potentially reduce commuting time
- Choose roommates in aviation, healthcare, or similar schedules so you're not clashing on sleep cycles

**Pro Tip:**

If you're in a region with other pilots in training or flight school students, consider co-renting a house and splitting rooms. You can create your own crash pad for half the cost of renting solo.

**Watch Out For:**

- Paying premium rent in an area you don't plan to live in long-term
- Furnishing a rental that you'll leave in under a year
- Getting locked into long-term leases with high breakage fees

**Option 3: Creative Housing Hacks**

**1. Rent-by-the-Room Models**

Apps and platforms like PadSplit, Bungalow, and even certain Facebook groups allow you to rent a single furnished room with all utilities included. This is a game changer for pilots on reserve or rotating through training centers.

**2. RV or Van Life**

Yes, some pilots actually live in RVs or converted vans. Parked near airports, shared with other pilots, or moved between gigs.

Pros:

- No rent (after purchase)
- Full mobility
- Great for nomadic phases

Cons:

- Upfront cost
- Maintenance
- Zoning and parking challenges

**3. Host Homes**

Some pilots connect with locals who offer spare rooms for rent at reduced rates, especially near flight schools or regional bases. It's like Airbnb meets house-sitting.

Ask:

- In flight school Facebook groups
- Through flight instructor networks
- At the front desk of your training center or airport

**4. Living with Family (Temporarily)**

It might feel like a step back, but if you're in a heavy debt-repayment phase, moving in with parents or family for 6–12 months can accelerate your savings rate like nothing else.

Just make sure you:

- Set boundaries
- Contribute financially or with chores
- Have a clear exit strategy

**Pros and Cons: Rent vs. Own as a Pilot**

**Renting Pros:**

- Flexibility
- No maintenance
- Lower up-front costs
- No risk if base changes or contract ends

**Renting Cons:**

- No equity building
- Rent can increase yearly
- Limited control over the property

**Owning Pros:**

- Equity and appreciation
- Tax deductions
- Potential rental income (Airbnb or long-term if you commute)

**Owning Cons:**

- Maintenance costs
- High upfront expense
- Tied to a location (bad if your base moves)

**Pilot-Specific Ownership Risk:**

Buying too early in your career—before your base, schedule, and income stabilize—is one of the most common mistakes new pilots make.

If you plan to move in 2–3 years? Rent.

If you're locked into a major carrier hub and plan to stay for 5+ years? Consider buying.

**Real-Life Scenario: Kevin, 30, Regional First Officer**

Kevin was commuting from Tampa to Newark and paying $1,200/month for an apartment he used less than 10 days a month. He switched to a crash pad for $350/month, banked the difference, and paid off $9,000 in student loans in under a year. Now he's planning to buy his first home—in the city where his fiancé lives, not where his airline is based.

**Financial Action Steps**

- Audit your housing cost: what are you actually paying per day of use?
- Calculate the cost of commuting vs. living near your base
- Research crash pads or pilot room rentals near your base on Facebook, Reddit, or pilot forums
- If renting, negotiate: ask for lease flexibility, free utilities, or furnished options
- Create a 12-month housing plan: Will your base change? Is a move coming? Is now the time to lock into a mortgage?

**Plain-Language Lessons Nobody Taught You**

- You don't need a "real apartment" to be a real adult. Your goals aren't everyone else's.
- Crash pads aren't forever. They're a season.
- Housing is your biggest controllable expense. Optimize it early.
- Never buy a house just because it "feels like the next step."
- You can be homeless on paper and still be 100% in control of your life.

**Call to Action:**

Before you take off tomorrow:

- Research 3 housing alternatives near your base
- Check how much you're spending per night you're actually home
- Email your chief pilot or instructor and ask what housing hacks they used early in their career

Just one move. Then another next week. Your housing costs don't have to hold you down.

**Final Word:**

This isn't just about saving on rent. This is about buying time, buying peace of mind, and building runway.

You're not supposed to have it all figured out at 25, 30, or even 40. You're supposed to make smart, temporary decisions that serve your long-term vision.

If that means sleeping in a twin bed surrounded by snoring first officers for six months while you pay off a chunk of debt or hit 1,500 hours, so be it.

You're not doing it wrong.

You're doing it smart.

Own your space. Fly your finances.

Your future self will thank you.

So will your crew.

So will your sanity.

# Chapter 7: Credit 101 for Pilots – How to Build It and Use It

Let's clear the air right up front: credit is not the enemy.

Used poorly, yes—it can wreck your finances, your stress levels, and your sleep. But used properly? Credit is one of the most powerful tools you can have in your flight bag. It can help you qualify for housing in a new base, secure a car when your schedule changes, or even save thousands in interest over the life of a mortgage or student loan refinance. And as a pilot with fluctuating income, unusual tax documents, and an unconventional lifestyle, having great credit isn't just nice to have—it's mission-critical.

This chapter is here to demystify credit, kill the shame, and give you a strategy you can actually stick with. Whether you're a 20-something CFI with one secured card or a 50-year-old captain trying to finally clean up a credit mess from early in your career, this chapter is your pre-flight briefing on credit.

No judgment. Just tools.

**Start Here: What Is Credit and Why Does It Matter to Pilots?**

Your credit score is a three-digit number that lenders, landlords, and even some employers use to judge your financial trustworthiness. It ranges from 300 to 850.

A high score means:

- Lower interest rates

- Higher approval odds
- More flexibility when relocating, buying, or refinancing

As a pilot, you'll often:

- Move between cities or states
- Rent short-term apartments or crash pads
- Need car loans or home loans with fluctuating income
- Fly contract jobs or receive 1099 pay instead of W-2

Having excellent credit means you won't get penalized for having an unconventional lifestyle.

**The 5 Factors That Affect Your Credit Score**

1. **Payment History (35%)**

- Do you pay your bills on time? Even one late payment can drop your score 50+ points.
- Set autopay. No exceptions.

1. **Credit Utilization (30%)**

- How much of your available credit are you using?
- Ideal: Use less than 30% of your total limit. Bonus points for under 10%.
- Example: $1,000 limit, try not to carry more than $300.

1. **Length of Credit History (15%)**

- How long have you had credit?
- Keep old cards open, even if you don't use them often.

1. **New Credit Inquiries (10%)**

- Too many hard pulls in a short time hurts your score.
- Space out applications. Avoid store cards.

1. **Credit Mix (10%)**

- Having a mix of credit types helps: credit cards, student loans, car loans, etc.
- Don't open loans just for mix. Let it happen naturally.

**Building Credit from Scratch (or Rebuilding After a Crash)**

**Start with a Secured Credit Card**

- Deposit $200–$500
- Use it for small monthly expenses (fuel, groceries)
- Pay in full every month

**Next Steps:**

- Apply for a second unsecured card after 6–12 months of on-time payments
- Ask for a credit limit increase every 6 months (with no hard pull)
- Keep usage low, pay on time, and be patient

**Bonus Move:**

- Become an authorized user on a trusted friend/family member's card (only if they have great credit and low balances)

**What to Do with Existing Debt**

If you already have credit cards:

- List balances, interest rates, due dates
- Prioritize the highest-interest cards first (avalanche method)

- Always make minimums
- If you're stretched, call and ask for a temporary hardship program

**Avoid:**

- Only making minimum payments forever
- Carrying balances over 30% of your limit
- Applying for multiple cards during financial stress

**Understanding the Pilot Lifestyle and Credit Strategy**

- **On reserve?** Keep an emergency fund in place so you don't rely on cards
- **Commuting?** Use a travel rewards card that gives you cash back or airline points
- **Crash pad living?** Use credit only for fixed expenses, not to inflate your lifestyle
- **In training?** Avoid taking on new debt unless absolutely necessary

**Best Credit Cards for Pilots**

**1. Chase Sapphire Preferred**

- Great for travel rewards
- Solid insurance perks for delayed/cancelled trips

**2. Discover It Student or Secured**

- Cash back on basic expenses
- Reports to all three bureaus

**3. American Express Blue Cash Preferred**

- Good for pilots with families and higher grocery/gas spending

Always research annual fees, sign-up bonuses, and rewards categories before applying.

**Common Credit Mistakes Pilots Make**

- Closing old accounts (this shortens your credit history)
- Co-signing for roommates or friends
- Maxing out a card for flight gear or emergency expenses
- Ignoring credit during years of training or low income

Your financial turbulence now doesn't have to follow you forever. But you do have to take control.

**Real-Life Scenario: Hannah, 29, Regional FO**

Hannah had three maxed-out cards, a $610 credit score, and couldn't get approved for an apartment near her new base.

She called her lenders, negotiated payment plans, and paid $50 over the minimum each month. In 12 months, her score jumped 117 points.

She got approved for a Chase card with a $2,000 limit and started using it only for gas. She's on her way to financial altitude.

**How Credit Affects Major Milestones**

**Apartment:**

- Credit score often required above 650
- May need a co-signer or extra deposit with poor credit

**Car Loan:**

- Lower credit = higher interest
- Example: 720 score = 4% APR, 600 score = 14% APR

**Mortgage:**

- 740+ gets best rates
- Under 620? Many lenders won't approve

**Refinancing Loans:**

- Excellent credit can cut your interest in half
- Even a 20-point improvement may save you thousands

**Action Steps**

- Pull your credit report for free at AnnualCreditReport.com
- List all open credit accounts with limits and balances
- Set autopay for minimums
- Pay down highest-interest card first
- Request a credit limit increase (if you've made on-time payments for 6+ months)

**Plain-Language Credit Lessons Nobody Taught You**

- Credit is not evil. It's a tool.
- You don't have to carry a balance to build credit. In fact, you shouldn't.
- One late payment is worse than a maxed-out card. But both hurt.
- Opening lots of store cards tanks your score.
- A $500 secured card used responsibly can unlock thousands in savings later.

**Call to Action:**

Before you go wheels-up tomorrow:

- Set up autopay on every card you own
- Review your credit usage and drop below 30%
- Pick one card to pay $50 extra toward this month
- Check your credit score through your bank or credit card app

One move today. One more next week. Climb steadily.

**Final Word:**

You didn't spend years chasing ratings and flight hours just to let a three-digit number dictate your options.

You're already trusted with lives at 30,000 feet. You can be trusted with credit.

Don't fear it. Master it. Use it to build freedom, not friction.

Your future self will thank you.

So will your crew.

So will your sanity.

# Chapter 8: Your First Aviation Paycheck – What to Expect

So, you finally did it.

After years of training, studying, grinding, building hours, and likely eating more gas station burritos than you care to admit—you got the job. You signed the contract. You earned the wings. And now you're staring at your very first aviation paycheck. The moment you've been waiting for.

And yet… it doesn't feel like the life-changing windfall you imagined.

This chapter is going to walk you through what to actually expect from your first aviation paycheck, how to make sense of it, what to do with it, and most importantly, how to make it work for you—not just for your landlord, loan servicer, or grocery bill. Because the real power of a paycheck isn't the number on it.

It's how you use it.

**Expectation vs. Reality**

When you sign your offer letter, the airline recruiter might talk about $60,000 per year. Maybe $70,000. Maybe more. But when that first direct deposit hits your account, you're wondering where half of it went.

Welcome to the world of:

- Taxes
- Union dues
- Insurance premiums

- 401(k) deductions
- Training pay vs. line pay
- Per diem confusion

That "$60K" job? Might look more like $2,100 net every two weeks.

That doesn't mean you got ripped off. It just means you need to learn how to read your paycheck like you read a METAR—carefully, consistently, and with context.

**Understanding the Anatomy of an Aviation Paycheck**

Your first pay stub will likely include a few things:

- **Base Pay:** Your guaranteed hourly wage times your monthly guarantee (typically 75-80 hours/month)
- **Per Diem:** A non-taxable daily food and travel allowance, usually around $1.50 to $2.50/hour away from base
- **Overtime or Extra Flying:** Hours above guarantee
- **Training Pay:** Often lower than line pay, especially during initial operating experience (IOE)
- **Deductions:** Federal and state taxes, Social Security, Medicare, union dues, retirement contributions, health insurance, and more

Each airline has its quirks. But here are some common truths:

- You don't get paid for all your time
- Per diem is not "extra money"
- You often won't see a full paycheck until your second or third pay cycle

**Training Pay is Humbling**

Most regional airlines and some majors start you on training pay. It might be a flat weekly rate. It might not include per diem. And it's usually the lowest pay you'll earn in your entire flying career.

If you're making $500/week during training, and staying in a crash pad or hotel, most of that will go toward survival.

This is the time for:

- Budgeting to the dollar
- Meal prepping or grocery runs
- Holding off on large purchases

Don't assume your "real paycheck" will start immediately.

**The Magic of Per Diem (And the Trap)**

Per diem is one of the most misunderstood parts of pilot pay.

It is:

- Non-taxable income
- Based on hours away from base
- Usually paid out separately from hourly pay

It is NOT:

- A bonus
- Guaranteed
- A substitute for budgeting

Many new pilots spend their per diem as if it were part of their salary. Then tax season hits, and they're confused why they owe money.

Smart move? Treat per diem as savings, debt payments, or emergency fund fuel.

**What to Expect in Deductions**

Here's what might come out of your check:

- **Federal income tax**: Based on your W-4 elections
- **State income tax**: Depends on your state of residence
- **Social Security and Medicare**: 7.65% combined
- **Union dues**: Varies, but often around 1.5% of gross pay
- **401(k) contributions**: Optional, but some airlines auto-enroll

- **Health/dental/vision insurance**: Pre-tax deductions

Before you spend, understand what you're keeping.

**Why Your Pay Might Fluctuate**

Your pay isn't always steady.

Variables include:

- Number of hours flown
- Trip trading
- Delays, cancellations, sick calls
- Reserve vs. line holder status
- Deadhead vs. credit time
- Training or check rides

Learn your pay protections. Ask your union rep. Use scheduling apps. The more you understand how pay is calculated, the more you can plan your income.

**Common Mistakes with a First Paycheck**

- Blowing the first full check on a new headset, watch, or sunglasses
- Failing to account for taxes and deductions
- Forgetting to save for quarterly estimated taxes (if 1099)
- Assuming pay will stay high year-round
- Neglecting to budget because "I finally made it"

Don't mistake your first real paycheck as financial arrival. It's just the start.

**Real-Life Example: Jordan, 28, New First Officer**

Jordan got his first paycheck and saw $3,200 in his account. He paid off two credit cards, bought a new flight bag, and treated himself to a weekend trip. Then his next check came in at $1,475 after a slow reserve month.

Lesson learned? Don't spend off your highest check. Budget for your average.

**Action Plan for Your First Three Months of Paychecks**

**Month 1:**

- Open a high-yield savings account
- Transfer $200 from every paycheck to it
- Track every expense with an app or notebook
- Don't touch per diem

**Month 2:**

- Start an emergency fund (goal: $1,000 minimum)
- Automate minimum payments on all loans
- Review paycheck deductions and benefits

**Month 3:**

- Contribute to 401(k) if employer matches
- Begin paying down highest-interest debt
- Budget based on your lowest monthly check, not your highest

**How to Read Your Pay Stub Like a Pro**

Every pay stub is different, but look for:

- **Gross Pay**: Before deductions
- **Net Pay**: What hits your account
- **Credit Time**: Hours paid vs. hours flown
- **Pay Rate**: Make sure it matches your contract
- **Per Diem**: Track separately

If it doesn't make sense? Ask your union rep or payroll department. Never blindly accept what you don't understand.

**Plain-Language Breakdowns Pilots Need to Know**

- Your paycheck isn't your pay. It's what's left after everyone else takes a cut.

- Per diem is non-taxable. That's why it feels like a boost.
- Budget like you're on reserve even if you're not.
- Automate good behavior before bad habits set in.

**Action Steps**

- Log into your payroll portal. Download your pay stub. Read every line.
- Start a spreadsheet or app to track monthly income
- Create a "low-pay budget" and a "full-pay budget"
- Set up auto-transfers to savings and debt each pay cycle

**Call to Action:**

Make one smart move with your next paycheck:

- Save $100
- Pay $50 extra toward debt
- Open your 401(k)
- Review and adjust your W-4

Just one move. Then another next week. Fly your finances like you fly your plane: deliberately, skillfully, and with full awareness.

**Final Word:**

Your first aviation paycheck is a milestone. It's proof that your hard work is paying off. But it's also a test.

Will you use it to build a foundation, or burn it on lifestyle inflation?

This isn't about guilt. It's about choice.

Your paycheck is your fuel. Spend it with intention, and it will carry you to financial altitude.

Your future self will thank you.

So will your crew.

So will your sanity.

# Chapter 9: Understanding Taxes Early in Your Career

If there's one topic that triggers more confusion, anxiety, and outright avoidance than any other in a pilot's financial journey, it's taxes.

And it's no wonder. You go from living off loan money during training to earning actual income, possibly with per diem, training pay, reserve flying, or 1099 contract work all mixed in. Then tax season comes around and you're staring at a stack of unfamiliar forms and wondering how you can owe money when you barely feel like you made any.

This chapter isn't about turning you into a tax accountant. It's about making sure you don't get caught off guard, overpay, underpay, or miss opportunities that could save you thousands.

If you're early in your career, this chapter might be the most important financial decision point you face in the next five years.

**Start Here: The Basics of Income Taxes**

Let's lay the foundation. As a pilot, your income is taxed at the federal level, and often at the state and local levels too.

If you're a W-2 employee (working for an airline or charter company), your employer withholds taxes from each paycheck.

If you're a 1099 contractor (some instructors, ferry pilots, corporate pilots), YOU are responsible for withholding and paying taxes on your own.

**What taxes are we talking about?**

- Federal income tax
- State income tax (unless you live in a no-tax state)
- Local/city income tax (some areas)
- Social Security (6.2% of wages)
- Medicare (1.45% of wages)

If you're 1099, you'll also pay:

- Self-employment tax (15.3%, which includes both halves of SS/Medicare)

**Know Your Income Types**

- **Base Pay:** Guaranteed hours x hourly wage
- **Per Diem:** Not taxable
- **Overtime Pay:** Fully taxable
- **Bonuses:** Fully taxable
- **1099/Contract Pay:** Fully taxable, no automatic withholding

If you don't know what kind of income you have, stop now and check your most recent pay stub.

**How Per Diem Works**

Per diem is beautiful because it's **non-taxable**.

It's considered a reimbursement for meals and incidentals while you're away from base. It's paid separately and not reported as income on your W-2.

That means:

- It doesn't increase your tax bill
- It doesn't count toward loan applications or 401(k) contributions

Some pilots make the mistake of budgeting as if per diem were guaranteed income. Don't. Use it as savings, travel fund, or debt payoff fuel.

**How to Read a W-2**

If you're W-2, your employer will send you a W-2 each January. Key boxes to understand:

- **Box 1:** Taxable wages
- **Box 2:** Federal income tax withheld
- **Box 12:** Pre-tax deductions (401(k), HSA)

If Box 1 looks lower than your actual gross pay, it's likely due to pre-tax deductions or per diem not being included.

**If You're 1099: Welcome to Self-Employment**

You're responsible for:

- Tracking all income
- Saving for taxes (30% is a safe rule of thumb)
- Filing quarterly estimated taxes (April 15, June 15, Sept 15, Jan 15)

You can also deduct business expenses:

- Headsets, flight bags, fuel (if not reimbursed)
- Home office (if you do flight planning at home)
- Travel expenses for work trips (lodging, meals, mileage)
- Cell phone (portion used for work)

You must keep good records. Use a spreadsheet, QuickBooks, or an app like Everlance or MileIQ.

**Biggest Early-Career Tax Mistakes Pilots Make**

- Assuming your airline is withholding enough (they might not be)
- Ignoring 1099 income from side gigs
- Failing to file quarterly estimated taxes
- Spending a signing bonus without saving for the tax bill
- Forgetting that a bump in pay bumps your tax bracket

Just because you got a big refund last year doesn't mean you will this year. Especially if you went from training pay to full-line flying.

**State Tax Residency Matters**

Where you live for tax purposes determines whether you pay state income tax.

States with NO state income tax:

- Texas
- Florida
- Nevada
- Washington
- Alaska
- South Dakota
- Wyoming

If you live in one of these, you keep more of your paycheck. But your home address and domicile must align. Some states are aggressive about auditing pilot tax residency.

If you commute to another base, it does NOT automatically change your tax home.

**Estimated Taxes: What Pilots Need to Know**

If you are 1099, or your W-2 employer isn't withholding enough, you need to make quarterly payments.

Use IRS Form 1040-ES.

Missed a deadline? You could face a penalty, even if you pay in full at year-end.

**Best Practice:**

- Save 25–30% of every 1099 check
- Transfer to a separate savings account immediately
- Pay quarterly using EFTPS.gov

**Hiring a Tax Professional**

If you have any of the following, get a pro:

- Mixed W-2 and 1099 income
- State residency complexity
- Multiple base changes
- You bought or sold a home
- You want to deduct aviation expenses

Look for someone who understands:

- Per diem
- Union dues
- Pilot tax laws (not just general employment tax)

Ask your union, senior pilots, or online forums for CPA referrals.

**Smart Pilot Tax Strategies**

- Max out pre-tax 401(k) contributions ($23,000 in 2024 if under 50)
- Open and fund a Roth IRA (if eligible)
- Use an HSA if your health plan qualifies (triple tax benefit)
- Deduct flight gear and training costs (if 1099)
- Keep a digital file folder for all receipts, forms, and pay stubs

**Real-Life Scenario: Mark, 27, CFI and Contract Ferry Pilot**

Mark had $45,000 in income. $22,000 was 1099. He spent the year thinking he didn't make enough to owe.

He never filed quarterly estimates. He never saved for taxes.

At year-end, he owed $6,500 in taxes and penalties.

After that, he:

- Opened a dedicated savings account
- Transferred 30% of each 1099 check automatically
- Paid quarterly

- Kept detailed logs of every expense, down to flight bag purchases

He slept a lot better the next tax season.

**Plain-Language Lessons About Taxes Pilots Need to Hear**

- If you're 1099 and not saving for taxes, you're flying financially blind
- Per diem is a gift—use it wisely
- A tax refund isn't a bonus. It's your money you overpaid
- Filing late means penalties. Don't miss deadlines
- Your tax preparer isn't a magician. They can't fix what you didn't track

**Action Steps Before Your Next Paycheck**

- Check your W-4 settings (you may need to adjust withholding)
- Review your pay stub to see what's being withheld
- If 1099, open a tax savings account and transfer 30% from every gig
- Download a mileage or expense tracker
- Put quarterly tax dates in your calendar

**Call to Action:**

Make one move this week:

- Pull last year's tax return and actually read it
- Email your CPA or find one who understands pilot pay
- Open a folder for this year's tax documents
- Save your first receipt from a work-related purchase

Just one move. Then do another next week. Avoiding taxes doesn't make them go away.

**Final Word:**

Taxes aren't fun. But they don't have to be terrifying. With a little awareness, a few good habits, and the right help, you can stay ahead of the IRS and on course for financial freedom.

Don't let confusion or avoidance cost you money, peace of mind, or sleep.
You're already a professional in the sky.
Be one on the ground too.
Your future self will thank you.
So will your crew.
So will your sanity.

# Chapter 10: Avoiding Lifestyle Creep on Entry-Level Pilot Pay

Let's get something straight from the jump: lifestyle creep is real, sneaky, and dangerous—especially in the aviation world.

You go from years of scraping by on ramen, crash pads, and unpaid time building hours to finally earning a paycheck. And even if that paycheck isn't huge yet, it feels huge compared to what you were used to. So what happens next?

A new flight bag. A nicer watch. An upgraded car. Meals out on overnights. Weekend getaways to celebrate your new "real pilot" income.

Before you know it, your spending has ramped up just as fast as your pay—and your savings? Your debt payoff? Your financial runway? Still stuck on the tarmac.

This chapter is here to help you avoid that trap. Because while there's nothing wrong with enjoying your hard-earned money, there is something deeply wrong with flying yourself into financial turbulence for the sake of looking like a successful pilot.

We're going to break down what lifestyle creep looks like, how to spot it, and how to fight it with simple, practical, empowering strategies that keep you in control.

**What Is Lifestyle Creep, Really?**

Lifestyle creep happens when your expenses rise at the same pace—or faster—than your income.

It's not just buying flashy stuff. It's subtle.

- It's getting Starbucks every flight instead of brewing your own
- It's upgrading from a crash pad to a solo apartment before you can afford it
- It's increasing your Amazon spending every time your paycheck bumps

You tell yourself you deserve it. And hey—you probably do.

But deserving something and being able to afford it long-term are two different things.

Lifestyle creep doesn't just drain your account. It delays your goals. It derails your debt payoff. It puts pressure on your relationships. It steals your financial peace.

**Why Pilots Are Especially Vulnerable**

Aviation comes with a culture of appearances:

- Fancy watches
- Luxury luggage
- First-class perks
- Jet-setting lifestyle

Even if you're flying CRJs out of Paducah, the pressure to look the part is real.

Plus, your schedule is unpredictable. You eat on the go. You crash in hotels. You're constantly around higher-paid captains, making it easy to start mimicking their spending before you're on their level.

Add in the rapid income increases that can come with upgrades or airline changes, and you have a recipe for unsustainable spending habits.

**The Paycheck Illusion**

That first $2,500 deposit hits your account and you feel rich.

But you forget:

- Taxes already took a big cut
- Union dues and insurance deductions reduced your gross
- Per diem isn't part of your base salary

And yet, you start spending like you're clearing six figures.

Then:

- Car payments increase
- Rent creeps up
- Your social life starts costing more
- Travel becomes more spontaneous and expensive

Suddenly, your net worth hasn't moved in a year—even though your pay has.

**Real-Life Scenario: Caleb, 29, New First Officer**

Caleb went from flight instructing for $1,200/month to flying right seat at a regional carrier and earning $3,500/month.

Within six months, he:

- Leased a luxury car
- Rented a high-rise studio near the airport
- Got a $700 watch on a credit card

By the end of his first year, he had more debt than when he started. His credit card utilization was over 80%, and he had zero savings.

He was working hard. Flying well. Earning more. But his lifestyle was flying higher than his finances could support.

**How to Recognize Lifestyle Creep Before It Owns You**

- Your savings rate hasn't increased despite higher pay
- You have more subscriptions than you use
- You use "I'll pay it off next month" to justify purchases
- You eat out more than you cook
- You feel pressure to spend to keep up with colleagues
- You're always waiting for the next raise to feel secure

Creep is sneaky. It always feels justifiable. But it chips away at your financial lift until you're stalled.

**Ground Rules for Guarding Against Lifestyle Creep**

**1. Lock In Your Lifestyle Early**

Choose a modest lifestyle at your first job and stick with it for 1–2 years, even as your income increases.

**2. Automate Good Behavior**

- Auto-transfer 20% of each paycheck to savings
- Auto-pay $100 extra on your student loans
- Auto-contribute to your 401(k)

**3. Create a "Fun Budget"**

Don't cut yourself off. Give yourself a monthly allowance for fun. Stick to it.

**4. Avoid "Comparison Cockpit" Spending**

You don't know the captain's financial situation. Don't copy it blindly.

**5. Use Per Diem Strategically**

Treat it as bonus fuel:

- Save it
- Use it to pay off debt
- Invest it in your Roth IRA

**6. Plan Purchases, Don't Justify Them**

Want a new iPad? Cool.

But plan for it. Save for it.

Don't swipe and justify it as a "career necessity" without a plan.

**Lifestyle Upgrade Checklist: Yes or No?**

Before you upgrade anything, ask:

- Can I pay for this in full without touching savings?
- Will this increase my monthly fixed costs?
- Is this a want or a need?

- Am I buying this to impress or to improve?
- Have I hit my savings and debt goals this month?

If you answer no to two or more—wait.

### Lifestyle Creep Red Flags

- You get nervous checking your bank account
- You have multiple Buy Now, Pay Later (BNPL) balances
- Your credit card balance keeps increasing
- You avoid budgeting because "it stresses you out"
- You keep saying, "It'll be fine once I upgrade/pay off that one thing/-make captain"

## The Creep-Proof Pilot's Plan

### Budget Like You're Still a CFI

Not forever. But for your first year. Pretend your pay didn't jump. Funnel the difference into wealth.

### Create a Lifestyle Ceiling

Pick a monthly living expense cap. Stick to it. Only raise it when you increase your savings rate first.

### Practice "Delay and Review" Spending

Wait 48 hours before buying anything over $100. Review your budget. If it still feels smart, green light it.

### Track Your Financial Climb

Use a net worth tracker. Watch your assets grow, not just your paycheck. That's how you know you're actually leveling up.

### Choose One Celebration Per Raise

When your income increases, allow one small lifestyle upgrade. Just one. Then funnel the rest toward goals.

### Empowering Reminders for the Sky and Ground

- You don't owe anyone an expensive lifestyle
- The best flex is financial peace, not a Rolex

- Growing your wealth is quieter than spending it
- You can live well without spending wildly
- You're not being cheap. You're being strategic

**Action Steps to Take Right Now**

- Write down your current monthly expenses
- Set a cap for rent, transportation, and food
- Auto-transfer 10% of your next paycheck to savings
- Cancel one subscription you don't use
- Delay one big purchase by 30 days and track how you feel

**Call to Action:**

Make one financial move before you go wheels-up tomorrow:

- Freeze your lifestyle spending
- Start a net worth tracker
- Set a lifestyle upgrade rule (one per raise)
- Talk with another pilot about how they avoid lifestyle creep

Just one move. Then another next week.

Don't fly blind with your money. Don't climb faster than your financial aircraft can handle.

**Final Word:**

Your first flying job should feel like the beginning of your freedom—not the beginning of a financial mess.

You didn't get into this industry just to spend your whole career catching up. You got here to take off, to climb, to build something bigger.

So enjoy your money. But don't waste your lift.

Live well. Spend smart. And never let your expenses fly faster than your plan.

Your future self will thank you.

So will your crew.

So will your sanity.

# Part II: Taking Off – Your Early Career in Aviation

This section is where flight becomes real—not just in the cockpit, but in your financial life. *Part II: Taking Off* guides you through the critical early stages of your aviation career, when your first real paychecks start arriving, your schedule shifts from training blocks to flight rosters, and your financial decisions begin shaping your future altitude.

These chapters are designed to meet you exactly where you are—earning your first income, paying off student loans, navigating crash pads, and wondering what to do with that new 401(k) enrollment form. We'll tackle taxes, budgeting, housing, credit, lifestyle creep, and the subtle financial habits that separate pilots who soar financially from those stuck circling the same paycheck-to-paycheck pattern.

This isn't about restriction. It's about structure. It's not about deprivation. It's about direction. Whether you're living on reserve, flying five-day trips, or commuting across states to build your hours, *Part II* will help you create a plan that supports your mission—without sacrificing your peace of mind or your financial potential.

Your wings are on. Let's make sure your money's flying with you.

# Chapter 11: Regional Airline Economics – Contracts, Pay, and Perks

You finally get the call.

After years of training, instruction, and check rides, you sign your first contract with a regional airline. You're in uniform, you're holding a schedule, and you're building hours toward the magic number: 1,500. But while your flying skills are leveling up fast, your understanding of your paycheck might be lagging behind.

This chapter is your straight talk on the economics of being a regional airline pilot. Because understanding the money side of the job isn't optional. It's part of being a professional.

You don't have to wait until you hit the majors to make smart financial moves. You just have to understand the landscape now—and how to fly it strategically.

Let's get you oriented.

**Understanding the Regional Airline Business Model**

Regional airlines don't operate independently in the way most passengers assume.

They typically fly under the branding of major carriers:

- SkyWest for United, Delta, and American
- Envoy for American
- Republic for Delta, United, and American

These airlines operate on a *Capacity Purchase Agreement (CPA)* model. That means the major airline pays the regional to fly routes under its brand. The regional earns money from the contract, not from passengers buying tickets.

Why does this matter?

- Regionals are cost-sensitive
- Pilot pay is historically lower than majors
- Schedules are tighter, training budgets leaner

Your job as a regional pilot is vital. But financially, you need to understand you're in a stepping stone role.

**Base Pay: Understanding the Hourly Rate Model**

Pilot pay is based on *flight hours,* not time on duty.

Here's the breakdown:

- You have a monthly minimum guarantee (typically 75–80 hours)
- You are paid a fixed hourly rate
- You are only paid when the aircraft door is closed and brakes are released

So if you sit in the airport on reserve for 5 hours, you get paid *zero* unless you get assigned a flight.

**First-Year Pay Example:**

- $50/hour x 75 hours = $3,750/month gross
- After taxes, union dues, insurance, etc.? Closer to $2,400–$2,800

**This is why budgeting matters.** That big pay bump you envisioned may take a couple years to show up.

**Training Pay: Your First Reality Check**

Most regional airlines don't pay full hourly rates during training.

Instead, you might get:

- Flat pay (e.g., $400/week)
- Reduced hourly rate
- No per diem until IOE starts

Training pay can last 2–3 months. Plan for this.

- Save in advance if possible
- Consider side gigs that don't interfere with studying or rest

**Per Diem: What It Is and Isn't**

Per diem is a fixed hourly allowance paid for time away from base.

- Typically $1.75–$2.25/hour
- Non-taxable
- Doesn't count toward overtime, 401(k), or loan applications

It's easy to spend per diem like regular income. But smart pilots treat it as fuel:

- Save it
- Use it for debt repayment
- Fund your emergency account

**Upgrades and Pay Progression**

Your first year will be the lowest pay of your flying career. But things ramp up quickly.

Example pay scale (approximate):

- Year 1 FO: $50/hr
- Year 2 FO: $60/hr
- Year 3 FO: $70/hr
- Year 1 CA: $85/hr
- Year 2 CA: $95/hr

- Year 3 CA: $105/hr

Upgrades depend on:

- Company growth
- Attrition to majors
- Union seniority lists

Don't plan around guaranteed upgrade timelines. Be flexible. But be ready.

**Bonuses and Incentives**

Regionals often use bonuses to attract or retain pilots.

Types include:

- **Sign-on bonuses**: $10K–$100K, often paid in installments
- **Retention bonuses**: Paid after 1, 2, or 3 years
- **Referral bonuses**: For bringing in other pilots
- **Upgrade bonuses**: When moving from FO to CA

**Important:** Bonuses are usually taxed at a flat 22% or more. Plan ahead.

Don't spend your entire bonus before you see the actual deposit. Treat it like irregular income. Prioritize savings and debt first.

**Contracts and Flow-Through Programs**

Some regionals have flow-through agreements with majors.

**Flow-through vs. Flow-by:**

- Flow-through = you're guaranteed a major airline spot after a set period (e.g., Envoy to American)
- Flow-by = you may get an interview or preference, but not a guarantee

Questions to ask before signing:

- How long is the flow timeline?
- Is it seniority-based?

- Are there performance gates?
- What can break the contract?

Know what you're signing. And always get a copy.

**Commuting vs. Living in Base**

Commuting adds complexity.

- You may need a crash pad ($250–400/month)
- You'll lose time off to travel
- Missed commutes can impact your schedule and pay

Living in base often improves quality of life, reduces cost, and improves sleep.

Do the math:

- Cost of housing in base vs. crash pad + flights
- Impact on rest, stress, and relationships

**401(k) and Retirement Options**

Regionals offer:

- 401(k) with employer match (some up to 13%)
- Profit sharing (rare but possible)

Start contributing as soon as you're eligible.

- Target at least the match
- Consider Roth vs. pre-tax based on income level

Don't delay investing just because pay is tight. Even $50/month counts.

**Healthcare, Insurance, and Union Dues**

Your contract will detail:

- Health, dental, and vision insurance premiums
- Short-term disability (sometimes optional)
- Loss of license insurance (usually optional but wise)
- Union dues (usually 1.5% of gross pay)

You can opt out of some benefits, but don't do it blindly. Ask:

- What's covered?
- What's the deductible?
- What if I get hurt off duty?

**Schedule Bidding and Pay Impact**

Seniority = pay control.

- New hires often get reserve
- Reserve may mean lower pay and irregular hours
- Line holders can pick more lucrative trips

Use scheduling apps and talk to senior pilots. Learn how to maximize credit.

Example:

- A 78-hour line with multiple overnights could yield 90+ hours of credit with proper planning

**Real-Life Scenario: Erin, 25, First-Year Regional FO**

Erin budgeted based on $60K/year. But her first few months included:

- $400/week training pay
- $0 per diem
- Unexpected hotel/food expenses

Her net income was $1,200/month until IOE started. She had to:

- Pause student loan payments
- Use a part-time delivery job
- Borrow from her emergency fund

Six months in, she stabilized and began contributing $100/month to her 401(k). Her story isn't uncommon.

**How to Fly Smart with Regional Airline Pay**

- **Budget low:** Plan for your lowest pay month, not your best
- **Save early:** Start a $1,000 emergency fund immediately
- **Avoid lifestyle creep:** Don't buy like a major airline captain on regional pay
- **Understand your paycheck:** Break down every deduction
- **Ask questions:** Union reps, mentors, and senior pilots are your co-pilots in learning

**Action Steps**

- Get a copy of your contract and read the pay section
- Create a "worst-case" monthly budget
- Save your first per diem instead of spending it
- Call HR and clarify 401(k) match policies
- Download your first pay stub and review every line

**Call to Action:**

Before your next trip:

- Ask one captain what they wish they knew about regional pay
- Save your next per diem deposit
- Make a list of financial goals for your first 12 months

Just one move. Then another next week.

You're not just building flight time. You're building financial altitude.

**Final Word:**

Being a regional airline pilot is often your first real flying job. But it's also your first real money job.

Use it wisely.

Yes, the pay will improve. But the habits you build now will follow you to the majors.

This isn't about surviving until upgrade. It's about thriving with what you have.

You're not flying for scraps. You're flying a strategy.

Your future self will thank you.

So will your crew.

So will your sanity.

# Chapter 12: Decoding Your Pay Stub – Per Diem, Duty Rig, and More

There are few moments more exciting for a new pilot than opening your first paycheck.

And yet, there are few moments more confusing, either.

Because what you *think* you're getting paid—and what actually shows up in your bank account—are often two very different numbers.

Why? Because pilot pay isn't like most jobs. It's not a simple salary. It's not just hourly. It's not just base pay. It's a complex mix of pay codes, rig protections, per diem, deductions, and contracts—each with its own rules and quirks.

And here's the truth: if you don't understand how you're paid, you'll never understand how to budget, negotiate, or optimize your income.

This chapter is your decoder ring. We'll walk through everything from per diem to duty rigs to the mystery of why "credit time" doesn't always mean "money in your pocket."

Whether you're brand new to aviation or a few years in but still fuzzy on the details, this chapter will help you read your pay stub like a checklist—and own every dollar you earn.

**Why This Chapter Matters**

- You can't manage your money if you don't understand how it's earned
- You'll miss opportunities to increase income if you don't know how rig protections work

- You'll budget better when you understand pay fluctuations
- You'll advocate smarter during contract negotiations if you know what each pay line means

**Start With the Basics: Your Airline's Pay Stub Format**

Every airline uses its own software. Some use legacy systems from the 90s. Others offer slick dashboards. But no matter what it looks like, your pay stub will typically show:

- **Pay Period Start/End Dates**
- **Pay Categories (Hourly, Per Diem, Training, Holiday)**
- **Credit Time (What you're being paid for)**
- **Deductions (Taxes, Insurance, Union Dues)**
- **YTD Totals (Helpful for taxes)**

Ask your payroll department or union rep for a pay stub walkthrough in your first 60 days.

**Base Pay: What Most Pilots Understand—Sort Of**

You're paid based on flight hours.

Your **hourly rate** x **credit time** = gross pay.

But here's the catch:

- **Flight hour** = only block time (brakes off to brakes on)
- **Credit hour** = what you're paid for (may include rigs or minimums)
- **Scheduled credit** is often higher than actual block time (that's good)

You have a **monthly minimum guarantee** (MMG)—typically 75 to 80 hours. If you're scheduled less, you're still paid the MMG.

**Example:**

- $50/hr FO rate x 75 hours = $3,750 gross pay

**Per Diem: The Most Misunderstood Pilot Benefit**

Per diem is non-taxable pay for time spent away from base. Typically:

- $1.75–$2.25/hour
- Begins at check-in, ends at release
- Not included in 401(k) contributions

It's not "free money," but it *is* valuable.

**Smart pilots treat per diem as:**

- A savings booster
- A debt-paydown weapon
- A travel/replenishment fund

**Pro tip:** Track your per diem hours monthly. It'll help when comparing schedules or negotiating trades.

**Duty Rig, Trip Rig, and Minimum Duty Periods – What They Mean for You**

These protections make sure your pay reflects your *time worked,* not just your *time flown.*

**Duty Rig:**

- Also called 1-for-2
- You get 1 hour of pay for every 2 hours on duty

**Trip Rig:**

- Also called 1-for-3.5
- You get 1 hour of pay for every 3.5 hours away from base

**Minimum Duty Period:**

- Guarantees minimum pay for short-duty days (e.g., 5-hour min for any day with flying)

**Why It Matters:**

If you have a 12-hour duty day with only 3 hours of flight time, a good duty rig ensures you don't walk away with 3 hours of pay—it could bump to 6.

**Reserve vs. Line Pay Differences**

**Reserve Pay:**

- Paid the MMG no matter how little you fly
- May get more with "ready reserve" or call-out premium
- Irregular schedule = pay fluctuation

**Line Holder Pay:**

- More control over hours, per diem, and credit time
- Can "bid" higher-paying trips
- Usually more stable pay, but no "free" hours like reserve

Know your contract. Some reserve systems pay better for certain trips or call-outs.

**Holiday Pay, Training Pay, and Special Premiums**

**Holiday Pay:**

- Extra credit for flying on designated holidays (varies by contract)

**Training Pay:**

- Often a flat weekly rate or lower credit
- Some airlines allow per diem, some don't
- Budget carefully during training months

**Premium Pay:**

- Incentives to pick up extra trips (usually 125%-150% of base pay)
- Some contracts pay double on short notice

Watch for open-time offers in your crew portal. These can add thousands to your yearly income.

**Understanding Deductions**

Your gross pay will be reduced by:

- Federal income tax
- State income tax
- Social Security (6.2%)
- Medicare (1.45%)
- Union dues (usually 1.5–2%)
- Health insurance premiums
- 401(k) contributions (pre- or post-tax)
- Optional benefits (vision, dental, HSA, disability)

Download your pay stub every month and check deductions.

Errors happen. Fix them early.

**Year-to-Date (YTD) and Taxes**

Pay stubs show YTD figures. Use these to:

- Estimate taxes owed
- Maximize 401(k) contributions
- Track per diem (not shown on W-2 but helpful for budgeting)

If you earn 1099 income elsewhere (instruction, ferry work), YTD helps you estimate your total income for tax planning.

**Real-Life Scenario: Luis, 31, Regional FO**

Luis thought he was being paid for 90 hours a month. But his net deposits varied wildly.

After reviewing his stubs:

- He realized he was only being paid 78 credit hours, despite flying 90 block hours
- Per diem fluctuated based on schedule (he had misjudged it as fixed)
- He wasn't contributing to his 401(k), missing out on $2,000 in free match money

He now tracks every pay stub, logs his flight hours, and reviews his schedule for premium opportunities. His income is the same—but his clarity is higher.

**Checklist: How to Decode Your Pay Stub Each Month**

1. **Confirm credit time matches your schedule**
2. **Track per diem separately**
3. **Review all deductions line by line**
4. **Compare YTD totals to your own records**
5. **Log discrepancies and follow up within 30 days**
6. **Download and store every pay stub in a secure folder**

**Plain-Language Takeaways**

- Pay and time are not the same
- If you don't understand a pay code, ask your union or payroll
- Rig protections can make or break your monthly income
- Don't guess at your paycheck—verify it
- Every hour away from home has value. Make sure it shows up in your pay

**Action Steps for This Month**

- Print and highlight your latest pay stub
- Create a pay stub decoder legend for your contract
- Build a spreadsheet for tracking hours, credit, and income
- Ask a senior pilot how they optimize pay and track rigs

- Set a calendar reminder to review stubs monthly

**Call to Action**

Make one money move before you go wheels-up tomorrow:

- Read your pay stub, line by line
- Identify one item you don't understand—and find out what it means
- Add your credit hours to a log
- Save a copy in your digital archives

Just one move. Then another next week.

You're not just flying planes. You're flying a career.

**Final Word**

Understanding your pay stub isn't about nitpicking dollars. It's about owning the flow of your income.

When you decode your pay stub, you take the mystery out of money. You stop flying blind. You start making choices based on real data.

This isn't about ego. It's about empowerment.

Your future self will thank you.

So will your crew.

So will your sanity.

# Chapter 13: Building an Emergency Fund With Irregular Income

In aviation, turbulence is expected. But when it hits your finances, it can knock you off course.

That's why you need an emergency fund.

Not a maybe fund. Not a "we'll see" savings account. A real, ready, reachable reserve that keeps you flying when life tries to ground you.

The problem? You don't have predictable paychecks. As a pilot, especially early in your career, your income changes month to month. You might be on reserve, trading trips, commuting across time zones, or juggling W-2 and 1099 work.

So how do you build a safety net when your income feels like it's constantly in motion?

This chapter is your preflight briefing on how to create, maintain, and grow an emergency fund as a pilot with irregular income.

It's not about perfection. It's about preparation.

Because when your finances are secure, your mind is clear. And that's when you fly best.

**Why Every Pilot Needs an Emergency Fund**

You might feel like your income is too low to save. Or too unstable to commit to anything monthly.

But emergencies don't care what your schedule looks like.

And in aviation, these are common:

- Canceled classes or delays in training pay
- Union contract disputes
- Medical leave or FAA grounding
- Family issues that require time off
- Flight instructor downtime due to weather
- Aircraft damage or job loss in contract work

An emergency fund isn't a luxury. It's a flight instrument. When things go sideways, it keeps you upright.

**What an Emergency Fund Actually Is**

Not an investment account.

Not your checking account buffer.

Not a credit card.

An emergency fund is **cash** or near-cash in a **separate**, **dedicated** account that is:

- Easy to access (within 1–2 business days)
- Safe from market fluctuations
- Clearly defined for emergencies only

**How Much Do You Need?**

Standard advice says 3–6 months of living expenses.

But let's break that down for a pilot with variable income:

**1 month = your true monthly nut**

This includes:

- Rent or mortgage
- Utilities
- Insurance premiums
- Food and essentials
- Loan payments

It does **not** include:

- Travel
- Dining out
- Shopping
- Subscriptions

**3 months = minimum runway**

**6 months = optimal runway**

**12+ months = financial altitude**

If you're single, young, and have family backup, 3 months may work.

If you have dependents, debt, or fly 1099? Shoot for 6+.

**Step 1: Find Your Average Monthly Expenses**

Use your last 3 months of bank and credit card statements.

- Highlight essential expenses only
- Average them out
- Round up to give yourself margin

**Example:**

- Rent: $1,200
- Utilities: $150
- Food: $400
- Insurance: $200
- Loan payments: $350
- Total: ~$2,300/month

3 months = $6,900

6 months = $13,800

This is your target.

**Step 2: Choose Your Emergency Fund Vehicle**

Keep it **liquid but not visible.** You don't want it in your checking account.

Best options:

- High-Yield Online Savings Account (HYSA)
- Money Market Account with ATM card (no checks)

Do NOT use:

- Investment accounts
- CD with long lock-up
- Checking account

**Pro tip:** Nickname the account "Emergency Fuel Reserve" in your banking app.

**Step 3: Build With Irregular Income**

This is where it gets real.

You don't have the same paycheck every month. So don't try to save the same amount every month.

**Use a percentage system.**

Every time you get paid, put **10–20%** of net income into your emergency fund.

**Example:**

- Get paid $2,400 → save $240
- Get paid $3,100 → save $310

This smooths the highs and lows.

**Step 4: Use Per Diem as a Secret Weapon**

Per diem is often overlooked. It's untaxed, feels like extra, and adds up. Use it to supercharge your fund.

- Bank 100% of per diem for 6 months
- Use a separate tracker to log it
- Funnel it into your emergency account at month-end

This alone could add $2,000–3,000 in a year.

**Step 5: One-Time Boosts and Found Money**

Jumpstart your fund with windfalls:

- Tax refund
- Flight school refund or incentive
- Signing bonus
- Extra trip pay

Split these:

- 50% to emergency fund
- 50% to whatever else you need

**Step 6: Protect the Fund Like Your License**

This is not a vacation fund.
This is not a new gear fund.
This is not a "just because I'm tired" fund.
Emergencies include:

- Job loss
- Major car repair
- Medical bills
- Family crisis
- FAA grounding

They do **not** include:

- Concert tickets
- New iPads
- Holiday gifts
- Vacations

Build a firewall. If you take from it, rebuild immediately.

**Real-Life Scenario: Rachel, 33, Commuting FO**

Rachel flew for a regional and commuted from home to base every week. One winter, weather delays caused 3 missed commutes and 2 cancellations.

Her per diem dropped. Her actual hours fell below guarantee. She earned $900 less than planned in February.

Because she had a $5,000 emergency fund, she:

- Covered her bills stress-free
- Didn't borrow on a credit card
- Didn't panic

That fund wasn't just money. It was calm.

**What If You Can't Save Yet?**

Start with a micro goal.

- Save $500
- Then $1,000
- Then one month's rent

Track your spending weekly.

Pause unnecessary expenses for 30 days.

Use cash envelopes for food or entertainment.

**Remember:** Progress > perfection.

**Stacking Other Buffers**

Once you have your emergency fund basics covered, consider:

- A "Job Buffer Account" (for transitions or long training)
- A "Reserve Month Account" (to cover light pay periods)
- A "Grounded Backup Fund" (for loss of license time)

All of these are next-level. But they start with your emergency fund.

**Action Checklist**

1. Calculate your essential monthly expenses
2. Choose a savings vehicle
3. Set up auto-transfer from each paycheck
4. Save 100% of per diem for 30 days
5. Add found money when available
6. Define what counts as an emergency
7. Don't stop until you hit your 3-month minimum

**Plain Language Reminders**

- Irregular income isn't an excuse. It's a reason to prepare.
- $1,000 beats $0.
- If you can fly across the country in bad weather, you can build a savings plan.
- Don't let shame stop your momentum.
- Your emergency fund is not for when things go wrong. It's so you can stay right.

**Call to Action**

Make one financial move before your next trip:

- Open a separate savings account
- Set up a $50 auto-transfer
- Calculate your monthly essentials
- Save your next per diem check

Just one move. Then another next week.

**Final Word**

You train for engine failures. You brief alternate airports. You wear redundancy like a badge of honor.

Apply that to your money.

An emergency fund is your financial alternate.

It's your plan B.

It's your no-stress reserve.

You didn't come this far to get grounded by a flat tire, missed checkride, or a surprise dental bill.

Build the fund.

Fly with confidence.

Your future self will thank you.

So will your crew.

So will your sanity.

# Chapter 14: Essential Insurance for New Pilots – Life, Renters, and Disability

As a new pilot, your career is climbing.

You're finally earning real income, building flight time, and making financial decisions with long-term implications. But there's one topic most pilots skip until it's too late:

**Insurance.**

The word itself sounds boring, maybe even unnecessary. Especially when your cash flow feels tight and you're just trying to get through training, commuting, reserve, or your first real bid line.

But here's the truth:

Insurance isn't about being paranoid.

It's about being a professional.

It's about protecting the time, money, and effort you've invested.

And it's about giving yourself and your family peace of mind if life throws turbulence your way.

In this chapter, we're going to walk through the three most essential types of insurance for new pilots:

- **Renters Insurance**
- **Disability Insurance (including Loss of License)**
- **Life Insurance**

We'll break down what each one is, why it matters, how to buy it, and how much coverage you actually need.

No jargon. No pressure. Just straight talk from one pilot to another.

**Start With Why: You Are the Asset**

You are your career.

More specifically: your body, your eyes, your hearing, your ability to pass a medical, and your pilot certificate *are* your earning power.

If something compromises any of those things—temporarily or permanently—your income takes a hit.

That's where insurance steps in.

**1. Renters Insurance: Protecting Your Stuff (and Your Liability)**

**What It Is:**

Renters insurance covers your belongings and personal liability when you rent a house, apartment, or even a crash pad.

**Why It Matters for Pilots:**

- You move a lot in early career stages
- Your airline might not reimburse you for stolen items during layovers
- Your landlord's insurance does **not** cover your belongings
- If you cause a fire, flood, or injury, you could be liable for thousands

**What It Covers:**

- Theft, fire, water damage (to your stuff)
- Liability if someone gets hurt in your unit
- Temporary housing if your place is damaged

**What It Costs:**

- $10–25/month depending on location and coverage level

**How to Get It:**

- Use online comparison sites (Lemonade, Policygenius, etc.)

- Bundle with auto insurance if you drive
- Choose replacement cost over actual cash value

**Coverage Amounts:**

- $20,000 to $50,000 personal property
- $100,000 to $300,000 liability

**Pro Tip:** Add scheduled coverage for flight gear if you keep it at home.

**2. Disability Insurance: Replacing Your Income If You Can't Fly**

**What It Is:**

Disability insurance replaces a portion of your income if you're unable to work due to illness or injury.

For pilots, this includes:

- Back injuries
- Vision or hearing loss
- Mental health conditions
- Heart or neurological issues

**Why It Matters for Pilots:**

- Your FAA medical is your gatekeeper to flying
- A single diagnosis can ground you
- Most employers don't offer enough coverage
- The likelihood of being disabled for 90+ days is higher than dying before age 65

**Types of Disability Insurance:**

**Short-Term Disability (STD):**

- Covers 0–90 days
- May be provided by your airline

- Covers 60–80% of income

**Long-Term Disability (LTD):**

- Covers beyond 90 days
- Can last 2 years, 5 years, or until age 65
- Replaces 50–60% of base income

**Loss of License Insurance:**

- Unique to pilots
- Pays a lump sum or monthly benefit if you permanently lose medical certification
- Offered through unions, private brokers, or pilot associations

**How Much Coverage Do You Need?**

- Enough to cover fixed expenses (rent, loans, food)
- Ideally, 60–70% of your current income
- Include extra if you have dependents

**What It Costs:**

- 1–3% of your annual income for a private policy
- Group policies may be cheaper (check with your union)

**Pro Tip:** Always ask if the policy is *own-occupation*. That means you're considered disabled if you can't fly—even if you can work another job.

**3. Life Insurance: Protecting Those Who Rely on You**

**What It Is:**

Life insurance pays a lump sum to your beneficiaries (partner, parents, children) if you die.

**Why It Matters for Pilots:**

- You travel frequently and face unique occupational risks
- You may have co-signed debt with family
- You may want to support aging parents, siblings, or future kids
- You might want to lock in rates while you're healthy

**Types of Life Insurance:**

**Term Life Insurance:**

- Coverage for a set period (10, 20, 30 years)
- Lower premiums
- No cash value
- Great for young pilots

**Whole Life (Permanent) Insurance:**

- Covers you for life
- Includes cash value component
- Much more expensive
- Often oversold to young professionals

**How Much Coverage Should You Get?**

- 10–12x your annual income (as a rule of thumb)
- More if you have dependents
- Less if you're single and debt-free

**What It Costs:**

- \$15–50/month for a 20-year, \$500,000 term policy in your 20s or early 30s

**Where to Get It:**

- Pilot unions (often offer group plans)
- Online brokers (Policygenius, Quotacy)
- Financial advisor (fee-only preferred)

**Pro Tip:** Get coverage while you're young and healthy. Lock in low premiums.

**Real-Life Scenario: Derek, 28, Regional Pilot**

Derek was commuting weekly and paying rent on a crash pad and a home base apartment. During IOE, he slipped on ice, tore his ACL, and couldn't fly for four months.

He had no short-term disability.

He had $1,800/month in fixed expenses.

He borrowed from family to stay afloat.

After recovery, he:

- Bought a $12/month renters policy
- Enrolled in loss of license insurance through ALPA
- Purchased a $500,000 20-year term life policy for $18/month

He now calls them his "financial seat belts."

**Plain-Language Rules of Thumb**

- If you rent, get renters insurance. No exceptions.
- If you rely on your FAA medical for income, get disability coverage.
- If anyone relies on your income, get life insurance.

And remember:

- Insurance is cheaper when you're healthy
- Employer policies disappear when you change jobs
- Group plans are great, but personal coverage = control

**Checklist for New Pilots**

1. Get a renters policy today
2. Review your employer's disability coverage
3. Shop for a private long-term disability policy
4. Compare loss of license options
5. If you have dependents or co-signed loans, get term life insurance
6. Keep all policies in a shared digital folder

**Action Steps This Month**

- Call your union rep and ask about group disability and loss of license
- Get a renters quote online
- Apply for a $250K–$500K term life policy (even if single)
- Review all policy exclusions (especially aviation-related)

**Call to Action**

Make one financial safety move before your next trip:

- Buy renters insurance
- Apply for term life coverage
- Ask about disability options

Just one move. Then another next week.

**Final Word**

Insurance isn't just paperwork.

It's peace of mind.

It's being ready for the unplanned.

It's a vote of confidence in your future and your ability to protect it.

You already plan for weather, alternates, fuel, and contingencies in the sky.

Do the same on the ground.

Your future self will thank you.

So will your crew.

So will your sanity.

# Chapter 15: Travel Credit Cards, Rewards, and Financial Discipline

For pilots, travel is your default mode. You know airports, hotels, and layovers like most people know their neighborhood coffee shop. So it only makes sense to start leveraging that lifestyle into financial rewards.

But here's the trap:

Just because you *can* earn miles, points, and perks doesn't mean you should dive headfirst into the travel credit card game without a plan. This chapter is here to give you the full picture—how to use travel rewards to your advantage without falling into the traps that leave so many pilots flying high on perks but crashing hard in debt.

We'll cover:

- The best types of cards for pilots
- How to pick the right one for your flying life
- How to use rewards without overspending
- The psychological pitfalls of chasing points
- How to stay disciplined while enjoying the benefits

This isn't about chasing status. It's about strategy.

Let's get you set up for smart, grounded, and profitable travel spending.

**Start With Why: What Travel Credit Cards Offer**

Travel credit cards can offer:

- Airline miles or points
- Hotel rewards
- Airport lounge access
- Free TSA PreCheck/Global Entry
- Statement credits for travel-related expenses
- Rental car coverage
- Lost luggage reimbursement
- Trip interruption insurance

All of that can sound like a dream come true. But here's the catch:

- Most premium travel cards come with high annual fees ($95 to $695)
- Rewards are only worth it if you *pay in full every month*
- It takes discipline to avoid chasing bonuses you don't need

So before you apply for anything, you need to know your **mission**.

**Common Travel Credit Card Profiles for Pilots**

**The Commuter**

- Goal: Rack up airline points
- Best: Airline-branded credit cards (Delta Amex, United Explorer, etc.)
- Key perks: Free checked bag, boarding priority, miles multipliers

**The Hotel Hopper**

- Goal: Offset crash pad or layover hotel costs
- Best: Hotel-branded cards (Hilton Honors, Marriott Bonvoy)
- Key perks: Free nights, upgrades, status bump

**The Lounge Seeker**

- Goal: Max comfort in airports
- Best: Premium cards with lounge access (Amex Platinum, Capital One

Venture X)

- Key perks: Amex Centurion Lounge, Priority Pass, Global Entry credit

**The Global Jetsetter**

- Goal: International rewards and travel flexibility
- Best: General travel cards (Chase Sapphire Preferred/Reserve, Venture X)
- Key perks: Points transfer to airlines/hotels, no foreign transaction fees

**The Minimalist**

- Goal: Simple rewards, no fees
- Best: No-annual-fee cards with basic travel points (Chase Freedom Flex, Amex Green)
- Key perks: Cash back or flexible points

**How Points and Miles Actually Work**

**Cash Back:**

- 1% to 5% on specific categories
- Best if you want simplicity

**Travel Points:**

- Earn based on card usage
- Transferable to airlines/hotels
- Redeem for flights, hotels, upgrades

**Miles:**

- Airline-branded points

- Can be redeemed through airline portal

**Point Values:**

- 1 cent per point is average
- Transferable points often more valuable
- Airline miles can fluctuate based on redemption strategy

**Important:** Points are not cash. They lose value if hoarded. Use them.

**Sign-Up Bonuses: The Siren Song**

You'll see:

- 60,000 points after $4,000 spent in 3 months
- 100,000 miles for new applicants

Sounds amazing. But read carefully.

**Pitfalls:**

- Spending more just to hit the bonus = loss
- Interest charges cancel out rewards
- Missed payments = credit damage

**Rule of Thumb:**

Only chase a sign-up bonus if:

- You already spend that much normally
- You can pay in full every month
- You don't already have credit card debt

**Annual Fees: Worth It or Waste?**

Premium cards can charge:

- $95 (moderate)

- $250 (mid-tier)
- $550–695 (premium)

**Is it worth it?**

Calculate like a pilot:

- Lounge access saves you $50/month?
- Free bags save you $120/year?
- $300 travel credit offsets fee?

If your **annual benefits > annual fee**, you're winning.

But only if you stay disciplined.

**The Flight Plan for Responsible Travel Card Use**

**1. Always Pay in Full**

- Rewards are wiped out by interest
- Use auto-pay to avoid mistakes

**2. Don't Let Points Control You**

- Spend based on *need,* not *points*
- Don't buy $300 worth of wine just to hit a category bonus

**3. Stick to 1 or 2 Cards**

- More cards = more temptation
- Confusion leads to missed payments

**4. Track Your Rewards Value**

- Keep a spreadsheet or use apps like AwardWallet

**5. Time Your Big Purchases**

- Hit spending thresholds naturally
- Pay bills, rent (if allowed), or insurance premiums strategically

**6. Redeem Smart**

- Book early for best rates
- Transfer to partners for high-value redemptions

**The Discipline Test: Real-Life Scenarios**

**Jared, 29, Regional FO**

- Got a premium card with 100,000 point bonus
- Spent $4,000 in 2 months, including a new iPad and upgraded luggage
- Carried a $2,000 balance at 20% interest

**Result:**

- Paid $400 in interest
- Negated the point value of his bonus
- Lowered his credit score due to high utilization

**Lesson:**

- Points are not profit if you're carrying debt

**Talia, 35, Major Airline Captain**

- Used travel card only for fuel, groceries, and hotel spend
- Paid off every month
- Used points to fly her family to Hawaii in off-season

**Result:**

- $1,200 flight value
- Zero debt
- Maintained 800+ credit score

**Lesson:**

- Strategy + discipline = win

**Credit Cards and Your Credit Score**

Good credit = better loan rates, insurance premiums, and job applications.

**Factors That Affect Score:**

- Payment history (35%)
- Credit utilization (30%)
- Credit history length (15%)
- Credit mix (10%)
- New credit/inquiries (10%)

**Tips:**

- Keep balances below 30% of limit
- Don't open too many cards at once
- Never miss a payment

**Your Go-Bag: Travel Card Essentials for Pilots**

**Recommended Toolkit:**

- 1 airline card for free bags and miles
- 1 general travel card for flexible points
- 1 backup no-fee card for emergencies

**Apps to Use:**

- AwardWallet: Track points
- Mint or Monarch: Track spending
- Credit Karma: Monitor credit score

**Keep It Simple:**

- One card for airfare/hotels
- One card for food/fuel

**Checklist for Smart Travel Credit Use**

1. Choose a card that matches your lifestyle
2. Set auto-pay to avoid missed payments
3. Track your monthly spend
4. Never carry a balance
5. Redeem points annually
6. Reassess annual fee value every year
7. Keep one low-limit card locked away for emergencies

**Plain Language Reminders**

- Points are not profits
- Status doesn't equal wealth
- You don't have to collect every shiny card offer
- Use cards to *enhance* your lifestyle, not inflate it

**Action Steps This Week**

- Review your current credit card habits
- Calculate how much you'd earn from a travel card (realistically)
- Compare 2-3 cards side by side
- If you open one, set up auto-pay immediately
- Plan 3 redemptions this year that support real life, not social media

**Call to Action**

Make one financial move before your next trip:

- Set a rule for how you use your card
- Cancel a card that's costing more than it's worth
- Redeem points before they expire
- Set a credit utilization goal (under 10%)

Just one move. Then another next week.

**Final Word**

Travel cards can be powerful co-pilots in your financial life—but only if you're the one flying the plane.

Treat points like a bonus, not a goal.

Treat your budget like a flight plan.

Treat discipline like an instrument rating—it may not feel glamorous, but it'll save your life in bad conditions.

Your future self will thank you.

So will your crew.

So will your sanity.

# Chapter 16: Managing Relationships and Money on a Pilot's Schedule

Being a pilot doesn't just affect how you fly.

It affects how you live.

The schedule. The stress. The time zones. The crash pads. The bidding system. The unpredictable income early in your career. The long stretches away from home. And yes, the tension that can build between partners, roommates, family, and even yourself when money and time never seem to align.

So this chapter isn't just about budgeting or communication.

It's about making your money work for your relationships—not against them.

It's about navigating love, roommates, friendships, co-parenting, and long-distance dynamics when your lifestyle is anything but routine.

And it's about learning to build financial trust, respect, and clarity with the people who matter most.

Because you didn't earn your wings to lose peace at home.

Let's talk honestly.

**Start With the Reality: Your Schedule Is Not Normal**

- 4-on, 3-off rotation
- Red-eyes and 5 a.m. call times
- Reserve status, crash pads, commuting days
- Last-minute reroutes or delays

- Bidding systems that affect every other part of your life

All of this makes it hard to:

- Split bills evenly
- Attend consistent couple's money check-ins
- Plan family time or vacations
- Share tasks like budgeting, childcare, or meal planning

And when that tension is mixed with financial stress? It can spiral fast.

**Part I: Money and Romantic Relationships**

### *Know Your Communication Pattern*

Every couple has a default communication style:

- **Avoiders:** Don't talk about money until it explodes
- **Managers:** One person runs the finances, the other goes along
- **Debaters:** Constant negotiations, sometimes hostile
- **Partners:** Transparent, goal-focused, regular check-ins

Your schedule makes it easier to fall into avoidance or delegation.

But the healthiest long-term model is partnership.

**What Partnership Looks Like:**

- Shared logins and account access
- Regular "money dates" every month (video call if needed)
- Budget apps both can view (Monarch, YNAB, Mint)
- Agreement on big decisions and boundaries

### *Discuss the Big Questions Early*

- Who pays for what?
- How will we save?
- What happens if one of us gets grounded?
- Are we both contributing to retirement?
- How do we handle family support or obligations?
- Do we want joint accounts, separate, or hybrid?

If you can fly a plane, you can talk about money.

Just start.

### *When One Person Makes More*

This is common in pilot partnerships. Especially when one partner is still building hours or working outside aviation.

Resentment can build if you:

- Don't acknowledge the imbalance
- Tie financial power to relationship power
- Avoid conversations about shared goals

**Solution:**

- Proportional contributions (e.g., each pays 30% of income)
- Joint savings accounts with shared goals
- Acknowledge that time, emotional labor, and household management *are* valuable

## Part II: Long-Distance or On-the-Road Relationships

You might be married and based in different cities.

You might be dating someone who isn't in aviation and doesn't understand the lifestyle.

You might be a parent who shares custody.

All of it adds stress.

And money decisions get wrapped in emotional decisions.

**Strategies That Help:**

- Budget for travel visits if long-distance
- Build in margin for missed flights, delays, or overnights
- Use shared apps to track shared goals or expenses
- Talk openly about what "quality time" looks like when you're together

### *Don't Let Guilt Control Your Wallet*

When you're gone a lot, it's tempting to:

- Overcompensate with gifts or expensive outings
- Avoid saying "no" to a financial ask
- Skip budgeting conversations to keep the peace

But that builds long-term resentment and short-term debt.

Instead, use your absence to focus your goals:

- Save together for something meaningful
- Leave a budgeted gift or note before a trip
- Create rituals around your return

## Part III: Roommates, Crash Pads, and Shared Spaces

Living with other pilots (or non-pilots) in a crash pad or base city adds another layer of complexity.

**Set Clear Expectations:**

- What's included in the rent?
- Who pays utilities? Cleaning?
- How are late payments handled?

**Use Tools:**

- Venmo/PayPal for reimbursements
- Shared Google Sheet or Splitwise for expenses
- Keep receipts and payment records

**Be Professional:**

- Treat your crash pad like a co-working space
- Don't take advantage of quiet roommates
- Respect boundaries, schedules, and fridge space

Financial chaos at home affects your performance in the cockpit.

Create calm where you can.

**Part IV: Parenting and Co-Parenting on a Pilot Schedule**

If you have kids—whether you live with them full-time, part-time, or co-parent—your schedule adds pressure.

But your money decisions matter more than your miles.

**Tips for Pilot Parents:**

- Automate contributions to college or custodial accounts
- Schedule time monthly to check on child-related expenses
- Share access to a calendar with your parenting partner
- Discuss school costs, medical bills, travel logistics in advance

**Co-Parenting? Clarify:**

- Who covers what categories (clothes, tuition, travel)
- What to do when a schedule changes
- How you handle reimbursement

Kids don't need a rich parent.

They need a *reliable* one.

Start with financial clarity.

**Part V: Financial Boundaries with Family and Friends**

You might be the "successful one" in your family.

Or the first to leave your hometown.

Or the one with travel benefits.

That comes with:

- Requests for money
- Expectations for free flights or upgrades
- Jealousy, comparison, or resentment

Set boundaries lovingly:

- "I can list you for standby, but I can't guarantee a seat."
- "I want to help, but I need to stick to my budget."
- "Let me send you resources instead of cash."

And don't co-sign loans unless you're prepared to pay them off.

**Remember:** Love without boundaries leads to burnout.

Especially financial burnout.

**Part VI: Managing Money Together, Even When Apart**

You may be:

- Traveling different directions every week
- Missing key family events
- Living on different schedules entirely

Money can feel like one more thing you *don't* do together.

Make it collaborative again:

- Use shared finance apps (YNAB, Monarch, Honeydue)
- Keep a joint email folder for financial docs
- Set a recurring "money check-in" on your shared calendar

Even a 15-minute FaceTime to review budgets can reset trust and teamwork.

**Part VII: When It's Not Working**

Money stress breaks many relationships. Especially when combined with distance, fatigue, and unclear expectations.

**Watch for Warning Signs:**

- One partner hiding purchases
- Frequent overdrafts or credit card debt
- Feeling like you're on different teams
- Avoiding financial conversations

**Solutions:**

- Couples therapy or coaching
- Meeting with a financial planner together
- Reading a money book as a couple
- Resetting shared goals

You can reroute. You can realign. But only if both people are willing to fly the same direction.

**Plain-Language Rules for Healthy Money + Relationships**

- Don't avoid money talks just because you're tired
- Don't spend to cover up distance or guilt
- Schedule clarity like you schedule flights
- Share access, logins, and expectations
- Don't be the only one doing the financial lifting

**Checklist: Strengthening Money and Relationships on Your Schedule**

1. Schedule a monthly 15-minute money check-in with your partner
2. Clarify who pays for what in every shared space

3. Set travel or parenting boundaries clearly and early
4. Open a shared finance app
5. Create a joint emergency fund if partnered
6. Be honest about what you *can't* afford right now

**Call to Action**

Make one relational money move this week:

- Start a money date with your partner
- Message a roommate to split a bill more clearly
- Update your will or insurance beneficiary
- Automate a co-parenting expense transfer

Just one move. Then another next week.

**Final Word**

Flying is a solo job.

But financial peace is a shared responsibility.

Your flight plan at work doesn't guarantee calm at home. But with communication, consistency, and care, you can build a money system that supports both your *career* and your *connections*.

You deserve wealth that doesn't isolate you.

You deserve love that respects your profession.

You can have both.

Your future self will thank you.

So will your crew.

So will your sanity.

# Chapter 17: Side Hustles and Supplemental Income for Pilots

Let's get honest:

You don't need a side hustle because you're lazy.

You need a side hustle because being a pilot, especially early in your career, often means inconsistent pay, high debt, and big dreams.

Maybe you're grinding at a regional airline earning just enough to cover your crash pad, per diem meals, and student loan minimums.

Maybe you're a mid-career FO staring at $20K/year in daycare costs.

Maybe you're a senior captain who just wants to make your exit strategy smoother.

Wherever you are in your aviation journey, one thing is clear:

Your schedule is irregular.

Your income might be unpredictable.

But your ambition? That's steady.

This chapter is here to help you find smart, sustainable ways to earn more—without crashing your time, your mental health, or your career goals.

Let's talk about:

- The *why* of pilot side hustles
- Income streams that match your schedule
- Business ideas that build on your aviation knowledge
- Passive income strategies

- What to avoid
- How to protect your license and career while earning extra

Because you shouldn't need to choose between flying and financial security.

You can have both.

**Why Pilots Need Supplemental Income**

**1. Early Career Income is Tight**

Regional FOs and CFIs often earn $20K–$40K/year.

Crash pads, student loans, and travel eat up most of it.

**2. Lifestyle Inflation Happens Fast**

Once you hit six figures, it's easy to start spending like it.

Side income can support intentional upgrades (house, family, travel).

**3. Unpredictable Schedules Mean Unpredictable Pay**

Trip cancellations, weather delays, union disputes—they all hit your paycheck.

**4. You Want to Build Wealth Faster**

Side hustles can fund your IRA, emergency fund, or down payment.

**5. You Want an Exit Plan**

Whether you want to retire early, buy a business, or leave aviation someday—you need an income bridge.

**The Rules of Smart Side Hustling for Pilots**

1. It must work around your schedule.
2. It must not violate FAA or airline rules.
3. It must not interfere with your duty time, rest time, or health.
4. It must be something you can *pause* if needed.
5. It must feel energizing—not exhausting.

Side hustles should feel like supplemental fuel.

Not an engine failure.

**Types of Pilot-Friendly Side Hustles**

### *1. Flight Instruction (CFI/CFII/MEI)*

- Great for regional pilots or those building hours
- Schedule control
- Earn $25–80/hr
- Use downtime productively

**Caution:**

- Protect your rest time
- Avoid burnout

### *2. Real Estate Investing*

- Buy-and-hold rental properties
- Short-term Airbnb hosting
- REIT investing for passive income

**Pilot Perk:**

- You can self-manage from anywhere
- Good for couples or families where one partner is home more

**Start Small:**

- House hack a duplex
- Partner with someone experienced

### *3. Freelance Aviation Services*

- Checkride prep coaching
- Resume review for aspiring pilots
- Social media consulting for flight schools

### *4. Online Businesses*

- Start a pilot blog or YouTube channel
- Sell aviation merch or print-on-demand gear
- Build a course (weather theory, IFR skills, etc.)

**Pro Tip:**

- Build once, earn repeatedly (online courses, ebooks)

### *5. Affiliate Marketing*

- Recommend pilot gear, bags, sunglasses
- Use Amazon Associates or pilot-specific programs

**Easy Entry:**

- Start an Instagram or TikTok focused on pilot life

### *6. Freelance Skills (Non-Aviation)*

- Graphic design, web design, coding
- Video editing
- Copywriting or resume editing

**Platform Ideas:**

- Upwork
- Fiverr
- LinkedIn

### *7. Rideshare or Delivery (With Caution)*

- Uber, Lyft, DoorDash
- Flexible hours
- Watch fatigue rules

### *8. Part-Time Retail or Seasonal Work*

- Tax prep in Q1
- Retail in Q4
- Pick gigs that don't require long-term commitment

### *9. Contract Flying / Ferry Flights*

- Part 91 contract work
- Aircraft repositioning
- Short-term instruction gigs

### *10. Speaking and Training*

- Speak at schools, flight clubs, aviation camps
- Share your story and build a brand

**Real Pilot Profiles**

**Anthony, 26, Regional FO**

- Built a $5K/month CFI side business
- Paid off student loans in 4 years
- Now building his own Part 61 school

**Monica, 41, Major Airline Captain**

- Owns 3 rental properties in her base city

- Cash-flows $1,200/month after expenses
- Plans to retire from aviation at 55

**Trevor, 33, Cargo Pilot**

- Runs a TikTok page with 120K followers
- Sells pilot gear and earns affiliate income
- Just launched a course on IFR systems for students

**What NOT to Do**

- Don't violate rest rules by working another job during duty rest
- Don't invest in MLMs, crypto scams, or get-rich-quick ideas
- Don't overextend yourself and risk your medical
- Don't work with companies that don't understand pilot schedules

**How to Protect Your Aviation Career While Earning More**

**1. Disclose when required**

- Some airlines require approval for outside income
- Union handbooks often have guidance

**2. Schedule Smart**

- Block time for rest
- Plan side work only on scheduled off days

**3. Separate Brands**

- Don't use your airline name or logo without permission
- Keep business and personal content separate

**4. Pay Your Taxes**

- Side income = self-employment tax
- Set aside 25–30% of income
- Track expenses carefully

### 5. Save, Don't Just Spend

- Use side income to hit your financial goals faster
- Don't just inflate your lifestyle

### Tools to Make Side Hustling Easier

- **QuickBooks Self-Employed:** Track mileage, expenses
- **Canva:** Design merch or social posts
- **Stripe/PayPal/Venmo Business:** Accept payments
- **Calendly:** Schedule meetings or lessons
- **ConvertKit:** Email lists and newsletters
- **Gumroad/Teachable:** Sell digital products

### Checklist: Launching Your Pilot Side Hustle

1. Define your "why" – debt payoff, savings, freedom?
2. List 3 skills you can monetize
3. Block time on your off days
4. Choose your business model (service, product, content)
5. Register an LLC if needed
6. Open a separate bank account
7. Set a 90-day income goal
8. Tell someone for accountability

### Action Steps This Week

- Brainstorm your top 3 income ideas
- Do one hour of research on each

- Pick the best match for your current schedule
- Block one hour this week to get started
- Open a new savings account to hold your side hustle income

**Final Word**

You're not just a pilot.

You're a professional with leverage.

Your time is valuable.

Your brand is valuable.

Your perspective is valuable.

Don't hustle to survive.

Hustle to *thrive*.

Whether you're paying off debt, funding a dream, or just building some breathing room—you can earn more without burning out.

Start smart.

Build slow.

Stay consistent.

Your future self will thank you.

So will your crew.

So will your sanity.

# Chapter 18: Understanding Union Representation and Its Financial Impact

Union representation is one of the most powerful, complex, and sometimes misunderstood aspects of a pilot's career.

If you're just starting out, the word "union" might feel distant or bureaucratic.

If you're mid-career, you've probably seen firsthand how collective bargaining affects your contract, schedule, and pay.

If you're approaching retirement, you already know: your union helped shape the financial trajectory of your entire career.

But here's the truth: whether you love unions or question them, understanding *how* union representation impacts your finances is essential.

This chapter is not political. It's practical.

We'll explore:

- What unions do for pilots
- How contracts affect your pay, benefits, and retirement
- The role of union dues
- What to know during negotiations
- How to use union resources to your advantage
- What happens if there's a dispute, grievance, or strike

You're not just a line holder or reserve.

You're part of a collective crew, negotiating your worth.

Let's get clear.

**What a Pilot Union Actually Does**

At its core, a union is a group of employees working together to negotiate collectively with management.

For pilots, that means:

- Bargaining for pay, schedules, benefits, and retirement
- Representing members in disputes with the airline
- Protecting pilots during disciplinary or legal issues
- Providing support during negotiations, mergers, furloughs
- Educating members about rights, contracts, and options

The most well-known unions in aviation include:

- ALPA (Air Line Pilots Association)
- APA (Allied Pilots Association)
- SWAPA (Southwest Airlines Pilots Association)
- Independent unions (like NetJets or regional carriers)

**How Union Contracts Shape Your Financial Life**

Your contract (collective bargaining agreement or CBA) is your financial framework.

**Here's what it governs:**

- **Hourly pay rate and pay scale progression**
- **Minimum guarantee (monthly/annual)**
- **Trip and duty rig rules**
- **Per diem rates and reimbursements**
- **Vacation and sick accrual**
- **Retirement contributions (401(k), defined benefit)**
- **Insurance coverage (medical, dental, life, LTD)**
- **Profit-sharing, bonuses, stock options**

**Real Impact:**

Two pilots flying the exact same route at two different airlines can earn vastly different incomes because of union-negotiated contracts.

**Union Dues: What You Pay and What You Get**

Union dues typically range from 1% to 2% of your income.

That means:

- $80/month on a $96,000 salary
- $250/month on a $300,000 salary

**What you're paying for:**

- Negotiating teams (lawyers, economists, experts)
- Strike funds
- Legal representation
- Communications and member education
- Dues-funded disability and loss of license plans (some unions)

**Is it worth it?**

Ask yourself:

- Has my union negotiated raises in the last 3 years?
- Do I understand how to use my contract?
- Has the union protected me or a colleague in a dispute?

Often, even a small contract improvement (1–2% raise) offsets years of dues.

**Understanding the Value of Union Bargaining**

**Example: Pay Rate Negotiation**

- Pre-union raise: 1% annual cost of living
- Union-negotiated raise: 7% with retroactive pay
- That's thousands more in year-one earnings

**Example: Schedule Protection**

- Trip dropped incorrectly? Union enforces pay protection
- Reserve abuse? Grievance filed and contract clarified

**Example: Merger Protections**

- Seniority integration
- Protecting base domicile
- Maintaining scope clauses (avoiding outsourcing)

**Negotiations: How to Be Ready Financially**

Union negotiations can take months or even years.
Sometimes they stall. Sometimes they lead to strike votes.
**Your financial responsibilities during this time:**

- Stay informed
- Don't overspend based on projected raises
- Build an emergency fund (3–6 months minimum)
- Keep side hustle options warm
- Don't finance large purchases assuming contract changes

**If a strike is authorized:**

- You may lose income temporarily
- Strike pay may be limited
- Unions often have emergency funds, but not full salary replacement

Plan conservatively. Hope for resolution. Prepare for turbulence.

**Grievances and Disciplinary Support**

**What Happens When You're In Trouble?**

- Misfiled paperwork

- Sick time abuse accusations
- Failed checkride or SIM event

Your union rep is your first call.

They can:

- Advocate for you in hearings
- Ensure contract procedures are followed
- Help resolve issues before they escalate

Legal support from your union can save you tens of thousands.

**Pro Tip:** Document everything. Keep your logbooks, schedules, and communication organized.

**Union-Sponsored Benefits and Resources**

**1. Loss of License Insurance**

Some unions offer group plans with lower premiums

**2. Legal and Financial Help**

Free consultations or discounted services

**3. Retirement Planning**

Workshops, seminars, or access to fiduciary advisors

**4. Mental Health and Peer Support**

Pilot peer groups, substance abuse recovery, burnout prevention

**5. Contract Education**

Webinars, bulletins, contract guides to help you understand your rights

Use these. You're already paying for them.

**How Union Strength Impacts Airline Stability**

Strong pilot unions contribute to:

- Safer operations
- Better work-life balance
- Transparent communication

But also:

- Slower change adoption
- More friction during leadership transitions

**Financial takeaway:**

Choose your employer understanding how strong (or weak) their union representation is.

It affects your entire compensation trajectory.

**What to Do as a New Union Pilot**

1. Read your contract (even just the top 10 sections)
2. Join union briefings and communications
3. Know your base rep or council rep
4. Attend new-hire orientations or webinars
5. Ask questions when you don't understand something

**Plain-Language Examples of Union Financial Wins**

- $3/hour pay bump = $6,000/year
- Retirement match increase from 10% to 16% = $20,000+ annual boost
- Better trip rig or duty rig = 5–10 more paid hours/month
- Legal protection from wrongful termination = saves career, license, income

**Checklist: Financial Moves in a Unionized Airline**

1. Review your pay scale progression chart
2. Max out employer match (if enhanced via union deal)
3. Save extra when contract negotiations begin
4. Understand your grievance rights
5. Learn your schedule protection clauses
6. Join peer support or wellness programs

**Action Steps This Month**

- Find and read your CBA summary
- Talk to your union rep about retirement options
- Ask your fellow pilots how they use union resources
- Save 1 month of expenses in a strike fund

**Final Word**

You're not just a pilot.

You're part of a movement that has lifted safety, pay, and dignity across the entire industry.

Union representation is part of your wealth-building journey.

It's not perfect.

But it's powerful.

Your job is to engage, educate yourself, and use what's available.

You didn't come this far to leave money, support, or protection on the table.

Understand your contract.

Understand your rights.

And understand your value—together.

Your future self will thank you.

So will your crew.

So will your sanity.

# Chapter 19: Managing Multi-State Income and Tax Considerations

You fly across borders, but your money doesn't.

At least, not without consequences.

For pilots, the sky isn't the limit—but the tax code might be. When your schedule sends you to a dozen states in a week, your W-2 shows a home address in one place, and your crash pad sits in another, the question becomes: where do you really owe taxes? And how do you make sense of it all?

This chapter is your radar for navigating the complex, often confusing world of multi-state income and tax obligations. Whether you're a rookie first officer or a seasoned captain, understanding where you work versus where you live is the difference between avoiding audit turbulence and getting slammed with unexpected tax bills.

This is about clarity. This is about legality. This is about strategy.

**Why Multi-State Taxes Matter for Pilots**

Pilots often:

- **Live in one state (domicile or residence)**
- **Are based in another (crew base)**
- **Fly over or into many (source income states)**

Each of those states may claim the right to tax you.

And it's up to you to get it right.

**Why This Gets Tricky:**

- Not all states define residency the same way
- Some states want a slice of your income if you work there, even temporarily
- Not every airline withholds tax correctly for mobile employees

**Key Terms You Need to Understand**

- **Domicile:** Your legal permanent residence
- **Crew Base:** Where you start and end your trips (not necessarily your residence)
- **Source Income:** Money earned in a specific state, possibly taxable there
- **Reciprocal Agreements:** Agreements between states to avoid double taxation
- **Tax Credit:** What your home state gives you for taxes paid elsewhere
- **Per Diem:** Usually not taxable, but still must be tracked

**Scenario 1: The Classic Case**

You live in Texas (no state income tax), but your airline is based in California. Your paycheck says CA taxes withheld. You work flights that begin and end in California, but you commute from Texas.

**What You Need to Know:**

- You don't owe income tax to California if you aren't a CA resident or domiciled there.
- But you must file a non-resident return to claim back withheld CA taxes.
- Keep detailed records proving your Texas domicile.

**Scenario 2: The Crash Pad Confusion**

You live in Florida, but you have a crash pad in New Jersey and fly mostly

East Coast routes out of a New York base.

**Risk:** States like New York and New Jersey are aggressive about taxing anyone who works within their borders.

**Solution:**

- File non-resident returns in NY/NJ only if income was sourced there
- File your domicile return in Florida (no income tax)
- Avoid giving NY/NJ any indication that you've "moved in" (driver's license, lease, etc.)

**How to Track State Income Accurately**

- Keep a **flight log** of duty days and layovers by state
- Use apps like **TripLog**, **Everlance**, or a custom Google Sheet
- Maintain boarding passes, bid schedules, and hotel receipts
- Save your company pay reports, especially if they show duty location

**Best Practices for Filing Multi-State Taxes**

1. **Know Your State Residency Rules**

- Some require 183+ days of presence
- Others look at voter registration, home ownership, or driver's license

1. **File Non-Resident Returns When Necessary**

- Only in states where income was earned AND taxes withheld

1. **Claim Tax Credits to Avoid Double Taxation**

- Your home state may let you credit what you paid another state

1. **Consider Pro Help**

- Hire a CPA who works with pilots or flight crew
- Ask if they understand Public Law 95-430 (see below)

**The Law That Protects Pilots: Public Law 95-430**

This law says:

> *An individual regularly assigned to perform duties on a mode of transportation in two or more states shall only be subject to income tax in their state of residence.*

**Translation:** If you're a pilot or flight crew, and you live in one state but work in many, *only* your state of residence can tax your income.

**Caveat:**

- Your airline must withhold taxes based on your residence
- You must clearly establish your domicile

**What About Per Diem?**

- Per diem is **not taxable** if it's below the federal daily meal/lodging allowance and not reimbursed directly
- It is usually excluded from W-2 wages
- You cannot double-deduct per diem if you receive a tax-free reimbursement

**Action Step:** Track it anyway. It helps validate your travel for tax and audit purposes.

**How to Establish and Defend Your Domicile**

States may try to argue you owe them tax if you:

- Own property in-state
- Spend 183+ days in-state
- Use an in-state address for your W-2

- Have a crash pad lease in your name

To prove your true state of domicile:

- Register to vote and maintain license in your home state
- File state tax returns (even if $0)
- Keep your mailing address consistent
- Avoid using your crash pad address for bills or IDs

**The States That Create the Most Confusion**

**1. California:**

- Aggressive tax enforcement
- Wants a piece if you live there, own property, or fly into CA bases often

**2. New York:**

- Even a crash pad can raise flags
- Sends audit notices based on W-2 and bid schedules

**3. New Jersey and Illinois:**

- Similar to NY; can target commuters

**4. Texas, Florida, Washington:**

- No income tax. Safer domiciles, but still must prove residence

**What Happens If You Get Audited?**

- State will ask for proof of residence
- You'll need calendars, boarding passes, expense reports
- They may compare your W-2 with layover logs

- If you're unprepared, you may owe taxes + interest + penalties

**How to Avoid It:**

- File consistently
- Match W-2 address to your true home state
- Don't claim residency in a no-income-tax state unless it's legit

**Military and International Pilots**

- Deployed military pilots may keep domicile in one state
- Expat pilots must follow **foreign earned income exclusion** rules
- May need to file FBARs if foreign bank accounts exceed thresholds

**Best Practice:** Work with a tax advisor who handles multi-national tax issues for aviators

**Tax Withholding Tips for Pilots**

- Confirm your airline is withholding state tax based on your residence
- Review each W-2 box for correct state info
- Adjust withholding if needed (W-4 and state equivalent)
- Don't assume the airline gets it right—it's on you

**Checklist: Managing Multi-State Income Like a Pro**

1. Know your true state of domicile
2. Track your layovers and flight activity by state
3. File non-resident returns only when necessary
4. Use tax credits to avoid double taxation
5. Read Public Law 95-430 and discuss it with your CPA
6. Keep consistent records (bids, logs, travel receipts)
7. Never list a crash pad as your primary address

### Action Steps This Week

- Download your bid history and organize by state
- Compare your W-2 withholding to your actual domicile
- Set up a folder labeled "Tax Defense" with supporting documents
- Make an appointment with a CPA who specializes in airline crew
- Log your next trip's duty days and layovers by state

### Final Word

Flying across state lines doesn't mean you should pay taxes in all of them.

But it *does* mean you need a system.

Don't let your tax life drift. Keep it on course.

You earned your wings to fly planes, not fight the IRS.

Create clarity. Avoid surprises. Stay compliant. Fly smart.

Your future self will thank you.

So will your crew.

So will your sanity.

# Chapter 20: Setting Financial Goals for the First Five Years

The moment you step into the cockpit professionally, everything changes.

You're no longer just chasing hours.

You're chasing altitude—financial altitude.

The first five years of a pilot's career are among the most financially defining of their entire journey. Why? Because this is when you set the tone. It's when habits are formed. It's when you either get ahead, get stuck, or start playing catch-up.

Let's be honest: pilot pay in the early years isn't glamorous. You might be scraping by, flying regional, sleeping in a crash pad, or grinding through reserve duty. But that doesn't mean you can't build a solid financial foundation.

This chapter is your flight plan. It will help you:

- Prioritize your money goals year by year
- Avoid lifestyle creep
- Build buffers and savings
- Crush debt
- Invest early and often
- Set up financial systems that grow with your career

It's not about being perfect. It's about being intentional.

**Year 1: Survive and Stabilize**

Your priorities:

- Emergency fund
- Budget
- Basic debt management
- Financial education

**Goal 1: Build a $1,000 emergency buffer.**

This isn't your full emergency fund yet. But it's a fuel reserve. If your crash pad rent goes up, your car breaks down, or you lose a bid, you'll be glad it's there.

**Goal 2: Track your money.**

Use an app or spreadsheet. Know where every dollar goes. Flying 75 hours doesn't help if you leak money on takeout and gadgets.

**Goal 3: Know your numbers.**

How much student loan debt?

Interest rates?

Minimum monthly obligations?

**Goal 4: Start your financial education.**

Read one money book. Listen to one podcast. Follow a few pilot-savvy financial pages. Awareness is lift.

**Action:**

Automate your rent, bills, and minimum debt payments.

Set calendar reminders for each payday.

**Year 2: Attack High-Interest Debt + Build Emergency Fund**

Your priorities:

- Expand your emergency fund to 3 months of expenses
- Knock down debt with interest rates >7%

**Goal 1: Build up to a real emergency fund.**

If you get grounded or furloughed, you need a financial runway. Start with 1 month of expenses. Then 2. Then 3.

**Goal 2: Pay down high-interest debt.**

Target credit cards, personal loans, and private student loans. Use the avalanche method (highest interest rate first) or snowball method (smallest balance first).

**Goal 3: Learn your benefits.**

Are you eligible for a 401(k)?

Does your union offer a retirement match?

Is there a loss-of-license plan?

Start reading your pilot contract and benefits manual.

**Action:**

Make one extra debt payment this year.

Start a side hustle if needed.

**Year 3: Start Investing and Get Strategic**

Your priorities:

- Contribute to retirement
- Begin investing consistently
- Protect your income

**Goal 1: Open a Roth IRA (if eligible).**

Set up automatic monthly contributions. Even $100/month adds up.

**Goal 2: Contribute to employer retirement plan.**

If your airline offers a match, hit it. That's free money.

**Goal 3: Get basic insurance coverage.**

- Term life insurance (if anyone depends on you)
- Renter's insurance
- Disability insurance (if not already provided)

**Goal 4: Run a net worth statement.**

Assets minus debts. Do this yearly. Watch it grow.

**Action:**

Schedule a 15-minute money check-in every Sunday.

This is your preflight briefing for your financial life.

**Year 4: Optimize and Automate**

Your priorities:

- Cut costs
- Increase income
- Set long-term financial goals

**Goal 1: Build systems.**

- Use automatic transfers to fund savings
- Split paychecks into checking + investment + emergency fund

**Goal 2: Revisit student loan repayment.**

Should you refinance?

Use income-driven repayment?

Apply for forgiveness?

**Goal 3: Upgrade your savings strategy.**

- Open a high-yield savings account
- Start a "big life fund" for house down payment, wedding, travel

**Goal 4: Add income streams.**

Can you teach? Invest in real estate? Create content?

**Action:**

Pick one "optimize" goal to focus on this year—expenses, income, or savings rate.

**Year 5: Build Wealth Intentionally**

Your priorities:

- Maximize retirement savings
- Lay foundation for long-term wealth

- Align money with values

**Goal 1: Increase retirement contributions.**

If you're not maxing your 401(k), start increasing by 1–2% annually.

**Goal 2: Open a taxable brokerage account.**

This is where you build wealth beyond retirement. Set long-term goals: early retirement? House? Starting a business?

**Goal 3: Define your big financial goals.**

Where do you want to be in 10 years? What does financial freedom mean to you?

**Goal 4: Review your estate plan.**

Do you need a will? Beneficiary designations?

Have you chosen a power of attorney?

**Action:**

Start documenting your personal financial plan. Not perfect. Just real.

**Sample 5-Year Financial Timeline for a Pilot**

**Year 1:**

- $1K emergency fund
- Budget created
- Student loan payments automated

**Year 2:**

- 3-month emergency fund
- $5K paid toward high-interest debt
- Roth IRA opened

**Year 3:**

- $6K invested in Roth IRA
- 401(k) contributions started
- Net worth tracked quarterly

**Year 4:**

- Side hustle launched
- $10K in taxable investments
- Refinance student loans

**Year 5:**

- 401(k) at 10%+ contribution
- Financial goals defined
- Will created and beneficiaries updated

**Real-Life Pilot Scenarios**

**Jason, 29, Regional FO**

- Lived off $2K/month
- Paid down $40K of student loans in 4 years
- Built $25K emergency fund before joining a major

**Sasha, 35, Charter Captain**

- Saved 20% of every check automatically
- Invests in index funds monthly
- On track to be work-optional at 50

**DeShawn and Maria, pilot couple in their 40s**

- Use Sunday money dates
- Budget in YNAB (You Need a Budget)
- Teaching their kids about money early

**Common Pitfalls in the First 5 Years**

- Upgrading lifestyle too quickly after first big check
- Ignoring retirement because it feels far away
- Putting off building an emergency fund
- Overestimating how much per diem is "extra money"
- Not understanding union benefits or how to use them

**Checklist: Your First 5 Years Financial Pre-Flight**

- Emergency fund: $1K → 3 months
- Track every dollar for 30 days
- Understand your debt
- Open a Roth IRA
- Contribute to 401(k) if eligible
- Learn your pilot contract benefits
- Add term life and disability insurance
- Calculate your net worth yearly
- Automate your savings
- Start a side hustle or additional income stream

**Final Call to Act**

Don't wait for perfect timing.
Don't wait until you're making more money.
Don't wait for permission.
Make one money move before wheels up tomorrow.
Just one.
Set a savings goal.
Open a retirement account.
Cancel a subscription.
Download a budgeting app.
Then do one more next week.
You don't need to have it all figured out.
You just need to take off in the right direction.
Because the first five years aren't just about survival.

They're about setting a course.

You're not flying solo.

You're building a career, a life, and a legacy.

Your future self will thank you.

So will your crew.

So will your sanity.

# Part III – Mid-Flight Adjustments: Growing Income, Growing Responsibilities

Welcome to the cruise altitude of your aviation career—the years when your income starts to climb, your responsibilities expand, and the financial decisions get more complex. Part III is about managing the transitions that come after the early grind: upgrading from regional to major airlines, navigating lifestyle changes, building wealth beyond just saving, and making smarter choices with bigger paychecks.

This section helps you avoid the turbulence of financial complacency. As your schedule stabilizes and your compensation grows, so do the stakes. You'll learn how to manage taxes with higher earnings, prepare for family responsibilities, upgrade your insurance intelligently, invest like a pro (not just dabble), and avoid the lifestyle creep that sidelines so many pilots in their peak earning years.

Whether you're entering your 30s with new goals or your 40s with real momentum, this is your financial flight plan for maturity, mastery, and intentional money growth. You're no longer just holding altitude—you're navigating toward long-term freedom.

# Chapter 21: Upgrading to Major Airlines – What Changes Financially

You made it. You're trading in your regional call sign for a major airline uniform. This isn't just a career milestone—it's a financial inflection point.

For years, you were flying lean, grinding it out on reserve, making the most of per diem, and budgeting every meal. Now the numbers on your paycheck start to look like something you only dreamed about as a CFI or regional FO. But here's the thing:

More money doesn't mean less pressure.

In fact, the transition from regional to major airline comes with one of the biggest financial learning curves in aviation. You need to understand not just what changes—but what *should* change in how you manage, invest, save, insure, and plan.

Let's walk through the key areas where your financial world will shift once you take that step up.

**1. Your Paycheck Grows—But So Do the Expectations**

You might go from making $50K to $120K+ within a year. That's huge. But if you don't have a plan for that increase, it'll disappear faster than a hot turn in Chicago.

**Real Talk:**

- Taxes hit harder in higher brackets
- Bigger checks = bigger temptations (new car, nicer apartment, weekend

trips)
- Loan officers and credit card companies will suddenly be *very* interested in you

**Action:**

Before your first major paycheck hits, set automatic transfers to:

- Emergency fund
- Retirement accounts
- High-interest debt

The trick isn't to deny yourself. It's to delay lifestyle inflation long enough to build financial momentum.

**2. You'll Likely Move from Hourly Confusion to Contract Clarity**

Your pay scale will be more transparent. Seniority drives everything. Raises are baked in.

**Financial Wins:**

- More guaranteed hours (monthly or annually)
- Predictable upgrades in pay scale
- Higher minimum guarantees

**Watch For:**

- Higher union dues (worth it, but budget for it)
- Potentially less per diem vs. regional if schedules tighten

**Pro Tip:**

Ask your union rep to walk you through how duty rigs and trip pairing affect your *actual* pay, not just your base hourly rate.

**3. Benefits Get Better—If You Know How to Use Them**

At major airlines, your benefits package is serious. But complexity increases.

**Upgraded Options May Include:**

- Company 401(k) match or profit-sharing
- Group term life insurance (optional additional coverage)
- Long-term disability
- Medical, dental, and vision plans
- Loss of license insurance

**Action Plan:**

- Contribute at least enough to get the full employer match in your 401(k)
- Learn the vesting schedule
- Compare union loss-of-license with private policies

**Warning:** Many pilots underutilize their benefits simply because they don't understand them. Ask. Read. Review annually.

**4. Your Taxes May Get More Complex**

Higher income = higher tax bracket. Also:

- Stock options or profit sharing may be taxed differently
- You may now owe AMT (Alternative Minimum Tax)
- Multi-state income reporting still matters

**What to Do:**

- Get a CPA with airline experience
- Review W-4 withholding annually
- If married, review how dual income affects tax filing status

**Pro Tip:** Keep a digital tax folder by year. Include W-2s, trip logs, bonus statements, and any real estate or side hustle docs.

**5. You Might Relocate or Commute Differently**

New base? New commute? New zip code?

**That Means:**

- Cost-of-living may shift dramatically
- You may face crash pad costs again
- Time away from home = added pressure on budget, relationships, and stress

**What to Do:**

- If relocating, avoid buying a home immediately
- Calculate true commuting cost (time + money + mental load)
- Set boundaries for spending while on the road

**6. Your Schedule Improves (Eventually)—Use That Time Wisely**

With seniority, you may:

- Drop into better schedules
- Avoid red-eyes and junk pairings
- Fly less for more money

This is the moment to:

- Invest in financial planning
- Take on a side hustle (if that fits your lifestyle)
- Work toward financial independence

**Financial Discipline = Flight Deck Confidence**

The less financial stress you carry, the more clarity you bring to every flight.

**7. Your Retirement Timeline Gets Real**

Before: retirement was a distant dream.

Now: you see the runway.

**What Changes:**

- You can max out 401(k) contributions ($23,000+ annually depending on your age)
- Some major airlines offer additional deferred comp plans
- You need to start estimating your retirement number

**Questions to Ask:**

- How many more years do I *want* to fly?
- What does financial freedom look like to me?
- Am I on pace for a $2M+ retirement nest egg?

**Pro Tip:** Use a retirement calculator tailored to pilot schedules and pensions. Or better, sit down with a fee-only financial planner who works with pilots.

**8. Lifestyle Creep Becomes a Real Threat**

You're earning six figures. You can finally afford the nice car, better hotel, or watch you've always wanted.

Nothing wrong with celebrating.

But be careful. One raise = many new habits.

**How to Avoid Financial Drift:**

- Set a rule: 50% of any raise goes to savings/debt, 50% to lifestyle
- Use a separate account for "treat yourself" money
- Reevaluate subscriptions, expenses, and spending yearly

**9. Union Involvement Matters More Than Ever**

At the majors, your union has real negotiating power.

Your CBA (Collective Bargaining Agreement) affects:

- Retirement plans
- Health insurance premiums

- Scheduling rights
- Safety protections

**What You Should Do:**

- Attend union briefings
- Read your contract (at least the financial sections)
- Know your union rep by name

Understanding your contract = protecting your paycheck.

**10. Your Mindset Needs to Shift From Survival to Strategy**

This isn't about getting by anymore.

This is about building wealth, protecting your time, and designing a life that serves you.

**You Now Need To:**

- Have long-term goals (when do you want to stop flying?)
- Track your net worth annually
- Build an investing strategy (not just throw money in a target-date fund)
- Decide what kind of financial legacy you want to leave

**Real Pilot Stories**

**Jake, 32, former regional captain, now Delta FO:**

"I tripled my income overnight. But I didn't upgrade my lifestyle. I upgraded my investing. Five years later, I have a paid-off car, $150K in retirement accounts, and I'm house shopping with 20% down already saved."

**Alyssa, 40, Southwest Captain:**

"I made the mistake of assuming my big pay bump meant I could spend big. After two years, I had no savings, two car loans, and credit card debt. I pulled back, hired a financial coach, and now I max my 401(k) and have peace of mind."

**Checklist: Financial Moves After Joining a Major**

- Adjust your budget based on new income
- Max your 401(k) match ASAP
- Review all employer benefits and insurance options
- Update your emergency fund target
- Get term life + disability coverage if needed
- Run a new tax projection with a CPA
- Set financial goals for the next 5 years
- Automate investing into Roth IRA or brokerage
- Update beneficiaries on retirement accounts
- Schedule an annual financial check-up

**Final Call to Action**

You didn't upgrade just your title.

You upgraded your entire financial runway.

So now you need to fly like it.

Make one money move before wheels up tomorrow.

Just one.

Then do one more next week.

The major airline paychecks are real. But so are the risks.

And the opportunities.

Chart your course with intention.

Build with strategy.

And take pride in the legacy you're creating.

Your future self will thank you.

So will your crew.

So will your sanity.

# Chapter 22: Airline 401(k), Profit-Sharing, and Stock Plans Explained

You trained for years. You built hours. You clawed your way from CFI to FO. You earned your seat at a major airline.

And now you're earning real money—finally.

But here's the thing: how you *invest* what you earn will do more for your long-term financial health than any number of flight hours.

The good news? Airline retirement plans have the power to make you a millionaire.

The not-so-good news? Many pilots don't take full advantage of them because the language feels like turbulence: vesting, profit-sharing, ESPPs, catch-up contributions. You didn't go to flight school to become a retirement plan expert.

That's why this chapter exists.

Let's break down the most powerful wealth-building tools in your career: the 401(k), profit-sharing plans, and stock-based compensation. We'll treat each like an airplane system: understand how it works, what to monitor, what to tweak, and what to never touch without guidance.

**401(k) Plans: The Core of Your Financial Autopilot**

At most major airlines, the 401(k) plan is your primary retirement vehicle.

**What Is a 401(k)?**

It's a tax-advantaged retirement savings account offered by your employer.

**Two Versions:**

- **Traditional 401(k):** You contribute pre-tax, reducing taxable income now. Taxes are owed when you withdraw in retirement.
- **Roth 401(k):** You contribute after-tax, but withdrawals in retirement are tax-free (including growth).

**Why Pilots Should Care:**

- You likely have a high income. Reducing taxable income today can keep you out of a higher bracket.
- You may also be in a low-tax state *now* but retire in a high-tax one.
- Time is your co-pilot. Investing early in your career = compound interest on steroids.

**Key Features to Understand:**

- **Contribution Limit (2025):** Up to \$23,000/year (plus \$7,500 if you're 50+)
- **Employer Match:** Free money. Some airlines offer 3% to 16%+ of your pay
- **Vesting Schedule:** You only own *all* employer contributions after a certain number of years

**Action Step:**

If you're not contributing enough to get the full match, you're giving up free money. Increase contributions every year until you max out.

**Profit-Sharing Plans: The Airline Bonus Engine**

Many airlines offer annual profit-sharing bonuses, especially majors.

**What Is Profit-Sharing?**

A percentage of the airline's profits is distributed to eligible employees, usually based on compensation and seniority.

**How It Works:**

- Calculated annually
- Typically deposited into your 401(k) or paid out as a bonus check
- Amount varies: could be 5%, 10%, even 20%+ in great years

**What to Know:**

- It can fluctuate. Don't count on it for everyday expenses.
- You may owe taxes on it (unless deposited into 401(k))
- It grows your retirement account without effort

**Use It Wisely:**

- Treat it like a bonus, not a raise
- Use it to fund IRAs, pay down debt, or boost your emergency fund

**Pro Tip:**

In a good year, a profit-sharing deposit + 401(k) match can equal 30% of your base pay in retirement contributions.

**Airline Stock Purchase Plans (ESPPs): Your Ownership Opportunity**

Some airlines offer Employee Stock Purchase Plans.

**What Is an ESPP?**

A plan that lets you purchase company stock at a discount (often 10-15%) through payroll deductions.

**Why It Can Be Powerful:**

- Instant equity at a discount
- Often includes a "lock-in" window (e.g. 6 months)
- Can be sold for profit after the holding period

**But Be Careful:**

- You're already employed by the airline. Holding too much of their stock concentrates your risk.

- Stocks fluctuate. It's not guaranteed income.
- Taxes can be complicated (qualified vs. disqualified disposition)

**Guidelines:**

- Don't put more than 5-10% of net worth in company stock
- Sell ESPP shares regularly and reinvest into diversified funds
- Work with a CPA or advisor to navigate taxation

**Common Pitfalls Pilots Make With Retirement Plans**

1. **Not Starting Early Enough**

- "I'll invest when I upgrade to captain."
- Compound interest doesn't wait. Start with $100/month if needed.

1. **Chasing Hot Stocks in 401(k) Options**

- Your 401(k) isn't a day-trading account
- Stick to low-cost index funds or target-date funds unless you're confident

1. **Ignoring the Vesting Schedule**

- Leaving your airline before vesting could mean forfeiting tens of thousands
- Know your timeline

1. **Treating Profit-Sharing Like Lottery Winnings**

- Don't use it to upgrade your car
- Use it to upgrade your future

1. **Overconcentration in Airline Stock**

- Diversify. Your career, income, and stock shouldn't all hinge on one airline

**How to Maximize Your 401(k) as a Pilot**

- Contribute enough to get the full match (non-negotiable)
- Increase contributions with every raise or contract
- Use Roth 401(k) if early-career or in low tax bracket
- Use traditional 401(k) if high-income now, lower expected income in retirement
- Review allocations annually
- Roll over old 401(k)s to simplify

**Tax Strategies to Consider**

- **Backdoor Roth IRA:** For high earners above the Roth contribution limits
- **Mega Backdoor Roth:** If your airline plan allows after-tax contributions (rare, but powerful)
- **Health Savings Account (HSA):** Triple tax-free if available
- **529 Plans:** For kids' education (state tax deductions may apply)

**The Pilot's Retirement Timeline**

**Age 25-35:**

- Max Roth IRA
- Contribute to 401(k) up to match
- Build emergency fund + crush high-interest debt

**Age 35-45:**

- Max 401(k)
- Invest in taxable brokerage
- Consider disability + term life insurance

**Age 45-55:**

- Project retirement needs
- Catch-up contributions
- Rebalance portfolio conservatively

**Age 55-65:**

- Consult with CPA or advisor annually
- Prep for RMDs
- Build withdrawal strategy

**Real-Life Scenarios**

**Mark, 34, United FO**

- Contributes 16% to 401(k)
- Received $18K profit-sharing last year
- Invests 5% of pay in ESPP, sells annually
- Net worth: $280K

**Linda, 41, Alaska Captain**

- Rolled old 401(k) into IRA
- Uses HSA to pay medical costs in retirement
- Targets $2.5M retirement portfolio by 60

**Devon, 28, Delta FO**

- Uses Roth 401(k)

- Puts profit-sharing toward student loans
- Planning to open brokerage for early retirement fund

**Checklist: Navigating Your Retirement Benefits**

- Review your airline's 401(k) plan document
- Contribute at least enough to receive full employer match
- Choose your 401(k) investments intentionally
- Understand your vesting schedule
- Know when profit-sharing is paid and how it's taxed
- Decide if ESPP is right for you (and how much to invest)
- Track your total retirement savings annually
- Rebalance investments every 6-12 months
- Consider working with a CFP who understands airline compensation

**Final Call to Action**

You wouldn't skip your preflight.

Don't skip your financial planning.

Your 401(k), profit-sharing, and stock plan are more than benefits.

They're engines.

Engines that can power your freedom, your family's future, and your ability to step away from the cockpit when *you* decide.

So make one move before you go wheels-up.

Just one.

Check your contribution percentage.

Open a Roth IRA.

Schedule a call with a financial advisor.

Then do another next week.

Because when your money works while you sleep (or fly), you're finally free to fly on your terms.

Your future self will thank you.

So will your crew.

So will your sanity.

# Chapter 23: Roth vs. Traditional – Making Retirement Contributions Wisely

If you're a pilot who's already figured out how to juggle cross-country overnights, minimum rest periods, and seniority-based bidding systems, you're clearly capable of navigating complex systems. But there's one system that often trips pilots up—not because it's harder than flying, but because nobody ever taught us how to read the instruments.

Retirement planning.

And specifically, choosing between Roth and Traditional retirement contributions.

This chapter is your flight manual for that decision. Whether you're contributing to a 401(k), 403(b), 457(b), or IRA, the core question is the same:

**Should I pay taxes now, or later?**

Let's dive deep into this, layer by layer, so that by the end of this chapter, you can answer that question confidently.

**What Is the Difference Between Roth and Traditional Contributions?**

It all comes down to taxes.

**Roth Contributions**

- You pay taxes on the money *before* you contribute.
- The money grows tax-free.

- You can withdraw it *completely tax-free* in retirement (if certain conditions are met).

**Traditional Contributions**

- You contribute *before* paying taxes.
- The money grows tax-deferred.
- You pay taxes when you withdraw it in retirement.

**Quick Analogy: Roth vs. Traditional**

Roth is like buying your plane ticket now and flying for free later.

Traditional is like flying now but paying the ticket price when you land.

Depending on the route, the ticket price at landing (i.e. your future tax bracket) could be more or less than what it costs today.

**Why This Decision Matters So Much for Pilots**

Your income as a pilot will likely rise dramatically over time. You might start out making $40K to $60K as a regional FO, then make $150K+ as a captain at a major airline, and potentially end your career in the $250K+ range with seniority, overtime, and profit sharing.

Because your income trajectory is steep, so is your tax bracket.

**That means:**

- In your **early years**, Roth might make more sense.
- In your **peak earning years**, Traditional might be better.

But it's not that simple.

Let's explore the variables that matter.

**When Roth Makes Sense**

1. **You're in a lower tax bracket now than you expect to be later.**

- This is common early in your career.

1. **You want tax-free income in retirement.**

- Especially if you expect to have other taxable sources (pension, social security, rental income).

1. **You want to avoid Required Minimum Distributions (RMDs).**

- Roth IRAs (but not Roth 401(k)s) don't have RMDs.

1. **You want flexibility in retirement.**

- Having both Roth and Traditional gives you more levers to pull for tax planning.

1. **You expect taxes to rise in the future.**

- This is a big-picture guess, but many believe federal tax rates will climb.

**When Traditional Makes Sense**

1. **You're in a high tax bracket today.**

- If you're already paying 32%+ on federal income taxes, you might want the deduction now.

1. **You expect to be in a lower bracket in retirement.**

- Common for pilots who plan to retire early or live lean.

1. **You want to reduce your Adjusted Gross Income (AGI).**

- Contributing to a Traditional 401(k) can reduce your AGI, which can help with:

- Qualifying for student aid (for your kids)
- Lowering Medicare premiums later
- Avoiding phase-outs on deductions and credits

1. **Your employer contributes to a Traditional plan only.**

- Employer match or profit-sharing is always pre-tax, so you'll likely have Traditional money anyway.

**What Pilots Actually Do (and Why It Matters)**

Most pilots do one of the following:

- **Start Roth early** and **switch to Traditional** as income grows.
- **Split contributions** (50/50 or some mix).
- **Use Roth for IRAs** and **Traditional for 401(k)s**.

This hybrid approach is called **tax diversification**.

It gives you optionality in retirement.

**Example: First Officer Alex**

- Age 29, making $85,000/year
- Contributes 15% to Roth 401(k)
- Maxes Roth IRA separately
- Wants to retire early at 55

**Why Roth makes sense:**

- Still in a moderate tax bracket
- Long runway for growth
- Wants tax-free income later when withdrawing early (can use Roth contributions penalty-free)

**Example: Captain Lisa**

- Age 46, making $260,000/year
- Already has $400K in 401(k)
- Using Traditional 401(k) to reduce current taxes
- Starting to fund a backdoor Roth IRA

**Why Traditional makes sense now:**

- In a high tax bracket
- Wants to lower AGI
- Planning partial Roth conversions in early retirement before RMDs kick in

**Strategies to Consider**

1. **Backdoor Roth IRA**

- If your income is too high to contribute directly to a Roth IRA, contribute to a Traditional IRA and convert it.

1. **Mega Backdoor Roth**

- Some airline 401(k) plans allow after-tax contributions beyond the standard limit, which can then be converted to Roth.

1. **Roth Conversions**

- In years where income drops (furlough, sabbatical, early retirement), convert Traditional dollars to Roth at a lower tax rate.

1. **Roth Contributions During Military Leave or LOA**

- If your income is temporarily reduced, Roth contributions are more favorable.

1. **Use Roth for Estate Planning**

- Roth IRAs can be passed to heirs tax-free (with some RMD rules depending on relationship).

**How Taxes Really Work in Retirement**

Let's say you retire with:

- $1.5M in a Traditional 401(k)
- $300K in a Roth IRA
- $100K in brokerage accounts

You want $100K/year to live.

By pulling from different buckets, you can keep yourself in a lower tax bracket.

This is called **tax bracket management**.

Having both Roth and Traditional gives you more flexibility than just one or the other.

**Psychological Factors to Consider**

- **Do you like certainty?** Roth gives you peace of mind: what's in the account is yours, no surprises later.
- **Do you like minimizing taxes today?** Traditional scratches that itch.
- **Do you fear higher taxes later?** Roth feels like pre-paying for peace.

**Final Considerations**

1. **Roth 401(k)s do have RMDs.**

- But you can roll them into a Roth IRA before RMD age to avoid them.

1. **Employer match is always Traditional.**

- Even if you contribute Roth, their match goes in as pre-tax.

1. **Track your contributions.**

- Especially Roth IRA contributions (you can pull them out tax-free anytime).

1. **Use calculators and simulators.**

- Many retirement platforms let you model Roth vs. Traditional outcomes.

1. **Work with a CPA or financial planner.**

- Especially as your income and assets grow.

**Checklist: Choosing Roth vs. Traditional Wisely**

- What's your current tax bracket?
- Do you expect to be in a higher or lower bracket in retirement?
- Do you qualify for Roth IRA contributions?
- Does your airline allow Roth 401(k)?
- Are you already maxing your 401(k) and want to do more?
- Do you understand your employer's vesting and match structure?
- Are you planning for early retirement or standard age?
- Would you benefit from tax diversification?

**Final Call to Action**

This isn't just about math.

It's about *choice*.

Having a blend of Roth and Traditional accounts gives you choices in retirement: choices about how much tax you pay, when you take distributions, and what legacy you leave behind.

So pick one thing to do today:

- Increase your Roth 401(k) contribution by 1%
- Open a Roth IRA if eligible
- Talk to a financial planner about your future tax brackets
- Run a simulation comparing Roth and Traditional outcomes

Your job requires precision, preparation, and confidence.

Your financial life should too.

So let's get your money flying in the right direction.

Your future self will thank you.

So will your crew.

So will your sanity.

# Chapter 24: Real Estate Decisions for Pilots – Own, Rent, or Invest Remotely?

If you're a pilot, chances are you've lived out of a suitcase, stayed in a crash pad, or called more than one city "home" in the same year. The flexibility and mobility that come with your career can be a dream. But when it comes to real estate, that same mobility makes everything more complicated.

Should you rent or buy near your base?

Should you invest in real estate in a different city altogether?

Should you even bother with real estate at all early in your career?

This chapter is your navigator for one of the biggest financial decisions you'll face outside the cockpit.

Let's get clear, grounded, and strategic.

**The Real Estate Realities of a Pilot's Life**

Before we talk dollars, we have to talk *life*.

Your life.

Pilots often:

- Commute to their base by jumpseating
- Change domiciles based on seniority or company growth
- Live in crash pads to save money early in their careers
- Work odd hours that make traditional homeownership logistically stressful

Translation: you don't always have the same stability as a 9-to-5 land-dweller. That changes how you think about *where* and *how* you live.

And it should change how you think about real estate too.

**Option 1: Renting Near Your Base**

**Pros:**

- Flexibility to move with job changes or base swaps
- Lower upfront costs
- No responsibility for maintenance or property taxes
- Easy exit if your schedule or lifestyle changes

**Cons:**

- Rent can rise over time
- You don't build equity
- You have less control over your space (noise, restrictions, lease terms)

**Ideal For:**

- New regional pilots building hours
- Pilots with uncertain base assignments
- Anyone on a shorter-term contract or anticipating life changes (relationships, family growth, etc.)

**Tips for Renting Wisely:**

- Negotiate lease length for flexibility (e.g. 6-month lease)
- Look for proximity to airport and public transport
- Calculate total cost: rent + commuting costs + crash pad if needed

**Option 2: Buying a Home Near Your Base**

**Pros:**

- Build equity over time
- Fixed-rate mortgage protects against inflation
- You have control over your space and upgrades
- Potential tax deductions on mortgage interest and property taxes

**Cons:**

- High upfront costs: down payment, closing costs, inspections
- Less flexibility if your base or airline changes
- Homeownership comes with maintenance, insurance, and property tax obligations

**Ideal For:**

- Pilots with stable bases
- Families wanting school district stability
- Senior pilots with long-term placement in a desirable city

**Tips for Buying Wisely:**

- Use a mortgage broker familiar with pilot income (which can be complex)
- Don't stretch your budget—consider housing as *one* part of your total financial plan
- Be cautious of HOA rules that might affect your travel lifestyle

**Option 3: Living Elsewhere, Commuting In (a.k.a. Crash Pad Life)**

**Pros:**

- You can live where you *want* and work where you *need*
- Lower cost of living in your chosen home city
- You may be near family or better lifestyle options

**Cons:**

- Commute time and fatigue
- Crash pad costs and inconvenience
- Limited home presence can strain relationships

**Ideal For:**

- Pilots with a strong preference for one city
- Those with roots in a specific area (spouse job, family, etc.)
- Anyone prioritizing lifestyle and long-term investment over short-term convenience

**Tips:**

- Evaluate all-in costs: flights, crash pad, car storage, time away from home
- Be strategic with seniority and bid options to minimize commute days
- Factor in mental fatigue from commuting on top of flying

**Option 4: Investing in Real Estate Remotely**

You don't have to live in the house to profit from it.

**Remote investing** is increasingly popular among pilots. Here's why:

**Pros:**

- Buy in affordable markets while living elsewhere
- Generate rental income
- Leverage real estate appreciation
- Create future retirement housing options

**Cons:**

- Need reliable property management

- Financing can be trickier for investment properties
- Risk of vacancy or repairs

**Ideal For:**

- Pilots with extra savings and strong credit
- Anyone interested in long-term passive income
- Those with limited ties to expensive base cities

**Tips for Investing Remotely:**

- Work with a real estate agent and PM who know the local market
- Run conservative cash flow projections
- Be sure you can cover the mortgage if your tenant moves out
- Consider starting with a duplex: live in one, rent the other

**Real Estate vs. Your Career Trajectory**

Let's walk through the timeline:

**Flight School or CFI:**

- Renting is almost always the move.
- Keep overhead low and mobility high.

**Regional Airline FO (Years 1-3):**

- Still likely renting, maybe doing a crash pad + weekend home combo.
- Consider saving aggressively for future down payment.

**Captain or Major Airline FO (Years 4-8):**

- This is when buying becomes viable.
- You've got stability, income, and options.

**Mid-Career (Years 8-20):**

- Evaluate real estate not just as housing, but as part of your wealth strategy.
- Explore rentals, second homes, and income-producing properties.

**Senior Captain or Pre-Retirement (20+ Years):**

- Think about location for retirement.
- Pay off mortgages or downsize.
- Turn properties into retirement income or sell for lump-sum equity.

**Pros and Cons Summary Table**

| Option | Pros | Cons |
|---|---|---|
| Renting | Flexibility, low upfront cost | No equity, rising rents |
| Buying | Equity, stability, tax perks | Maintenance, less mobility |
| Crash Pad/Commute | Choose your home city | Travel fatigue, cost layering |
| Remote Investing | Passive income, long-term wealth | Risk, property management |

**Action Steps**

1. **Run a break-even analysis.** How long would you need to live in a property to offset buying vs. renting?
2. **Create a "housing mission plan."** Where do you want to live in 1, 5, and 10 years?
3. **Talk to a mortgage broker who understands pilot pay.** Per diem,

reserve pay, bonuses—you need someone who gets it.

4. **Track your crash pad, hotel, and commuting costs.** They add up fast. Know your numbers.
5. **Build a down payment fund.** Even if you don't buy for 3 years, you'll be ready.
6. **Explore REITs (real estate investment trusts)** if you want exposure to real estate without owning physical property.

### Real-Life Stories

#### Captain Mike, Age 48

- Bought in Atlanta early, rented it out when moved bases.
- Turned into a long-term wealth asset.

#### FO Jessica, Age 30

- Still renting in a crash pad. Bought a duplex in her hometown.
- Her mortgage is covered by renters.

#### Retired Captain Ana, Age 65

- Sold her paid-off home near base. Moved to a lake house paid in cash.
- Her real estate appreciation funded her retirement.

### Final Thoughts

Pilots don't have traditional lifestyles. So your housing decisions shouldn't follow traditional formulas either.

You don't *have* to buy a house to be smart with money.

You don't *have* to rent forever just because you fly for a living.

You *do* need to:

- Understand your goals
- Know your numbers

- Stay flexible
- Build equity in *some* form

Your wings give you freedom. Let your real estate decisions reflect that same power.

**Final Call to Action**

Make one move today:

- Open a down payment savings account
- Schedule a call with a mortgage broker
- Research remote real estate markets
- Ask other pilots what they've done and what they regret

Your future self doesn't need another layover.

Let's get your housing game cleared for takeoff.

Your crew will thank you.

Your bank account will thank you.

Your peace of mind will thank you.

# Chapter 25: Buying a Home With an Irregular Schedule

For most people, buying a home involves researching neighborhoods, attending open houses on weekends, and coordinating with realtors and lenders during 9-to-5 hours. For pilots? That's laughable. Your schedule isn't just non-traditional—it's the antithesis of traditional.

Your job demands long stretches away from home, early call times, reroutes, and layovers. You live out of suitcases and iPads. So how are you supposed to navigate one of life's biggest financial decisions when you can barely predict what city you'll be in next week?

This chapter is your guide to buying a home when your schedule doesn't follow the rules.

**Understand the Unique Challenges of Buying as a Pilot**

You're not just busy. You're unavailable at traditional times.

You're not just earning a salary. Your income is variable, with per diem, overrides, bonuses, and reserve.

You're not just choosing a home. You're making a base decision, a commute decision, a family decision, and a tax decision all at once.

This means:

- You need more planning time
- You need more support
- You need to be crystal clear on your goals

**Pre-Flight Check: Are You Ready to Buy?**

Before you book a showing, check these indicators:

1. **Stable Base** – Are you likely to stay at your current domicile for the next 3-5 years?
2. **Savings** – Do you have enough for a down payment, closing costs, and an emergency fund?
3. **Credit** – Is your score at least 700+ to qualify for favorable mortgage terms?
4. **Debt Load** – Are you handling student loans and credit cards responsibly?
5. **Schedule Stability** – Are you able to attend key meetings and signings, either virtually or in person?

If any of those feel shaky, pause. You can always buy later. But once you close, you're locked in.

**Set Your Mission Profile**

Ask yourself:

- Is this a primary residence or future rental?
- Is this a solo purchase or joint with a spouse?
- Will you be commuting to your base, or is this a base city property?
- Will your schedule allow for upkeep, repairs, and household management?

The answers will shape what, where, and how you buy.

**Getting Pre-Approved (Without Blowing Up Your Schedule)**

Step 1: Work with a mortgage broker who understands aviation pay.

Your base pay, per diem, bonuses, and profit-sharing need to be explained properly to underwriters. Some lenders won't count all forms of pilot income unless it's well-documented.

Step 2: Get a digital-friendly lender.

Many lenders now offer e-signatures, online portals, and mobile uploads.

Make sure your mortgage process is compatible with airport Wi-Fi.

Step 3: Lock in the rate.

With your variable income, it's tempting to float for a better deal. But schedule unpredictability could mean missing key windows. Lock when you're comfortable.

**House Hunting With a Flight Schedule**

Coordinate with your realtor in advance:

- Block time during off days
- Ask for video walkthroughs if you're away
- Use a shared Google Drive for contracts, comps, and disclosures
- Trust a realtor who moves fast and respects your time constraints

If you're buying with a partner, they may need to be your in-town boots on the ground.

**Making an Offer While You're in the Air**

This is where preparation pays off.

- Ensure you have electronic access to all pre-approval documents
- Use a power of attorney if needed for physical closings
- Clarify with your agent how offers will be submitted if you're unreachable

This isn't rare. Many pilots buy homes mid-trip. But don't wing it—have a communication plan.

**What Kind of Home Works With a Pilot Lifestyle?**

Consider these features:

- **Airport Access** – Proximity to your base or to a major hub if you commute
- **Low Maintenance** – Townhomes or condos with HOA-covered exterior
- **Security** – Gated communities, security systems, and packages that

won't sit unattended

- **Storage** – Enough room for gear, uniforms, rollerboards, and extra crew bags
- **Noise and Light Control** – You sleep during the day. Blackout curtains and quiet neighborhoods matter.

This is not just about square footage. This is about function.

**Should You Buy Alone or With a Partner?**

If you're single:

- You must have systems in place for when you're gone
- Consider a smaller property or one with a low-maintenance exterior

If you're buying with a spouse or partner:

- Discuss household roles (who handles mail, maintenance, bills, etc.)
- Set expectations: your irregular presence can create emotional and logistical gaps

**The Down Payment Question**

- 20% down is ideal to avoid PMI and lower your mortgage rate
- 5-10% is more common for pilots early in their careers
- Consider using a combination of savings, bonuses, or equity from other properties

Also consider:

- VA Loans (if military background)
- Physician/Professional loans (some lenders extend these to pilots)
- State-specific first-time buyer programs

**Emergency Fund for Homeowners**

You cannot afford to be house-poor in this profession.

You need:

- 3-6 months of full expenses
- Additional $5K for unexpected repairs (furnace, appliances, etc.)

Because when you're on reserve and a pipe bursts? You'll thank yourself.

**The Mortgage Timeline and Your Bid Schedule**

Plan around:

- Mortgage approval (2-4 weeks)
- Appraisal and inspection timelines
- Closing (30-45 days after contract)

If you have vacation coming up, schedule showings then. If you're switching airlines or seats, wait until that change is official.

**Buying in a Crash Pad City vs. Your Real Home**

This is the double-life dilemma.

**Buy near your base if:**

- You want to end the crash pad phase
- You expect to be at this base for 5+ years
- You want to cut hotel/commute costs

**Buy in your hometown if:**

- You prefer commuting
- Your family is rooted there
- You see long-term equity or lifestyle upside

Some pilots eventually buy *both* (a primary residence and a small studio at their base).

**Real Estate and Your Overall Wealth Plan**

Buying a house is not just about shelter.

It impacts:

- Cash flow
- Tax deductions
- Credit utilization
- Net worth trajectory

Make sure this fits within:

- Your investment strategy
- Retirement plan
- Career mobility outlook

**Pilot Stories: Real-Life Lessons**

**Captain Laura, 43**

Bought her first house solo. Overwhelmed at first, she automated everything: bills, lawn service, security system. It became her sanctuary.

**FO Marcus, 30**

Bought a duplex. Rents out one unit. Covers the mortgage while building equity.

**Retired Captain Dave, 65**

Moved three times in his career. Bought in his final base city and paid it off before retirement.

**Plain Language Breakdown: Fixed vs. Variable Mortgages**

- **Fixed:** One rate forever. Easy to budget. Better for pilots who want stability.
- **Variable (ARM):** Lower initial rate, but it changes. Riskier if you might stay long-term.

Most pilots choose fixed.

**Plain Language Breakdown: Escrow**

- It's a holding account for taxes and insurance.
- The lender manages it.
- Budget for it—your mortgage payment is *principal + interest + escrow.*

## Final Thoughts

You don't need a perfect schedule to make a smart housing decision.

You just need a plan.

Let your real estate moves match your career arc.

Think like a captain, not a passenger.

Plan for the turbulence. Pack for the future.

Buying a home isn't a detour from your flying career.

It's part of the flight plan for financial independence.

**Final Call to Action**

This week:

- Pull your credit score
- Schedule a call with a mortgage broker
- Create a "home readiness checklist"
- Block your next set of days off for touring

Don't wait for a perfect schedule. It may never come.

But your future address? It's waiting for clearance.

Let's help you land it.

# Chapter 26: Planning for Kids and Family as a Traveling Professional

Being a pilot is one of the few careers that regularly takes you away from home, not just for hours, but for days at a time. It's a profession that demands sharp focus at 36,000 feet—and then asks you to shift into full-on spouse or parent mode the second you walk through the door. There is no taxiing into your family life. You land directly in it.

And when you're also trying to plan financially for that family? It adds an entirely new layer of complexity.

This chapter is about how to plan for kids and family when you work in a metal tube, live by bid schedules, and carry the weight of other people's lives—in the air and at home.

**Section 1: The Financial Reality of a Flying Parent**

Let's start with honesty. You are not like your friends who are home every night at 6 p.m.

Your parenting costs are not just daycare, groceries, and college savings. You're dealing with:

- Extra childcare for overnights
- Higher travel costs for reunions, family events, and holidays
- Lost wages during unpaid leave if your schedule shifts unexpectedly
- Possibly one partner opting out of the workforce to create stability at home

This is not a standard budgeting problem. This is pilot-specific financial planning.

## Section 2: Building a Two-Cockpit Household

If you're raising kids with a partner, communication is your co-pilot. Create a shared family flight plan:

- **Split the responsibilities.** Who handles the kids' bedtime routines, school drop-offs, and pediatric appointments?
- **Build in buffers.** Assume delays, reroutes, or reschedules. Keep a backup childcare plan in place 100% of the time.
- **Money talks matter.** What are you prioritizing as a family? Debt payoff, home upgrades, college savings, or lifestyle experiences?
- **Automate together.** Use joint calendars and shared financial apps to track bills, investments, and important dates.

## Section 3: Budgeting for Children in a Flight-Based Lifestyle

You can budget for a child on a pilot's income. But you must be strategic:

- **Childcare:** Night nannies, extended daycare hours, or backup babysitters cost more than standard 9-to-5 setups.
- **Schooling:** Are you buying in a district for quality public schools? Or will you need private tuition or tutoring to support your travel?
- **Travel:** When you want to bring the family to your layover or base city, flight benefits help, but hotels and time off do not.
- **Gifts and Guilt:** Many flying parents overspend on birthdays and holidays trying to make up for lost time. Build this into your budget so love isn't measured in swipe volume.

## Section 4: Insurance, Guardianship, and Protecting Your Family

If you're gone often, you must plan for what happens if you don't come back.

- **Life insurance:** Term insurance is usually best. Consider 10-20x your annual salary if you have dependents.

- **Disability insurance:** Protect your income in case you can't fly.
- **Loss of license insurance:** A must-have if you're the primary earner.
- **Wills and guardianship:** Who raises your kids if something happens to you? This is the checklist no one wants to face but must complete.
- **Emergency contacts:** Make sure your airline, your spouse, your union, and your financial advisor know the plan.

**Section 5: Family Planning & Leave in Aviation**

Pilots face unique leave challenges:

- Not all airlines offer paid parental leave.
- Maternity leave may bump you from a seat or base.
- FMLA is an option—but unpaid.
- Commuting with a new baby at home is emotionally draining.

What to do:

- Save aggressively in advance if you're planning to expand your family
- Understand your union-negotiated benefits and deadlines for seat freezes
- Decide how long you realistically want to be off work

**Section 6: Saving for College (and Keeping Your Sanity)**

A few college saving routes:

- **529 Plans:** Tax-advantaged savings
- **UTMA/UGMA accounts:** Great for gifts, but count as child's asset on FAFSA
- **Brokerage account in your name:** More flexibility, fewer tax perks

Remember:

- Start small but start early
- Automate contributions monthly (even $50/month grows)
- Talk to your kids early about the cost of education and their role

**Section 7: Teaching Your Kids Financial Literacy (Even While You're Gone)**

You don't need to be home daily to raise money-smart kids.

- Leave video messages explaining saving and budgeting
- Assign allowance via apps like Greenlight or GoHenry
- Share your pay stub and explain how taxes and retirement work
- Celebrate their wins (saving for a toy, donating to charity)

Parenting isn't about perfection. It's about intentional presence—even if you're doing it from a hotel room in Denver.

**Section 8: Emotional and Relationship Budgeting**

Let's be real. Money isn't your only budgeting challenge. Your time and energy are scarce resources too.

- Block out dates for family time and protect them like a flight assignment
- Budget for time with your partner—not just money
- Use group chats, video calls, and handwritten notes to stay close
- Pay for help if it protects your sanity (cleaning service, grocery delivery)

A pilot's love language might just be an Amazon gift card and pre-scheduled therapy. Normalize the help.

**Section 9: Real Pilot Families Share Their Tips**

**Jake, FO, 34:**

"We keep a family shared Google Calendar with my entire bid schedule. My wife adds school stuff, and we plan everything on Zoom on Sundays."

**Captain Maria, 41:**

"I max out my HSA and 401(k) because I know we're already paying a lot in daycare and preschool. Those tax savings are huge."

**Retired Captain Drew, 62:**

"I bought a second home near my final base. We raised the kids there and sold it after I retired. That second property was the best financial and emotional decision we ever made."

**Section 10: Final Descent – Your Family Flight Plan**

- Start with open conversations about money, time, and roles
- Save early and automate often
- Protect your family legally and financially
- Adjust your expectations as the seasons shift (infants, toddlers, teens)
- Forgive yourself for the missed games or recitals

Your flying life won't look like anyone else's. That's the point.

But with the right plan, your family can feel more secure than most.

**Final Call to Act**

- Schedule a financial planning session with your partner this month
- Review your insurance and guardianship documents
- Open a 529 or kids' savings account
- Block out three dates for family time this quarter

Flying is your job.

Family is your flight plan.

Make sure your career lifts your household—not just your altitude.

You've got this, Captain.

And your family knows it.

# Chapter 27: Marriage and Money – Pre-Nups, Post-Nups, and Transparency

Marriage is one of the most beautiful commitments two people can make to one another—but it also comes with serious financial implications, especially when one or both spouses are professional pilots. Long hours in the air, unpredictable schedules, and income that fluctuates with contract cycles, seniority, or global demand make it crucial for pilots to approach marriage with the same level of planning and communication that they bring to the cockpit.

This chapter is not here to scare you. It's here to empower you to make clear-eyed, heart-forward decisions that protect your relationship and your financial future.

Let's take off.

## Why This Chapter Matters

You've earned your wings, your salary, and your independence. But whether you're newly married, engaged, thinking about proposing, or decades into a committed relationship, understanding the financial framework of marriage is non-negotiable.

Pilots face unique stressors: long-distance dynamics, variable income, sudden layoffs, furloughs, disability concerns, career shifts, and pension nuances. Add in another person's financial past, spending habits, goals, and assumptions about money, and you've got a complex situation that demands transparency, structure, and intentional conversations.

Marriage is a legal contract. It impacts:

- How your income is taxed
- Who owns what
- What happens if one of you dies
- What happens if the marriage ends
- And whether you have a plan in place to protect your kids, legacy, and earnings

Let's unpack all of it.

## Pre-Nuptial Agreements: A Flight Plan for Your Financial Future

### *What Is a Pre-Nup?*

A prenuptial agreement (or pre-nup) is a legal contract created before marriage that outlines how assets, debts, income, and property will be handled during the marriage and in the event of divorce or death.

Think of it like a well-thought-out safety briefing. You hope you never need it. But if turbulence hits? You're glad it's there.

### *Pros of a Pre-Nup*

- Protects pre-marriage assets (401(k), real estate, inheritance)
- Clarifies how income and expenses will be handled
- Helps define marital vs. separate property
- Can prevent costly, drawn-out legal disputes
- Offers clarity and reduces financial surprises
- Supports open, intentional money conversations before marriage

### *Cons (or rather, emotional hurdles)*

- Can feel unromantic or accusatory
- May be difficult to discuss if financial imbalance exists
- Can be challenged if not properly executed

### *When Should You Consider One?*

- You have substantial assets or debts entering the marriage
- This is your second marriage or you have kids from a previous relationship
- You own a business or plan to in the future
- You're entering marriage later in life with an established financial life
- You're marrying someone with significantly different earning potential or money mindset

### *Pilot-Specific Considerations*

- Flight school debt: Who is responsible if marriage ends?
- Per diem pay and tax treatment: Who benefits from your work expenses?
- Retirement plan and vesting timelines: What's yours vs. shared?
- Airline bonuses, profit-sharing, and stock options: Are they marital income?

## Post-Nuptial Agreements: Adjusting the Course Mid-Flight

### *What Is a Post-Nup?*

A postnuptial agreement is like a pre-nup, but created *after* you're already married.

It may outline the same details:

- Division of assets
- Income structure
- Debt responsibilities
- Inheritance or trusts

Post-nups are often triggered by major life changes:

- A big promotion or windfall
- One spouse taking time off to raise kids
- A sudden illness or diagnosis
- Moving to a new state with different marital property laws
- Infidelity or a desire to rebuild trust with financial clarity

*Pilot-Relevant Examples*

- You become a captain and now make triple what your spouse earns
- You or your spouse want to start a business
- You're considering early retirement or stepping back for family

A post-nup gives your financial strategy a tune-up. It allows you to update plans with mutual respect, not panic.

## Transparency: The Bedrock of a Strong Financial Relationship

Money isn't just math. It's emotional. It's historical. It's personal.

And for pilots, the stakes are even higher because of high income potential, sudden changes in employment, and the very real emotional toll of time away from home.

### *Key Topics to Discuss Openly with Your Partner*

1. **Current Debt:** Student loans, credit cards, car loans, mortgages
2. **Spending Habits:** Are you a saver? A spender? Where do you differ?
3. **Financial Goals:** Retirement age? Dream home? Supporting family?
4. **Income & Bonuses:** When, how much, and how it's used
5. **Emergency Fund Philosophy:** How much is enough?
6. **Account Access:** Will you share accounts or keep some separate?
7. **Estate Planning:** Wills, powers of attorney, beneficiaries
8. **Insurance Coverage:** Disability, life, long-term care, loss of license

### *Tools to Help Facilitate These Talks*

- Schedule monthly "Money Date Nights"
- Use budgeting apps with shared views (like YNAB or Monarch)
- Keep a shared document with account logins and financial plans
- Consult a neutral third party (like a financial advisor or coach)

Transparency isn't about control. It's about trust.

## What Happens If You Don't Plan?

Let's say you skip the pre-nup. You never talk about the money. And then something happens:

- Divorce
- Death
- Disability
- Career-ending injury
- Family lawsuit

What happens next is determined by **state law** if there is no legal agreement in place. And state law might not reflect your values, preferences, or family structure.

You worked too hard to let your financial life get tossed to the wind.

## Real-Life Stories

**Case Study 1: The Early-Career Climb**

A first officer marries a schoolteacher. No pre-nup. Within five years, the pilot earns five times their spouse's salary. They buy a home together, open joint accounts, and eventually divorce. The spouse claims half the pilot's profit-sharing and stock grants accrued during the marriage. The pilot is stunned. Had they created a pre-nup or post-nup, expectations would have been clearly defined.

**Case Study 2: The Second Marriage Reboot**

A senior captain remarries after raising kids from a first marriage. They want their pension and real estate to go to their children, not their new spouse. A pre-nup and updated estate plan allow that to happen—preserving peace, clarity, and trust.

**Case Study 3: Partners in Flight and Finance**

Two pilots meet at flight school, marry, and navigate the ups and downs of career building together. They use monthly financial check-ins, alternate who contributes to the 401(k), and create a family budget that supports both flying and future planning. They don't have a pre-nup but do have a post-nup and a shared vision.

## Questions to Ask Yourself (and Each Other)

1. If we broke up tomorrow, how would we divide our finances?
2. Do we have shared financial goals? Or are we on different runways?
3. Are we clear on what's mine, yours, and ours?
4. Have we talked about kids, childcare costs, and parental leave?
5. What happens to our finances if one of us can't fly?
6. Do we have enough insurance coverage?
7. What legacy do we want to leave?

## Action Steps for Pilots in Any Relationship Stage

- **Single but serious?** Educate yourself on your state's marital property laws. Begin documenting your assets.
- **Engaged?** Start the prenup conversation early. Focus on fairness, not fear.
- **Newly married?** Set up joint systems with transparency. Consider a post-nup if major financial shifts are coming.
- **Established couple?** Schedule regular financial conversations. Keep things updated. Plan your legacy.

## Final Descent: This Isn't Just Paperwork. It's Peace of Mind.

Talking about marriage and money is emotional. It requires courage. But the reward is massive: confidence, clarity, and calm.

Remember, love is the foundation. Communication is the engine. Legal clarity is your autopilot. And trust? That's the jet fuel.

Your marriage deserves honesty, structure, and respect—especially when your career already demands so much time away. Having a financial plan that supports your relationship means fewer surprises, fewer resentments, and more room to build the life you both want.

You fly better with a flight plan. Your financial life is no different.

Make one financial move before you go wheels-up tomorrow. Just one. And do another next week.

Because the only thing worse than flying blind—is doing it with someone you love in the jumpseat beside you.

Let's fly smart. Let's fly together.

# Chapter 28: Creating a Pilot-Friendly Budget System That Works

Pilots live and breathe checklists. Preflight. Takeoff. Climb. Cruise. Descent. Landing. Every phase has a protocol, a rhythm, and a safety net. But when it comes to personal finances, that same sense of order often goes missing. Why? Because most pilots were never handed a checklist for money.

This chapter is your flight manual for budgeting — written for your lifestyle, your irregular income, and your need for both control and flexibility. It's not a lecture. It's not a guilt trip. It's a systems-based approach to cash flow built by someone who respects the work you do and the life you're trying to build.

Whether you're flying legs for a regional airline, enjoying layovers in Europe with a major carrier, or juggling per diem with side gigs, this is your go-to guide for finally feeling confident about how your money moves.

## Why Budgeting Feels So Broken for Pilots

Let's start with the obvious: most standard budgeting advice isn't written for people who live on irregular schedules and unpredictable paychecks.

- You get paid monthly, biweekly, or per trip — and sometimes those paychecks vary.
- Per diem feels like free money… until it quietly disappears into airport

snacks and rideshares.
- Crash pads, commuting costs, layovers, and inconsistent schedules make it hard to predict fixed vs. variable expenses.
- You're often on the go, so tracking spending on the fly (pun intended) feels impossible.
- You get hit with random expenses: uniform upgrades, medical exams, ATP checkride fees, or the dreaded unexpected move to a new base.

This chapter respects that reality. But it's also here to challenge the idea that you're stuck living paycheck-to-paycheck just because you're in the early phases of your flying career.

## The Goal: Calm Cash Flow, Not a Punishing Spreadsheet

A good budget isn't about deprivation. It's not about tracking every single dollar. It's about:

- **Predictability**: Knowing what bills are coming and when
- **Clarity**: Understanding where your money's going
- **Power**: Having a plan for savings, debt, and spending that aligns with your goals

You don't need 47 budget categories and a spreadsheet that updates by the hour. You need a system that runs like a well-trimmed aircraft: smooth, steady, and low-stress.

Let's build it together.

## Step 1: Know Your Net (Not Just Your Gross)

Your hourly rate or salary doesn't mean much until you see what actually hits your account. That's your **net income**, and it's the real number you can plan around.

Break down your monthly take-home like this:

- **Base pay**: What shows up consistently
- **Per diem**: Separate it. It's tax-free and variable — treat it like a bonus, not a guarantee
- **Overtime/Premium flying**: Track averages if you fly extra regularly, but don't budget around it unless it's stable
- **Deductions**: Union dues, medical premiums, 401(k) contributions, etc.

Create a document or app that tracks your average monthly net over the last 3–6 months. That's your launch pad.

## Step 2: Create Your Financial Checklists (3-Account Budget System)

Here's the core system that works for pilots:

**1. Fixed Ops Account (Auto-Pilot Bills)**

This is where your stable, recurring bills get paid automatically:

- Rent or mortgage
- Car payment and insurance
- Utilities
- Cell phone
- Minimum student loan payments
- Union dues or professional fees

**2. Variable Ops Account (Manual Control)**

This is your debit/checking account for flexible expenses:

- Groceries
- Gas
- Layover spending
- Restaurants
- Entertainment

- One-off purchases

**3. Reserve Tank (Emergency + Goals)**
Your savings account(s) should include:

- Emergency fund
- Short-term goals (vacation, training costs, moving)
- Long-term savings (house down payment, Roth IRA contributions, future child expenses)

Direct deposit your paycheck to split between these three accounts based on predetermined percentages:

- 60% to Fixed Ops
- 25% to Variable Ops
- 15% to Reserve Tank

These percentages can shift as your career advances, but starting with this gives you structure without suffocation.

## Step 3: Set Up the Auto and the Manual

Think of your Fixed Ops account like a fully automated flight system:

- All regular bills get paid from here
- Avoid mixing discretionary spending here — no Target runs, no Uber Eats
- You want to be able to glance at it and know: "Yes, my monthly life is covered."

Variable Ops is your fly-by-wire system:

- Use one debit card only for these expenses

- Once it's gone, it's gone — that's your signal to slow spending, not dip into other funds
- You can use apps like YNAB (You Need A Budget), GoodBudget, or simple spreadsheets to track if needed

## Step 4: Include Layover Funds in the Budget

Layovers are where cash slips away. Use one of the following strategies:
**Option A: Envelope System**

- Budget $100–$200/month specifically for layovers
- Load it onto a separate card or app (like Cash App, Venmo, or even a prepaid card)

**Option B: Per Diem Fund as Bonus Savings**

- Bank 100% of your per diem and let it stack
- Use it for mini-vacations, gear upgrades, or debt payoff

**Option C: "Layover Wallet" Line Item**

- Treat layover spending like a regular budget item — it's real and recurring. Budget for it accordingly.

## Step 5: Build Your Runway — Emergency Fund and Buffers

Budgeting without buffers = turbulence ahead.
Set these short-term goals:

- **$1,000 starter emergency fund**: Use this for car repairs, hotel reroutes, and surprise fees
- **1 month of expenses**: Build toward this next
- **3–6 months of expenses**: Once you're making consistent money at a

major or legacy carrier

Use high-yield savings accounts or money market accounts to store these funds — not your main checking.

## Step 6: Automate Wealth, Not Just Bills

You don't need to think about savings every day. You need it to happen without drama.

Set up automatic transfers:

- From your main income account to savings the day after each paycheck
- From savings to Roth IRA or brokerage accounts (monthly or quarterly)
- Consider split direct deposit to route money to different banks/accounts automatically

When wealth is automated, it doesn't feel like a loss. It just becomes part of how you fly.

## Step 7: Adjust Per Season, Base, and Career Phase

Your budget won't be static:

- **Moving bases?** Expect a spike in crash pad costs or relocation fees
- **Training phase?** You'll have more per diem, but fewer hours — adjust Variable Ops spending
- **New contract?** Update Fixed Ops and long-term savings percentages
- **Got married?** Combine the budgeting system — but preserve autonomy with personal "fun money" accounts for each partner

The goal is flexible structure — not budgeting jail.

## Real Pilot Scenarios

**Scenario 1: Sam, Regional FO with $42K Base Pay**

- Per diem: ~$4,500 annually
- Side hustle: DoorDash during off days
- Strategy: Uses per diem to pay off student loans aggressively while budgeting fixed expenses tightly

**Scenario 2: Dani, New Major Airline Pilot**

- First year: Jump in pay from $45K to $92K
- Action: Doubled retirement savings, built 3-month emergency fund in 9 months, and froze lifestyle inflation

**Scenario 3: Marcus and Jen, Dual-Pilot Couple**

- Shared "house fund" and separate fun accounts
- Use Sunday "money huddle" to go over schedules and review budget flow

## The Pilot's Budget Philosophy

You don't have to track every dollar to be successful.
You just need to:

- Give every dollar a job
- Keep spending in alignment with your values
- Avoid mixing personal spending with fixed bills
- Create enough margin to breathe

When you master your budget, your confidence on the flight deck starts showing up in your bank account.

## Call to Action

Make one change tonight:

- Open a second checking account
- Review your last 90 days of spending
- Build a pilot-specific spending template

Don't overthink it. Just fly the next leg. Then the next.

Every hour in the air builds toward your rating. Every dollar you assign builds toward your financial independence.

**So go ahead: make your money fly smoother.**

You've got the controls. Now let's keep climbing.

# Chapter 29: TInvesting Beyond Retirement Accounts – Brokerage Accounts and Index Funds

You've spent years thinking about your 401(k). Maybe you're even making regular contributions. That's a good start.

But if you stop there, you're missing a huge piece of the long-term wealth equation.

This chapter is about what happens after you check the retirement contribution box. It's about the next level of investing—the kind that builds flexibility, opportunity, and power.

It's about learning how to invest outside of retirement accounts, through taxable brokerage accounts. And doing it in a smart, consistent, pilot-friendly way.

This is not about stock-picking. This is not about gambling on the next hot tech IPO. This is about smart, diversified investing using simple tools that even the busiest pilot can manage.

Let's start with a simple truth: If your only investments are inside tax-advantaged accounts like your 401(k) or Roth IRA, you may be setting yourself up for long-term success—but you're limiting your short- and mid-term flexibility.

A taxable brokerage account gives you freedom. Freedom to:

- Invest money you might need before age 59 ½
- Harvest gains or losses for tax planning

- Fund big-ticket goals (a home, a sabbatical, helping your kids)
- Build true wealth that doesn't rely on government rules or withdrawal schedules

## *What Is a Brokerage Account?*

A brokerage account is an investment account that you open with a financial institution (like Fidelity, Schwab, Vanguard, or a robo-advisor like Betterment or Wealthfront) that allows you to buy and sell investments: stocks, ETFs, bonds, mutual funds, and more.

Unlike a 401(k), there are no tax advantages going in. You invest with after-tax money. And you pay taxes on dividends, interest, and capital gains along the way.

But that's the trade-off for flexibility.

## *Why Index Funds?*

You have hundreds of investment options in a brokerage account. But let's be honest—most of them are noise.

Index funds cut through that noise. An index fund is a type of investment that aims to mirror the performance of a market index—like the S&P 500. They are:

- Low-cost
- Broadly diversified
- Tax-efficient
- Consistent
- Easy to understand

Translation: They're the workhorse of modern investing. They don't try to beat the market. They try to *be* the market. And over long periods of time, that's more than good enough.

## *Pros and Cons of Brokerage Accounts*

**Pros:**

- Liquidity: You can access your money anytime.
- Flexibility: No age restrictions on withdrawals.
- Tax strategies: Can harvest losses to reduce your tax bill.
- Simplicity: No rules about required minimum distributions (RMDs).

**Cons:**

- No tax deduction for contributions
- You pay taxes on dividends and realized gains
- Requires more discipline—because it's easy to withdraw

## *The Pilot's Advantage*

Pilots have a unique income arc: low in the early years, steep rise mid-career, and potentially very high later.

Your income is also tied to bidding, bases, union negotiations, and seniority. You might have great years and lean years.

A brokerage account can act as a stabilizer. It gives you a pot of money that isn't tied to job benefits, tax rules, or government timelines.

And because you travel, you might have low-cost housing or per diem that frees up extra income. Don't spend it all—invest some of it.

## *How to Start*

1. Open an account at a reputable brokerage (Schwab, Fidelity, Vanguard, etc.)
2. Fund it automatically—even $250/month adds up
3. Choose a target allocation (e.g., 70% stocks / 30% bonds)
4. Use low-cost index ETFs (e.g., VTI, VXUS, BND)

5. Reinvest dividends
6. Review once per quarter (not daily)

### *What to Avoid*

- Stock picking
- High-fee mutual funds
- Emotional trades (panic selling, chasing gains)
- Neglecting tax implications

### *Tax Smart Moves*

- **Tax loss harvesting:** Selling losing investments to offset gains
- **Qualified dividends:** Often taxed at lower rates
- **Holding long term:** Avoid short-term capital gains

### *Scenario: Meet Jordan*

Jordan is a 32-year-old first officer. She maxes out her 401(k) and Roth IRA. She has $800/month extra after bills.

Rather than park it in a savings account, she opens a brokerage account. She invests in VTI (total U.S. stock market), VXUS (international), and BND (bonds).

After 10 years, she has $130K in this account. She uses $30K for a home down payment. The rest continues to grow. She didn't time the market. She just kept flying and investing.

### *Final Thoughts*

This is the investing chapter for when you're ready to grow beyond retirement accounts.

This is how pilots build flexibility, options, and freedom.

This is your tool to prepare for the unexpected.

You're not just flying planes. You're building a financial flight plan that can take you anywhere—no turbulence, no grounding, no delays.

Start small. Start smart. Stay consistent.

**Call to Act:**

Open a brokerage account. Fund it this month. Choose one index fund. Start your financial preflight.

The only thing worse than flying blind is waiting too long to get off the ground.

# Chapter 30: Automating Your Finances for Peace of Mind

Flying demands precision, repetition, and preparation. Pilots don't freestyle a flight plan. Every route, checklist, and protocol exists to reduce chaos, protect safety, and increase efficiency. Your finances deserve that same kind of flight plan. The truth is, most pilots aren't failing financially because they're reckless. They're failing because they're trying to fly their money manually in a world that rewards autopilot.

That's what this chapter is about—creating a system that removes stress, reduces error, and protects your wealth-building journey. Automation is your financial co-pilot. It's not about being lazy. It's about being smart enough to know that systems beat willpower, and clarity beats chaos. You're not just buying peace of mind—you're buying back mental bandwidth, which is gold for someone navigating time zones, reserve lists, bidding wars, and unexpected schedule changes.

Let's build your financial autopilot.

SECTION ONE: THE CASE FOR AUTOMATION

You already trust automation with your flight deck. Now let's trust it with your checking account. Here's what automation solves for:

- **Missed bill payments** that lead to late fees and credit dings
- **Inconsistent saving habits** that delay your goals
- **Overdrafts** from trying to track it all in your head
- **Emotional investing** or overspending during slow months or bonus

months

- **Mental fatigue** from trying to manually manage every dollar

Pilots don't have consistent 9-5 lives. Your cash flow varies, your downtime is erratic, and your mental focus needs to be sharp for safety and performance. Automation eliminates the background noise of money management.

SECTION TWO: HOW TO BUILD YOUR SYSTEM

Step 1: Open Two Checking Accounts

Think of this like having two flight decks for different missions:

- **Primary Checking**: The account where your paycheck hits and where fixed bills are paid (rent, insurance, subscriptions).
- **Lifestyle Checking**: Your "personal allowance"—groceries, restaurants, Amazon, fun. You'll transfer a fixed amount here every week or month.

Why it works: You never have to guess how much is safe to spend. You're not pulling from your rent money when you splurge on sushi.

Step 2: Add a High-Yield Savings Account

Label it with the goal: "Emergency Fund," "New AirPods Fund," "2026 Iceland Trip."

Why it works: Naming goals makes them real. Keeping savings separate from checking avoids temptation.

Step 3: Schedule Your Paycheck Flight Plan

When your paycheck arrives:

- 401(k) and HSA contributions come out automatically (more on that later)
- Debt payments and fixed bills auto-draft from Primary Checking
- A weekly allowance auto-transfers to Lifestyle Checking
- A fixed monthly savings amount goes to your High-Yield Savings

You can set this all up with your bank, credit union, or tools like Ally, SoFi, Capital One 360, or Fidelity.

Step 4: Monthly Review (But NOT Manual Control)

Every month (pick a date), do a 20-minute check-in:

- Are the transfers working?
- Did you overdraw?
- Do you need to raise or lower your weekly spending transfer?

This is like doing a pre-flight walkaround. You're just checking that the systems are doing their job—not flying the whole plane by hand.

SECTION THREE: CUSTOMIZING YOUR FLIGHT PLAN

Your career stage, schedule, and priorities will shape your system. Let's build some profiles:

**The New CFI with $120K in Loans**

- Income is tight, but structure is everything.
- Use free bank accounts. Set $10 a week to go to savings, just to build the habit.
- Make student loan payments automatic so they never fall through the cracks.
- Set up alerts to notify you if your checking drops below $200.

**The First Officer at a Major Airline**

- Your income just doubled, but your expenses might creep up too.
- Create three savings buckets: Emergency Fund, Travel, Down Payment.
- Automate transfers to each based on percentages.
- Automate a monthly Roth IRA contribution.
- Use your airline benefits portal to max out 401(k) contributions. Set it and forget it.

**The Senior Captain Planning for Retirement**

- Set up automation to draw from your pension, Social Security, or annuities into one centralized retirement account.
- Automatically fund a Health Savings Account if still eligible.
- Use rules-based investing for dividends and capital gains.
- Auto-pay all recurring bills from a designated account to minimize fraud risk.

SECTION FOUR: WHAT NOT TO AUTOMATE

Automation is powerful—but don't outsource critical thinking. Don't automate:

- Big purchases (review these manually)
- Financial advisor fees (watch what they charge)
- Charity donations over a certain amount (should be intentional)
- Annual bills (you might forget they're coming)

Automate the boring. Stay hands-on with the big, meaningful moves.

SECTION FIVE: WHY PILOTS NEED THIS MORE THAN MOST

You live on reserve. You fly during holidays. You're jet-lagged in a hotel in Detroit while your credit card payment is due. Automation protects you from the realities of pilot life.

Your lifestyle is non-linear. Your financial systems can't be built like a 9-5 worker's budget. Automate the repetitive and predictable, so you have capacity for the unexpected.

This is about confidence. It's about reclaiming time. It's about making smart moves with less stress.

Automating your finances isn't boring. It's brilliant.

END-OF-CHAPTER ACTION CALL:

"Make one financial move before you go wheels-up tomorrow. Just one. Set up a weekly transfer to your savings or split your paycheck between two checking accounts. And do another next week. The only thing worse than flying blind is staying grounded when you've got the power to soar."

This isn't just about bills.

This is about bandwidth.

This is about freedom.

This is about never again missing a financial opportunity because you were too tired, too behind, or too busy flying.

Financial automation is your flight plan to peace of mind.

Set it. Check it. And let it fly.

# Part IV: The Captain's Chair – Mastering Mid- to Late-Career Wealth

By the time pilots reach mid-career, they're no longer just flying aircraft—they're navigating life's biggest financial decisions at cruising altitude. This section is for those who've climbed the ranks, built a life, and now need to protect it, scale it, and prepare for smooth landings ahead. Whether you're a captain with a decade of seniority, a dual-income pilot household managing complex benefits, or a seasoned pro approaching retirement, this part speaks directly to your phase of life.

We'll explore how to maximize retirement contributions with strategic precision, leverage profit-sharing and stock plans without overexposure, and begin serious estate planning. You'll learn how to use your financial altitude to make investment decisions that reflect your values, risk tolerance, and timeline. We'll also dive into navigating divorce, second marriages, and legacy planning for children or charitable causes—all from a pilot's perspective.

This isn't just about big paychecks—it's about making them last. It's about building real wealth, maintaining optionality, and ensuring your hard work doesn't fly into a storm of poor planning. This is your financial cockpit, and you're in command.

# Chapter 31: Advanced Tax Planning – HSAs, FSAs, and Backdoor Roths

Let's talk about money moves that don't get discussed enough in flight school—or even on the flight deck. If you've made it far enough in your aviation career to start thinking long-term, chances are you've heard some jargon tossed around in crew lounges and pilot forums: "I max out my HSA," "I'm doing the Backdoor Roth thing this year," "I loaded up the FSA before open enrollment closed." But what do these really mean? More importantly, how can they fit into a pilot's lifestyle?

This chapter is about strategic tax planning—not the kind that sends you down Reddit rabbit holes or drowns you in tax code citations. We're breaking it down like a checklist: clean, clear, direct. Whether you're a regional pilot earning per diem and building hours or a widebody captain flying international routes, understanding these tools could save you thousands over your career.

Let's make your money fly with the same precision you bring to every landing.

**Section 1: Why Tax Planning Matters for Pilots**

When your pay is inconsistent, your schedule is erratic, and your benefits change depending on seniority or carrier, you can't afford to leave tax breaks on the table.

Tax planning isn't about loopholes. It's about knowing what tools exist, how to use them in the right order, and how to keep more of what you earn. Pilots often have complex income structures: base pay, per diem, duty rig, bonuses, profit-sharing, and sometimes 1099 income on the side. That complexity creates opportunity if you know where to look.

The three tools we'll cover—Health Savings Accounts (HSAs), Flexible Spending Accounts (FSAs), and Backdoor Roth IRAs—are especially valuable for pilots because they offer ways to:

- Lower taxable income
- Save for future healthcare or retirement needs
- Access tax-free growth on investments

Let's break each one down.

**Section 2: Health Savings Accounts (HSAs) – The Swiss Army Knife of Tax Planning**

HSAs are arguably the most tax-advantaged accounts available. You get three levels of tax benefits:

1. Contributions are tax-deductible.
2. Growth is tax-free.
3. Withdrawals are tax-free if used for qualified medical expenses.

**Who Can Contribute?**

You must be enrolled in a High Deductible Health Plan (HDHP). Many airline and union health plans offer an HDHP option, but not all. If you're married and your spouse's coverage isn't an HDHP, you may not qualify.

**Contribution Limits (2025)**

- Individual: $4,300
- Family: $8,650
- Add $1,000 if you're 55+

**How It Helps Pilots**

- Flight schedules and layovers mean healthcare expenses can hit unexpectedly. Having a tax-free fund gives you a cushion.
- You can invest your HSA like a retirement account—many custodians let you invest in mutual funds or ETFs.
- Once you hit 65, you can withdraw for *anything* (not just medical) without penalty—though non-medical withdrawals are taxable.

**Pro Tip**

Don't use your HSA for small expenses like Band-Aids or Tylenol. Pay out of pocket, keep the receipts, and let your HSA grow tax-free. You can reimburse yourself years later.

**Section 3: Flexible Spending Accounts (FSAs) – Use It or Lose It**

FSAs are like HSAs but with fewer freedoms and tighter rules.

**Types of FSAs:**

- **Healthcare FSA**: Covers medical, dental, vision, and other healthcare costs.
- **Dependent Care FSA**: Helps cover child care expenses for pilots with young families.

**Contribution Limits (2025)**

- Healthcare FSA: $3,200
- Dependent Care FSA: $5,000 per household

**Key Differences From HSAs**

- FSAs are employer-specific.
- Funds typically must be used within the plan year (some offer grace periods).
- FSAs don't roll over like HSAs.

**Why Pilots Use FSAs**

If you know your family will need braces, glasses, contacts, prescriptions, or daycare this year—use the FSA. You'll save roughly 25–40% depending on your tax bracket.

**Pro Tip**

Front-load your expenses early in the year. You can access your full FSA amount even if you haven't contributed it all yet.

**Section 4: Roth IRAs and the Backdoor Roth Strategy**

Most pilots earn too much to contribute directly to a Roth IRA. But there's a workaround.

**The Problem:**

- Roth IRA income limits phase out starting at ~$146K (single) or ~$230K (married) in 2025.

**The Solution: Backdoor Roth IRA**

Step-by-step:

1. Contribute to a non-deductible Traditional IRA.
2. Wait a few days (for record-keeping).
3. Convert that amount to a Roth IRA.

If you have *no other Traditional IRA assets,* there's little to no tax impact.

**Why It Works for Pilots**

- Many pilots have union pensions or 401(k)s but lack access to Roth options.
- This gives high earners access to tax-free retirement growth.

**Watch Out For:**

- The pro-rata rule. If you have pre-tax IRA balances, the IRS will apply taxes proportionally.
- Always consult a CPA before doing a Backdoor Roth.

## Section 5: Putting It Together – A Flight Plan for Advanced Tax Moves

Let's take three fictional pilots and see how they could use these tools:

**Scenario 1: First Officer Jenna, Age 32**

- Income: $130K
- Health Plan: HDHP with HSA
- Goals: Start investing outside her 401(k)

Jenna should:

- Max her HSA and invest it
- Use a Healthcare FSA for predictable expenses (like LASIK)
- Start a Backdoor Roth IRA for long-term tax-free growth

**Scenario 2: Captain David, Age 45**

- Income: $250K
- Family of four
- Spouse doesn't work

David should:

- Max the family HSA and invest it aggressively
- Use Dependent Care FSA to cover daycare or after-school care
- Execute annual Backdoor Roths for both himself and his spouse

**Scenario 3: Retired Pilot Lisa, Age 67**

- Uses HSA withdrawals to cover Medicare premiums and prescriptions tax-free
- Keeps prior receipts for tax-free reimbursement on past expenses

## Section 6: Avoiding Common Pilot Mistakes With These Accounts

1. **Using the HSA like a checking account**
2. Don't. Think of it like a Roth IRA with a medical twist.
3. **Letting FSAs expire**
4. Set calendar reminders for FSA deadlines. Some plans allow $610 to roll over, but most don't.
5. **Doing a Backdoor Roth without checking IRA balances**
6. If you have old pre-tax IRAs from past employers, roll them into your 401(k) first.
7. **Ignoring these options until tax season**
8. These moves must be made throughout the year—not when you're filing returns.

**Section 7: Final Checklist Before Takeoff**

- Enroll in a HDHP and open an HSA if eligible
- Set recurring contributions (monthly or per paycheck)
- Review open enrollment documents for FSA options
- Talk to HR or your benefits rep about how your plan integrates with these tools
- Use a spreadsheet or app to track HSA/FSA spending and receipts
- Book time with a tax advisor before doing any Roth conversions

**End of Chapter Call to Act**

Make one tax-smart move this month. Just one.

Open an HSA. Book a Roth IRA strategy session. Max out your FSA before it expires. Whatever it is—don't wait until next tax season.

Because when you're flying 38,000 feet above the ground, it's the systems you built *before* you took off that keep you safe.

Same goes for your money.

Let's not just fly—let's soar, tax-efficiently.

**Final Note**

This chapter wasn't about getting rich overnight. It's about using the systems the IRS already allows—to keep more of your hard-earned money, reduce risk, and fly with clarity.

You already know how to read a flight plan. Now you've got a tax plan too.

Your future self will thank you.

So will your crew.

So will your peace of mind.

# Chapter 32: Managing Deferred Compensation and Airline Stock Plans

Let's talk about the money that doesn't hit your checking account right away—and how it can be just as important, if not more so, than your direct deposit. Deferred compensation plans and airline stock programs can quietly become seven-figure wealth engines if you understand how they work, how to avoid common traps, and how to align them with your long-term financial plan. This chapter is for the pilot who wants to fly smarter—not just with a paycheck, but with legacy money.

**What Is Deferred Compensation?**

Deferred compensation is a portion of your earnings set aside to be paid at a later date—often when you retire, or leave the company. Airlines may offer this as an optional benefit to higher-ranking pilots or as part of retention or performance programs. Think of it like a paycheck with a parachute: it doesn't show up now, but it could soften your landing later.

**Why Deferred Comp Matters for Pilots**

- **Tax Timing**: You may be in a lower tax bracket in retirement, making deferred income more tax-efficient.
- **Retirement Gap Coverage**: Deferred comp can bridge the income gap between age 60-65 (when some pilots retire) and age 67 (when Social Security kicks in).
- **Compounding**: Deferred dollars can often be invested and grow over time—tax-deferred.

But it comes with strings. This money is technically an unsecured promise to pay. If the airline goes under, you might lose it. So let's break it down.

**Types of Deferred Compensation Plans You May Encounter**

- **Non-Qualified Deferred Compensation (NQDC)**: Most common. Contributions are made pre-tax, but you don't control the investment. You select a payout schedule (e.g. lump sum in 10 years, or 5-year payout post-retirement).
- **Supplemental Executive Retirement Plans (SERPs)**: Usually offered to senior captains and executives. These are company-funded and vest over time.
- **Equity Compensation (Stock Options, RSUs)**: Not always considered "deferred comp" formally, but in practice it functions similarly. Vesting schedules dictate when you actually own and can sell shares.

**How Airline Stock Plans Work**

If you work for a publicly traded airline, you may be offered one or more of the following:

- **Employee Stock Purchase Plans (ESPPs)**: Allows you to buy stock at a discount (usually 10-15%). Often payroll-deducted.
- **Restricted Stock Units (RSUs)**: Grants you stock after a vesting period. When they vest, you owe taxes on the fair market value.
- **Stock Options**: Gives you the option to buy shares at a set price. If the stock price goes up, you profit.

These tools can be a path to wealth—but only if you understand:

- **Tax triggers** (vesting vs. exercise vs. sale)
- **Concentration risk** (too much of your wealth in your employer's stock)
- **Liquidity windows** (when you can sell)

**Taxes and Timing: Where Pilots Get Tripped Up**

Let's say your RSUs vest this year. The IRS sees that as income. If you didn't plan for that, your tax bill could be a shock.

If you exercise stock options and don't sell them, you may still owe Alternative Minimum Tax (AMT).

If you defer $30K per year and take a lump sum in 10 years, that's $300K-plus growth—and a possible tax wall.

The solution? **Strategic planning**.

- Use tax software or a CPA to model outcomes.
- Stagger payouts to manage tax brackets.
- Use 401(k) and HSA contributions to offset tax spikes.
- Consider Roth conversions in low-income years to smooth future taxes.

**Building a Strategy Around Deferred Comp and Equity**

1. **Map the Timeline**: When will each plan pay out? What are the vesting dates?
2. **Layer It**: How does it interact with your pension, 401(k), Social Security, and other assets?
3. **Set Exit Rules**: Know when you'll cash out of stock to avoid emotional decisions.
4. **Don't Ignore Risk**: If your airline hits turbulence, your stock and deferred comp may drop in tandem. Diversify elsewhere.
5. **Align With Goals**: Are you retiring early? Saving for college? Planning charitable giving? Your strategy should reflect this.

**Real-World Scenarios**

- **Jason, Age 45, Senior Captain**: He defers $20K/year into NQDC, maxes out 401(k), and holds $100K in airline stock. Strategy: Begin annual sell-down plan to reduce stock exposure. Sets deferred comp payout to start at 62.

- **Sasha, Age 38, First Officer**: Has $30K in vested RSUs but no tax plan. Gets hit with unexpected tax bill. Strategy: Sets up withholding plan and sells a portion at each vesting event to cover taxes and rebalance.
- **Luis, Age 60, Nearing Retirement**: Deferred comp lump sum hits same year as pension. Strategy: Shifts some to 5-year payout and does Roth conversion in retirement year two.

**Action Steps for Pilots**

- Review your airline's benefit portal and summary plan descriptions.
- Talk to HR or your benefits rep to clarify details.
- Ask a financial planner to model your equity and deferred comp.
- Automate sells if appropriate to avoid holding too long.
- Use windfalls (RSU vests, option sales) to fund long-term goals—not lifestyle creep.

**Checklist Before You Lock In a Deferred Comp Election**

- Understand the payment schedule and your options
- Estimate your tax bracket at time of payout
- Coordinate with 401(k), pension, and other income streams
- Avoid overlapping large payouts in the same year
- Discuss with a tax professional and financial planner

**Call to Action**

Make one financial move before you go wheels-up tomorrow. Just one. Log in to your benefits portal and download your deferred comp plan summary. Highlight the payout options. Book 30 minutes with a financial advisor to review it.

Do another next week: Set a recurring calendar reminder to check stock plan activity every quarter. The only thing worse than flying blind is staying grounded when you've got the power to soar.

**Final Note**

Deferred compensation and stock plans aren't just executive toys. They're real tools for pilots who want to build wealth beyond their paycheck. But the difference between building wealth and building stress is your ability to plan ahead.

This isn't about complexity for complexity's sake. It's about dignity. It's about freedom. It's about using every lever available to you so you can retire confidently, support your family, and live with peace of mind at every altitude of your career.

You didn't earn your wings to feel weighed down by money.

You earned them to fly—fiscally, too.

# Chapter 33: Protecting Your Income – Loss of License and Long-Term Disability Insurance

You spent years chasing hours, studying for certifications, and passing medical exams just to earn your wings. You know that a steady hand and sharp mind keep planes safely in the air. But what happens when life grounds you? Not metaphorically. Literally. What happens when illness, injury, or unexpected life circumstances make flying impossible—temporarily or permanently? What if your license is suspended or revoked? How would you support yourself and your family?

If you're like many pilots, your identity is closely tied to your ability to fly. But your financial identity needs another co-pilot: protection. Specifically, Loss of License Insurance and Long-Term Disability Insurance.

This chapter is about one thing: protecting your income so that you never lose your financial altitude—even when turbulence hits.

Why This Chapter Matters

You've likely heard of life insurance. You probably even have it. But statistically, you're far more likely to suffer a disabling event than die prematurely. Especially in aviation, where your Class 1 medical is your golden ticket, even minor health issues can sideline you.

And while your company may offer some short-term or long-term disability coverage, it often doesn't cover your full earning potential—especially when you're younger and just building income.

If your ability to fly is your greatest asset, protecting that income is just as important as investing it.

Let's break this down, starting with the basics.

Part I: Understanding the Threats to Your Income

1. Medical Disqualifications

- Common medical issues that can cost you your license
- Mental health considerations
- Temporary vs. permanent loss of medical

1. FAA Medical Exams and the "Grounded" Reality

- The stress of renewals
- Medical deferments and AME reviews
- What counts as disqualifying

1. Industry Stats and Why Pilots Are at Risk

- Average age of medical disqualifications
- Real-world examples: what actually happens when a pilot can't fly

Part II: Long-Term Disability Insurance (LTD)

1. What It Covers

- Percentage of income (usually 50–70%)
- Elimination periods and benefit durations
- Own Occupation vs. Any Occupation definitions

1. Where to Get It

- Employer-sponsored policies
- Union-negotiated plans

- Individual private policies

1. Policy Traps to Avoid

- Taxable vs. non-taxable benefits
- Caps and exclusions
- Coordination with Social Security Disability

1. Pros and Cons

- Employer plans are cheaper, but less portable
- Private plans can be customized, but cost more

1. Action Steps

- Calculate your current income replacement gap
- Read your airline's group plan carefully
- Meet with a disability insurance specialist familiar with aviation

Part III: Loss of License Insurance (LOL)

1. What It Is

- Niche product designed for pilots only
- Kicks in when you lose your medical, not just can't work

1. Who Offers It

- ALPA and other unions
- Private aviation insurers (e.g., Petersen, Lloyd's of London)

1. Key Features to Compare

- Monthly benefit and maximum benefit
- Waiting period (often 90-180 days)
- Medical vs. non-medical loss

1. Cost and Underwriting

- Premiums based on age, aircraft type, and health
- May require additional medical screening

1. Pros and Cons

- Pro: Can kick in where LTD doesn't
- Con: Not always available depending on carrier/employer

1. Action Steps

- Talk to your union or insurance rep
- Price out supplemental LOL coverage
- Understand renewal rights and portability

Part IV: Coordinating LTD and LOL

1. Stacking Coverage Intelligently

- When to layer both policies
- Avoiding overlaps and coverage gaps

1. Real-World Scenarios

- Pilot A: Diagnosed with MS at age 36
- Pilot B: Temporarily grounded for heart surgery
- Pilot C: Long-haul COVID

1. Tax Implications

- Are your benefits taxable or tax-free?
- How to set up policies to avoid surprises

1. What to Do If You're Grounded

- Filing claims with LTD and LOL
- Doctor documentation and appeals
- Working with union or third-party advocates

Part V: The Psychology of Protection

1. Why Pilots Avoid This Topic

- Denial: "It won't happen to me"
- Shame: "If I lose my medical, who am I?"
- Financial Fear: "I can't afford more insurance"

1. The Reframe

- You insure your aircraft. You need to insure your career.
- This isn't fear-based planning. It's freedom-based.

1. Building Peace of Mind

- Knowing your family is covered
- Creating backup plans that reduce financial anxiety

Conclusion: Your Career Is Your Jet. Protect the Engine.

A lot of financial advice focuses on building wealth. And that's vital. But before you can grow your financial life, you need to defend it.

Disability insurance and Loss of License insurance aren't sexy. But they're serious. And they're powerful. They're your ejection seat if life ever forces an emergency landing.

You can always invest again. You can always build wealth again. But protecting your ability to earn is what makes everything else possible.

Final Call to Action:

"Make one financial move before you go wheels-up tomorrow. Just one. And do another next week. The only thing worse than flying blind is staying grounded when you've got the power to soar."

You didn't earn your wings to feel weighed down by money. Protect your income. Fly smarter. Your future self will thank you. So will your crew. So will your sanity.

# Chapter 34: Estate Planning Basics for Pilots – Wills, Trusts, and Healthcare Directives

Flying a plane requires a detailed flight plan, routine checks, and contingency preparation for unexpected weather or turbulence. Your financial life is no different—especially when it comes to estate planning. As a pilot, you understand the importance of preparation, precision, and responsibility. Estate planning is your financial preflight checklist for the unknown.

This chapter exists to bring clarity and confidence to a subject that most people delay until it's too late. You're not just preparing for the end; you're protecting your family's future, maintaining control of your assets, and ensuring your legacy reflects your life's work.

Let's walk through everything you need to understand—and act on—when it comes to wills, trusts, and healthcare directives. Whether you're a new hire grinding it out at a regional or a senior captain approaching final approach to retirement, estate planning matters. And it matters now.

**Section 1: Why Estate Planning Matters for Pilots**

Estate planning is not about being wealthy. It's about being responsible. You don't need a million-dollar home or an inheritance to justify it. You just need people you care about, assets you've worked hard for, or medical decisions you want to remain in control of. Pilots are in a uniquely high-risk, high-responsibility profession—and estate planning provides the structure to protect what you've earned and whom you love.

In aviation terms, think of estate planning as your autopilot system for your financial affairs when you can no longer manually fly the plane. You pre-program the headings. You chart the course. Your crew—your family, your executor, your healthcare proxy—will follow your plans, not guess your intentions.

No matter your net worth, you should care about:

- Who gets your assets
- Who makes decisions if you can't
- How to minimize confusion, court involvement, and conflict

**Section 2: The Will – Your Basic Flight Plan**

A will is a legal document that tells the world how you want your assets distributed and who should take care of any minor children. Without a will, your estate will go through probate, and the state will decide who gets what. That process can be time-consuming, expensive, and emotionally draining for your family.

**Key Elements of a Will:**

- **Executor:** The person responsible for carrying out your instructions.
- **Beneficiaries:** The individuals or charities you leave assets to.
- **Guardianship Provisions:** Who will take care of your minor children if something happens to you?
- **Asset Distribution:** Specific gifts or percentages you want allocated.

**Common Mistakes Pilots Make:**

- Not updating their will after marriage, divorce, or children.
- Naming outdated beneficiaries.
- Forgetting to include digital assets or airline-related benefits.

A will alone may not avoid probate, but it's a non-negotiable starting point.

**Section 3: Trusts – More Than Just an Upgrade**

If a will is your basic flight plan, a trust is your upgraded cockpit system—automated, precise, and efficient. A trust allows your assets to be distributed privately, often faster, and without the probate process.

**Types of Trusts Useful to Pilots:**

- **Revocable Living Trust:** You control the trust while you're alive. Assets avoid probate. You can update or dissolve it.
- **Irrevocable Trust:** Offers asset protection and potential tax benefits, but you give up control.
- **Special Needs Trusts:** Protects disabled dependents without jeopardizing benefits.
- **Minor Trusts:** Helpful for setting financial boundaries for children or dependents who aren't ready to inherit.

**Why Pilots Choose Trusts:**

- They want privacy (wills are public record).
- They want to protect assets from lawsuits, creditors, or remarriages.
- They want to plan for multiple generations (legacy planning).

**Section 4: Healthcare Directives - Who Makes the Call?**

As pilots, you're trained to make critical decisions quickly. But what if you can't? A healthcare directive ensures someone you trust is empowered to make medical choices on your behalf if you're incapacitated.

**Two Essential Documents:**

1. **Healthcare Power of Attorney (Proxy):** Designates who makes medical decisions for you.
2. **Living Will:** Lays out your wishes regarding life-sustaining treatment, resuscitation, and organ donation.

If you don't have these documents, hospitals may rely on laws that default to next of kin, which can delay decisions or cause unnecessary stress.

**Section 5: Digital Assets, Airline Perks, and Flight-Specific Considerations**

You're not a typical W-2 employee with a desk job. Your estate plan should account for the unique nature of aviation.

**Include in Your Plan:**

- Airline stock options or profit-sharing benefits
- Frequent flyer miles or travel pass benefits
- Airline life insurance policies (beyond personal policies)
- Digital logbooks or aviation-related intellectual property
- Secure access to online accounts (Dropbox, email, EFB apps)

**Pilot-Specific Tip:** Keep a sealed copy of your will and directives in your hangar or home office with clear labeling. Make sure at least two trusted individuals know where to find them.

**Section 6: Estate Taxes, State Rules, and Portability**

Federal estate taxes currently apply only to estates above $13 million (as of 2025), but that limit may change. States, however, often have much lower thresholds.

**What You Need to Know:**

- **Portability:** If married, unused federal exemption can transfer to the surviving spouse.
- **Step-Up in Basis:** Assets passed at death often receive a "step-up" in cost basis, minimizing capital gains for heirs.
- **Gift Limits:** You can give up to $18,000 per year (2025) per person tax-free.

Estate planning is not about tax dodging—it's about planning.

**Section 7: Common Scenarios Pilots Face**

**1. You're in Your 30s, Single, and Renting:**

You still need a basic will and healthcare directives. List beneficiaries for your 401(k), union benefits, and airline life insurance.

**2. You Have a Young Family:**

Establish guardianship in a will. Consider a living trust. Name contingent beneficiaries on your retirement accounts. Purchase term life insurance.

**3. You're a Senior Captain Near Retirement:**

Review your trust for legacy planning. Consider charitable giving vehicles. Consolidate accounts. Update your healthcare proxy.

**4. You Own Property in Multiple States:**

Trusts can help avoid probate in each state. Consult an estate planning attorney with multi-state expertise.

**Section 8: The Estate Planning Checklist**

1. Draft a will with a licensed estate planning attorney.
2. Set up a revocable living trust if privacy or efficiency is important.
3. Name a durable power of attorney for finances.
4. Complete a healthcare proxy and living will.
5. Update all beneficiaries on retirement accounts.
6. Review your airline perks and digital assets.
7. Revisit your plan every 3-5 years or after major life changes.

**Section 9: What It Costs, What It Saves**

**Attorney Fees:**

- Basic will: $300-$1,000
- Trust package: $1,500-$5,000

**Probate Costs if You Skip Planning:**

- 2-7% of estate value
- 6-12 months delay

Estate planning isn't expensive. Not having a plan is.

**Final Descent: What This All Means**

You're in a career built on systems, preparation, and training. Estate planning is an extension of that same mindset—one that ensures your family doesn't scramble in the worst moment. It gives you peace of mind, control, and a legacy that reflects a life of excellence.

This isn't about death. It's about leadership.

It's about passing on what you've built.

It's about making sure your crew is cared for, even when you're no longer at the controls.

So before your next takeoff, complete one step. One document. One conversation.

Fly smart. Live well. And plan like a captain.

**Call to Action:**

Make one financial move before you go wheels-up tomorrow. Just one. And do another next week. The only thing worse than flying blind is staying grounded when you've got the power to soar.

Your wings weren't meant to carry regret. Your legacy wasn't meant to be guessed.

Estate planning is your autopilot to peace.

Your future self will thank you.

So will your crew.

So will your sanity.

# Chapter 35: When a Financial Advisor Makes Sense – And What to Ask

Let's be honest—you didn't train for thousands of hours, fly through thunderstorms, memorize emergency procedures, and navigate the high-stakes world of aviation to lose sleep over Roth conversions or dividend reinvestments. And yet, here you are, sitting on a jumpseat of questions about your financial future. Should you hire a financial advisor? What do they even do? Are they worth the cost? How do you find one that won't steer you into turbulence?

Let's clear the runway.

This chapter isn't a sales pitch. It's a briefing—an honest, empowering flight plan to help you understand when a financial advisor makes sense for a pilot like you, what kind of advisor to look for, and exactly what questions to ask.

Because the truth is this: Some pilots absolutely benefit from hiring a financial advisor. Others don't need one—at least not yet.

Let's help you figure out which category you're in.

Part I: The Pilot Lifestyle = Unique Financial Complexity

You don't work 9 to 5.

You don't have a static income.

You may have per diem, profit sharing, stock plans, union pension benefits, a health savings account, and a base pay that varies by bid.

Add in:

- Crash pad expenses
- Possible 1099 income from side gigs
- Irregular pay stubs
- Retirement account options from two or more airlines
- Tax exposure in multiple states

You're not just a W-2 employee with a steady job and a 401(k).

You're a traveling professional with layers of complexity—and your financial planning should reflect that.

This is why financial advisors who understand the aviation industry can be so valuable.

But not all advisors are created equal.

Part II: What a Financial Advisor Can Do for You

Let's say you're a first officer or captain considering whether to outsource part of your financial management. What would you even hire someone to do?

Here's a checklist:

- Help you map out a comprehensive retirement plan
- Optimize your 401(k), Roth IRA, HSA, and profit-sharing benefits
- Plan for taxes—especially if you fly for multiple airlines, earn per diem, or pick up charter gigs
- Create a debt repayment plan, especially if you're still carrying flight school loans
- Run simulations to estimate your time to financial independence
- Design an investment portfolio aligned with your goals and risk tolerance
- Evaluate insurance coverage (including loss of license)
- Create college savings plans for your kids
- Set up trusts, wills, and estate documents
- Coach you through job changes, relocations, or side-business formation

A good advisor becomes your financial co-pilot. Someone who spots turbulence before you feel it. Someone who knows your mission and keeps you aligned with it.

But again: Not everyone needs that level of support.

Part III: When You Probably Don't Need an Advisor Yet

Let's be real. If you're a 27-year-old flying regional routes, still paying off your CFI loans, and have $1,200 in a Roth IRA and a crash pad bill each month, hiring a financial advisor might not make sense—yet.

You might benefit more from:

- Using a budget app
- Reading this book
- Opening a low-fee IRA with a robo-advisor like Betterment or Wealthfront
- Watching YouTube videos about index investing

You need time to build assets before paying someone to help you manage them.

That said, some advisors offer hourly or flat-fee planning for young professionals. That might be worth considering if you want a one-time check-up.

Part IV: When a Financial Advisor *Does* Make Sense

Here are some scenarios where working with a financial advisor is not just helpful—it's strategic:

1. You've transitioned from a regional to a major airline and your compensation jumped 50%+
2. You have over $150K in investments and want professional oversight
3. You're married (especially if your spouse has a different career/income structure)
4. You're a captain with stock options or a deferred compensation plan
5. You're within 5–10 years of retirement and want to ensure you're on track

6. You're dealing with multi-state taxes or want help with tax minimization
7. You're burned out on managing it all yourself
8. You've been burned before by bad investment decisions and want a fiduciary

If any of those apply to you, it may be time to find an advisor who understands your needs and speaks your language.

Part V: Fee Structures and Red Flags

There are three main ways advisors get paid:

1. **Fee-only (fiduciary)**
2. You pay them directly for their advice. They don't earn commissions. They're legally required to act in your best interest. Ideal for most pilots.
3. **Commission-based**
4. They make money by selling financial products—like life insurance or annuities. Some are ethical, but many have conflicts of interest.
5. **Fee-based**
6. This means they *can* charge fees *and* earn commissions. Ask tough questions.

**Red flags:**

- They push products before understanding your goals
- They won't sign a fiduciary oath
- They aren't transparent about fees
- They promise outsized returns with little risk
- They rush the relationship

Remember: You're the captain. They're not flying your plane. They're simply providing maps, forecasts, and advisory input. You decide the altitude.

Part VI: Questions to Ask in the First Meeting

Here are 10 questions to ask a potential advisor:

1. Are you a fiduciary 100% of the time?
2. How are you compensated?
3. Do you specialize in working with pilots or aviation professionals?
4. What services are included?
5. What's your investment philosophy?
6. Will you help with taxes, estate planning, and insurance?
7. Can I see a sample financial plan?
8. What happens if I need to pause the relationship?
9. What's your client-to-advisor ratio?
10. How often will we meet and how will we communicate?

If they dodge these questions or seem irritated, they're not the right advisor for you.

Part VII: How to Find a Great Advisor

Look for:

- CFP (Certified Financial Planner)
- Fee-only structure
- Experience with pilots, aviation professionals, or high-income earners
- Transparent, easy-to-understand communication

Places to start your search:

- NAPFA.org (National Association of Personal Financial Advisors)
- XYPlanningNetwork.com (great for Gen X/Y professionals)
- GarrettPlanningNetwork.com (hourly planners)
- Referrals from trusted colleagues or union reps

Avoid:

- Advisors who only sell insurance
- Those who speak in jargon and can't explain their recommendations simply
- Sales-first, strategy-second approaches

Part VIII: What a Healthy Advisor Relationship Looks Like

You should feel:

- Heard
- Respected
- Informed
- Never pressured
- Like you're gaining clarity and control

A great advisor helps you:

- Avoid expensive mistakes
- Reduce emotional decision-making
- Maximize your benefits
- Feel more confident about your future

They don't replace your responsibility. They amplify your control.

Conclusion: Hire a Co-Pilot for Your Financial Journey (When You're Ready)

No one becomes a great pilot alone. You train with mentors. You fly with instructors. You grow with captains who challenge you.

Finance is the same.

If you reach a point where your financial world gets too complex, too overwhelming, or too time-consuming—a trusted financial advisor can be the difference between flying blind and flying empowered.

Just make sure they're truly in your corner.

Make one financial move before you go wheels-up tomorrow. Just one. And do another next week.

Because the only thing worse than flying blind is staying grounded when you've got the power to soar.

This isn't just about money.

It's about control.

It's about peace of mind.

It's about the freedom to say yes to what matters and no to what doesn't.

Financial Literacy For Pilots isn't just a book.

It's your briefing manual for life.

Your future self will thank you.

So will your crew.

So will your sanity.

# Chapter 36: Creating a Financial Dashboard – Net Worth, Cash Flow, and More

If you're reading this chapter, it means you're ready to take full command of your financial cockpit. You want to see your entire financial life the way you see a flight deck—with clarity, control, and a deep understanding of every dial, switch, and system. You want to know exactly where you are, where you're going, and whether you have enough fuel to get there.

That's what a financial dashboard gives you.

A financial dashboard is not a luxury. It's essential.

Just like you wouldn't fly without checking your altimeter, airspeed indicator, and fuel gauges, you shouldn't go through life without knowing your net worth, cash flow, savings rate, debt levels, and investment growth. This chapter will show you how to create your own pilot-friendly financial dashboard—even if you're not a spreadsheet wizard or personal finance junkie.

It will become your pre-flight checklist for money.

Let's break it down.

Section 1: What Is a Financial Dashboard?

Think of your financial dashboard as your personal finance control panel. It pulls together key metrics so you can:

- Make smarter financial decisions

- Track progress toward your goals
- Adjust quickly when life or income changes
- Reduce financial stress by knowing your numbers

Your dashboard should answer:

- How much do I own?
- How much do I owe?
- What's my monthly cash flow?
- Am I saving or burning money?
- Am I on track for retirement?
- Where are my financial blind spots?

It should be visual, organized, and updated at least monthly.

Section 2: Core Components of a Pilot's Financial Dashboard

1. **Net Worth Tracker**

Net worth = what you own – what you owe.

Assets:

- Checking and savings accounts
- Retirement accounts (401(k), IRA, HSA)
- Brokerage accounts
- Real estate
- Vehicles (optional)

Liabilities:

- Student loans
- Mortgage
- Car loans
- Credit card debt

Track this over time—month by month, year by year. If it's going up, you're building wealth. If it's going sideways or down, it's time for a systems check.

1. **Monthly Cash Flow**

This is your income minus your expenses.
Income:

- Base pay
- Per diem
- Profit-sharing
- Stock compensation
- Side hustle income

Expenses:

- Fixed: rent/mortgage, insurance, utilities
- Variable: food, fuel, Amazon Prime, pilot gear
- Occasional: travel, holidays, maintenance

You want to create a clear picture of how much money is coming in and how much is leaking out.

1. **Savings Rate**

This is one of the most powerful metrics in personal finance.
Savings rate = total savings / gross income
Aim for:

- 15% minimum (basic retirement planning)
- 25%+ (fast-track financial independence)

Include contributions to:

- 401(k)
- Roth IRA
- HSA
- Brokerage accounts

Your savings rate tells you how much of your income is building your future versus fueling your lifestyle.

1. **Debt Snapshot**

You need to know:

- Balances
- Interest rates
- Minimum payments

Use this data to:

- Prioritize debt paydown (highest interest first)
- Decide when to refinance
- Know when to attack vs. hold steady

1. **Investment Allocation & Performance**

Your dashboard should reflect:

- Account balances
- Asset allocation (stocks, bonds, cash)
- Diversification (US, international, sectors)
- Year-to-date performance

You don't need to check this daily—but quarterly review is smart.

1. **Emergency Fund Level**

Quick-glance status:

- Target amount (3–6 months of expenses)
- Current amount
- Progress bar

1. **Retirement Projection**

Even a simple calculation like:
"If I keep saving $X/month and earn Y%, I'll have $Z by age 60."
This helps you:

- Make intentional lifestyle trade-offs
- Adjust your savings early (not too late)
- Avoid retirement surprise landings

Section 3: Building Your Dashboard (Low-Tech and High-Tech Options)
**Option 1: Spreadsheet**

- Google Sheets or Excel
- Use tabs for net worth, budget, cash flow
- Customize formulas to reflect aviation pay structure
- Free, flexible, and manual

**Option 2: Apps**

- Tiller (spreadsheets with live feeds)
- Monarch Money
- YNAB (You Need a Budget)

- Personal Capital / Empower (for investments)

**Option 3: Pen + Paper + Whiteboard**

- Old-school, but effective
- Especially useful for net worth snapshots or goal setting

Section 4: Automating Data Collection

Set up:

- Auto bank account syncs
- Auto categorize transactions
- Email summaries
- Monthly recurring reminders to review dashboard

Your job is to fly planes, not run reports all day. Use automation where possible.

Section 5: What Pilots Should Include That Most People Don't

1. **Per Diem Tracking**

- Untaxed income
- Can distort cash flow if not separated

1. **Bidding Schedules and Income Fluctuations**

- Create monthly income buffers
- Budget on your *lowest* expected month

1. **Crash Pad Costs vs. Home Base**

- Helps clarify true cost of housing
- Track both for tax and budgeting purposes

1. **Multi-State Tax Exposure**

- Flag state residency and filing considerations

1. **Loss of License / Disability Coverage**

- Review annually
- Add expiration dates to dashboard

1. **Travel Rewards & Credit Card Points**

- Optional but helpful
- Treat them like assets

Section 6: Real Pilot Examples (Scenarios)

**Pilot A:** 28-year-old regional FO, living in a crash pad, $120K in loans.

- Dashboard shows -$80K net worth
- Cash flow leak in eating out and travel
- Sets goal to break even net worth in 2 years

**Pilot B:** 40-year-old captain, married, two kids, 401(k) + ESPP

- Dashboard shows solid income, but cash flow neutral
- Spending review finds recurring charges bleeding $900/month
- Adjusts savings rate to 22%

**Pilot C:** 55-year-old senior captain nearing retirement

- Dashboard includes retirement projections, pension estimate, HSA drawdown strategy
- Meets with advisor to finalize estate documents

Section 7: Why Most Pilots Don't Do This – And Why You Must

Reasons pilots *don't* track this stuff:

- Too busy
- Feels overwhelming
- Shame or guilt
- Think they make enough to not worry

But even high-income pilots can end up:

- Broke in retirement
- Overextended in lifestyle
- Paying unnecessary taxes

Your dashboard keeps you honest.

It gives you awareness.

It gives you control.

It lets you fly smart.

Section 8: How Often to Update Your Dashboard

- Net Worth: Monthly
- Cash Flow: Monthly
- Savings Rate: Monthly/Quarterly
- Investment Allocation: Quarterly
- Retirement Projection: Annually
- Insurance Review: Annually

Conclusion: Your Dashboard = Your Control Panel for Wealth

This isn't about becoming a spreadsheet junkie.

It's about knowing what's really going on.

Once your dashboard is built:

- You'll feel calmer

- You'll make smarter decisions
- You'll spot problems early
- You'll set real goals based on real data

So don't fly blind.

Build your financial dashboard.

Review it often.

Adjust as needed.

And most importantly—let it help you fly free.

Make one financial move before you go wheels-up tomorrow.

Just one. And do another next week.

Because the only thing worse than flying blind is staying grounded when you've got the power to soar.

# Chapter 37: Balancing Travel with Family Wealth Planning

Let's begin by stating something pilots already know in their bones: your schedule is different. Your life runs on rotating bid cycles, fluctuating hours, and a constantly changing view out the window. And while that may make for great stories and Instagram-worthy sunsets, it can make financial and family planning feel like trying to hit a moving target in a headwind.

This chapter is about helping you find stability in motion. It's about how to build and protect wealth while balancing your aviation lifestyle and the people who matter most.

## *Section 1: The Financial Impact of a Pilot's Schedule*

Let's call it what it is: flying for a living is thrilling, but it also comes with real challenges. Time away from home means you miss key moments. You may not be the one signing the field trip permission slip, or attending every financial planning meeting. But that doesn't mean you can't lead the charge in building generational wealth.

Start by accepting two truths:

1. Your schedule is complex.
2. That complexity doesn't have to lead to chaos.

With systems, delegation, and regular check-ins, you can lead your family's financial journey even when you're on the other side of the country (or world).

## *Section 2: Building a Family Wealth Plan That Works in the Clouds*

You don't need a five-hour sit-down with a whiteboard and trust attorney every week. You need a living, breathing wealth plan that:

- Fits your lifestyle.
- Includes your family.
- Works when you're flying.
- Adjusts as your career evolves.

Here are the essential components:

1. Household Budget and Operating System

Your family should function like a well-run airline:

- Everyone knows the budget.
- Major expenses are reviewed in advance.
- You automate what you can.
- You set aside emergency fuel (your emergency fund).

Keep a shared document or app where your spouse or partner can track income, recurring expenses, savings progress, and upcoming big-ticket items. Even better? Automate as much as possible.

2. Short-Term and Long-Term Goals

- **Short-Term**: Pay off debt, save for a house, or plan that trip to Italy.
- **Mid-Term**: Fund kids' 529 plans, build investment accounts.
- **Long-Term**: Pay off the mortgage, retire with confidence, leave a legacy.

Set a quarterly "family check-in" and use your Sunday before a trip to review goals and progress.

3. Roles and Responsibilities

Just like in the cockpit, your household needs a captain and co-pilot. Define who handles:

- Bills
- Insurance renewals
- Investment decisions
- Estate plan updates

If you're the financial leader in your home, share your plan and empower your partner to manage if needed.

## *Section 3: Parenting While Flying*

One of the most difficult aspects of being a pilot parent is not being there for every birthday, school play, or important conversation about allowance. But you can still lead.

Teach Your Kids About Money

- Set up automatic transfers to their savings accounts.
- Schedule a "money talk" after your next trip.
- Show them your pay stub and explain taxes.
- Open a custodial brokerage account together.

Create Legacy Habits

- Leave hand-written notes when you're gone that include a "money tip of the week."
- Record short videos talking about the difference between needs vs. wants.
- Let them sit with you when you pay bills or rebalance your portfolio.

It's not about being perfect. It's about being present in a way that leaves a mark.

## *Section 4: Communication Is Your Co-Pilot*

Just like CRM (crew resource management), your family needs open communication, especially around money. The financial cockpit of your household can get turbulent without it.

Here's What Helps:

- A shared calendar for paydays, expenses, and family goals.
- Group text check-ins while on overnights.
- Sunday night Zoom calls when you're away longer than a few days.
- Email summaries of your budget or plans.

Talk early. Talk often. And talk without blame.

## *Section 5: Coordinating With Professionals While Flying*

You might not be able to walk into your CPA's office on a weekday. But you can:

- Schedule quarterly virtual meetings.
- Use a secure online vault for document sharing.
- Set reminders to review key deadlines (IRA contributions, tax filings, insurance renewals).

Put your financial team on your "crew list."

- Your wealth advisor = co-captain.
- Your CPA = your ATC.
- Your attorney = your weather radar.

They help you navigate so you can fly.

## *Section 6: Protecting What You're Building*

As your income grows, so do the stakes. Make sure your family wealth plan includes:

- Life insurance (term for most families).
- Long-term disability insurance (specific to pilots).
- Umbrella liability coverage.
- An updated will, healthcare directive, and power of attorney.

All of these should be reviewed annually with your spouse and attorney.

## *Section 7: What Pilots Get Wrong (and How to Fix It)*

- **They wait too long to involve their spouse.**
- **They try to do it all on layovers.**
- **They assume their income is their wealth.**
- **They avoid planning because it feels overwhelming.**

You don't have to be a financial expert. You just need a system.

## *Section 8: Sample Pre-Flight Wealth Checklist*

Before your next trip, make this part of your personal preflight:

- Contributions to 401(k) are automated
- Emergency fund is intact
- Family calendar is synced
- Bills are on autopay
- Upcoming big expenses are forecasted
- Spouse has access to key accounts

- You left a note for the kids
- You set a date for the next "money talk"

That's your wealth version of flaps, fuel, and flight plan.

### *A Clear Call to Act:*

Make one financial move before you go wheels-up tomorrow. Just one.

- Set up a shared money calendar.
- Start a 529 plan.
- Review your life insurance coverage.

And do another next week. The only thing worse than flying blind is staying grounded when you've got the power to soar.

### *Final Note:*

This isn't just about paychecks and pensions.

This is about dignity.

This is about freedom.

This is about having the financial lift to say "no" to burnout and "yes" to legacy, wealth, and balance.

You didn't earn your wings to feel weighed down by money.

*Financial Literacy For Pilots* is your permission slip to chart a flight plan for financial independence, clarity, and calm—at every altitude of your career.

Your future self will thank you.

So will your crew.

So will your sanity.

# Chapter 38: Giving Back – Supporting Aviation Nonprofits and Scholarships

When you spend your days cruising at 35,000 feet, you gain a perspective most people never experience. But even with the best views, every pilot knows: it takes a lot of people on the ground to get a plane in the air. In the same way, your financial success wasn't built alone. You had mentors, instructors, mechanics, family, fellow pilots—people who encouraged you, taught you, and supported you when your bank account said one thing and your ambition said another. Now that you're on more solid financial ground, maybe even thriving, it's time to ask:

How can I give back in a way that matters?

This chapter is about turning your altitude into impact.

It's about structured, strategic generosity that builds legacy.

It's about how pilots—yes, even with full schedules and unpredictable rosters—can support the next generation, fund scholarships, and fuel nonprofit missions in aviation.

And it's about how to do it smartly, so giving enhances your financial plan instead of draining it.

**Why Giving Back Matters More Than Ever**

You already know aviation is facing a talent crisis. We don't have enough pilots, instructors, or mechanics to meet future demand. But behind that headline are thousands of smart, driven students who could fill that gap—if they had the financial support to start flight school, finish training, or pass a final checkride.

That's where you come in. Supporting aviation nonprofits and scholarships isn't just an emotional decision; it's a strategic one. It protects the profession you love. It invests in the next generation of crew. And for many pilots, it helps heal the parts of the journey that were hard, lonely, or unsupported.

**Types of Aviation Nonprofits to Support**

Not all giving needs to go through a giant national organization. Some of the best impact happens locally, in tight-knit groups. Here are a few types of nonprofits to consider:

1. **Flight Scholarship Funds** – Local EAA chapters, women in aviation groups, or regional pilot associations often have scholarship funds.
2. **STEM & Youth Outreach** – Groups like OBAP (Organization of Black Aerospace Professionals), Girls in Aviation Day, or Young Eagles introduce kids to flight early.
3. **Military to Civilian Transition Programs** – These help veterans use their skills to build a second career in aviation.
4. **Mental Health for Pilots** – Some orgs help pilots quietly access therapy, peer support, or substance abuse treatment.
5. **Disaster Response Aviation** – Angel Flight and similar orgs use general aviation to transport medical patients or supplies.

Every nonprofit has a mission, and you have the power to help fund it.

**Strategic Ways to Give (That Also Make Financial Sense)**

Let's be honest. You don't have to be a billionaire to be a philanthropist. But you do want to give in ways that are tax-smart and aligned with your broader financial plan. Here are a few strategies:

- **Donor-Advised Funds (DAFs)** – You donate to a special account now, get a tax deduction this year, and give to charities over time. It's like a giving savings account.
- **Appreciated Stock Donations** – If you have airline stock that's grown

in value, donating it directly avoids capital gains taxes and gives the full value to charity.

- **Estate Planning** – You can leave a portion of your estate or retirement account to a nonprofit. It takes just a few clicks on a beneficiary form.
- **Scholarship Creation** – You can set up a named scholarship at your alma mater, flight school, or local aviation group. It doesn't always take as much money as you think.
- **Charitable Rollover from IRA (if over 70.5)** – You can transfer funds directly to a charity from your IRA to satisfy your RMD, tax-free.

**What If You're Not Ready to Give Big?**

That's fine. You don't have to donate five figures to make a difference. You can:

- Cover the cost of a headset for a student pilot
- Buy gas for a flight school discovery flight
- Offer to mentor a student weekly via Zoom
- Sponsor a Young Eagles flight day and pay for lunch
- Run a hangar talk at your FBO about real-world pilot life

Generosity isn't about amounts. It's about intention.

**Your Giving Checklist**

Before you write a check or create a fund, take these steps:

1. **Clarify your values.** What matters most? Youth? Diversity? Technical training?
2. **Set a giving goal.** What % of your income or net worth feels right?
3. **Talk to your advisor.** Make sure the giving strategy fits your tax and estate plans.
4. **Vet the nonprofits.** Use sites like Charity Navigator or GuideStar to check legitimacy.
5. **Document your impact.** Track what you gave, where, and what the result was. Celebrate it.

**Real Stories, Real Legacy**

There's a pilot in his 50s who quietly funds a $1,000 flight scholarship every year for a single mom in flight training. He was raised by a single mom who worked two jobs to support his dream.

There's a couple—both captains at major airlines—who decided not to have kids, but instead started a donor-advised fund that gives $25K per year to aviation schools around the country.

There's a retired freight pilot who mentors six students at his local airport, takes them to Oshkosh every year, and buys used uniforms for anyone who needs them.

You don't need a name on a building to change someone's life.

**Final Approach**

Supporting aviation nonprofits and scholarships isn't just about being generous. It's about being intentional.

You trained for years to get where you are.

Now imagine someone else just like you—young, hungry, broke, hopeful.

Be the tailwind that helps them lift off.

And do it in a way that reflects your values, protects your finances, and builds a legacy higher than any altitude you've ever flown.

**Call to Act:**

Choose one nonprofit or cause in aviation that speaks to your story. Give, volunteer, or mentor. Before your next trip, set up a recurring donation—even if it's just $25/month.

That small act may just be the first push that helps someone else reach V1.

Your generosity? It flies farther than you think.

**Let's help the next generation take off. Together.**

# Chapter 39: Avoiding Big Mistakes – Scams, Risky Investments, and Hype

Flying an aircraft requires precision, discipline, and adherence to checklists. Yet when it comes to managing money, even some of the most experienced pilots can find themselves veering off course. You train endlessly for flight emergencies—but are you prepared for financial turbulence?

This chapter is your no-nonsense briefing on how to avoid common (and costly) financial mistakes. It's not about perfection—it's about prevention. We'll look at real-world traps that pilots fall into, from shady investment deals to lifestyle inflation, and more importantly, how to sidestep them with confidence and clarity.

## The Appeal of the Shortcut

Every pilot knows the temptation of shaving time off a route. But shortcuts in aviation are dangerous—and the same is true in finance.

The promises are always seductive:

- "Double your money in six months."
- "Guaranteed returns with no risk."
- "This opportunity is only available to a few select insiders."

These phrases should trigger the same mental red flags as a cockpit warning light. If it sounds too good to be true, it almost always is.

## The Most Common Financial Mistakes Pilots Make

### *1. Falling for Investment Scams*

Scams prey on trust. And in the aviation community, trust runs deep. Whether it's a fellow pilot selling a "can't-miss" real estate fund or a friend-of-a-friend pitching a crypto startup, pilots are frequently targeted because of their high income and the camaraderie of the industry.

**What to Watch For:**

- Vague investment materials with no audited financials
- Pressure to invest quickly before "it's too late"
- High returns with zero risk
- Unregistered investment advisors or brokers

**How to Protect Yourself:**

- Ask for audited financials and legal documentation
- Check the advisor's FINRA or SEC registration
- Get a second opinion from a fiduciary advisor
- Trust your instincts—if something feels off, pause

### *2. Chasing Hype Over Strategy*

Every few years, a new investment trend makes headlines—crypto, meme stocks, NFTs, AI startups. While some of these may have merit, many pilots jump in without a clear understanding of the risks or how the asset fits into their long-term plan.

The result? Buying high. Selling low. Getting burned.

**Smart Strategy:**

- Stick to a diversified portfolio with clear goals
- Invest based on time horizon and risk tolerance
- Don't confuse speculation with investing
- Use "play money" (a small portion of your portfolio) for any high-risk experiments

### *3. Overleveraging in Real Estate*

Real estate can be a smart wealth-building tool—but it's not foolproof. Many pilots get excited about buying multiple properties, often in cities they barely know, and take on more mortgage debt than they can handle.

**Common Issues:**

- Vacancies and cash flow problems
- Unexpected repairs or tenant issues
- Illiquidity when you need to access cash

**Pro Tip:** Always stress test your real estate portfolio. Ask: Can you carry the mortgage and expenses for 6–12 months with no tenant?

### *4. Ignoring Insurance Until It's Too Late*

Loss of license. Long-term disability. Liability claims. These aren't just hypothetical risks—they're real financial threats.

Yet many pilots either:

- Don't have coverage
- Have the wrong coverage
- Overpay for the right coverage

**Fix It:**

- Review your policies with a qualified insurance planner

- Know the exclusions and definitions in your disability coverage
- Understand how a loss-of-license policy fits into your overall plan

### *5. Mixing Business With Friendship*

Pilots love to support each other—and that's a beautiful thing. But lending money, co-investing, or going into business with friends or fellow crew members can create messy entanglements.

**Set Boundaries:**

- Put everything in writing
- Treat financial partnerships like business partnerships
- Know when to say no (even to a friend)

## Red Flags: The Financial Version of a Cockpit Warning

Here's your quick checklist of red flags that scream "Danger Ahead!"

- Pressure to act immediately
- Guarantees of high returns with no risk
- Unclear or overly complex investment strategies
- Unlicensed or unregistered financial professionals
- Emotional appeals—fear of missing out (FOMO), guilt, loyalty

If you hear any of these, it's time to pull back the throttle and ask hard questions.

## The Emotional Side of Financial Mistakes

Let's be honest—money isn't just numbers. It's deeply emotional.

When you:

- Grow up with financial insecurity

- Feel behind your peers
- Are trying to prove yourself to your family or colleagues
- Tie self-worth to net worth

You're more likely to take risks you shouldn't.

Awareness is your tool here. Before making any major financial move, ask yourself:

- Am I doing this to impress someone?
- Am I trying to "catch up" or "level up"?
- Do I feel shame, fear, or ego around this decision?

Use logic to override emotion. Or better yet—have a personal financial checklist just like a preflight checklist.

## A Preflight for Your Finances: Questions to Ask

- Do I fully understand this investment/product?
- How does it fit into my overall financial plan?
- What are the risks, costs, and exit strategies?
- Is this advisor or salesperson licensed, and acting as a fiduciary?
- Would I be okay if I lost this money tomorrow?

If you can't answer these clearly—it's time to sit down with a trusted professional.

## Stories From the Jumpseat

**Mike, 38, First Officer:** Invested $100K in a "can't miss" energy fund pitched by another pilot. The company folded in 18 months. He never saw a dollar back.

**Sarah, 42, Captain:** Bought three rental homes in cities she barely knew. Tenants trashed one, another sat vacant, and the third had flooding damage.

She sold them all at a loss.

**Jorge, 45, Cargo Pilot:** Followed a Reddit thread into meme stocks. Made $40K in one month. Lost $60K the next.

These aren't rare stories. They're common. And preventable.

## The Power of Saying No

The best financial decision you'll make this year might be the one you don't make.

Say no to:

- Unfamiliar investments
- High-pressure sales tactics
- Friends who want you to co-sign or co-invest
- Emotional spending after a big raise or contract change

No is not negative. No is protective. No gives you room to say yes to smarter, safer moves down the line.

## Course Correction: What to Do if You've Made a Mistake

You're not alone. Every pilot has made a poor financial decision at some point. The key is recovery:

1. **Stop the Bleeding** – Don't double down on a bad bet.
2. **Assess the Damage** – Get honest about the loss or exposure.
3. **Seek Advice** – Talk to a CFP, CPA, or fiduciary advisor.
4. **Make a Plan** – Put steps in place to recover and move forward.
5. **Forgive Yourself** – Shame doesn't build wealth. Clarity and consistency do.

## The Long Game: Protecting Legacy and Confidence

Every dollar you protect today is one less dollar you'll need to earn again tomorrow.

Financial success isn't about finding the perfect investment. It's about:

- Avoiding major setbacks
- Protecting your downside
- Staying consistent through every season

A pilot who flies steady—avoiding turbulence and minimizing risk—ends the journey in better shape than one chasing shortcuts.

## Final Approach Checklist

- Trust but verify.
- Know what you're investing in.
- Avoid emotional decisions.
- Don't confuse income with wealth.
- Keep your long-term vision clearer than the short-term noise.

### *Call to Act:*

Make one financial move before you go wheels-up tomorrow. Just one. Review an investment. Cancel a pitch meeting. Ask a second opinion. Do another next week. The only thing worse than flying blind is staying grounded when you've got the power to soar.

### *Final Note:*

This isn't just about avoiding scams. It's about protecting your dignity. Your legacy. Your peace of mind. You earned your wings to soar, not to spiral.

Fly smart. Stay sharp. And never let hype hijack your financial flight plan.

# Chapter 40: Preparing for the FAA Age 65 Rule – Early Exit Strategy

You've spent your life defying gravity. You've fought through weather, fatigue, system failures, and schedule chaos—and still made it look easy. But there's one thing no pilot can override: the FAA Age 65 rule. When that clock hits, it's not a go-around. It's mandatory retirement.

The question is: will you glide into it like a perfect crosswind landing, or will you hit it like a tailstrike you didn't see coming?

This chapter is your financial flight plan for preparing for mandatory retirement with confidence. Whether you're 35 or 60, the earlier you prepare, the smoother your descent will be.

Let's talk legacy, liquidity, lifestyle, and life after the cockpit.

## Why the FAA Age 65 Rule Matters Financially

Unlike many careers where people can coast into semi-retirement or consult part-time indefinitely, commercial pilots have a federally mandated cutoff. No matter how healthy you feel or how sharp your skills are, you will be grounded.

For many pilots, flying is not just a job—it's their identity. When that identity is clipped, it creates not just emotional turbulence but financial risk.

*The Financial Risks:*

- Sudden loss of high income
- Pressure to draw down retirement savings too early
- Overreliance on pension projections that may be outdated or miscalculated
- Uncertainty about what's next—and how to fund it

If you haven't planned for this day, the moment your wings are clipped could feel like a free fall.

But with the right planning? You'll be on approach to the next chapter of your life, with financial systems fully coordinated.

## When to Start Planning: The Sooner, the Better

If you're under 40 and reading this chapter, congratulations. You're ahead of 90% of your peers.

If you're in your 50s and haven't really started, that's okay. You're not behind. But now is the time to act. Every year counts. Every dollar counts. And every decision you make compounds over time—for better or worse.

Start with one question: "What does life look like the day after I hang up my wings?"

Then build the plan backward.

## Step One: Know Your Numbers

Before you can glide into retirement, you need to know what you're flying with.

### *What to Track:*

- **Net Worth**: Total assets minus liabilities. Get brutally honest.
- **Fixed and Variable Expenses**: What will it cost to live your life once you retire?
- **Expected Retirement Income**:
- Social Security
- Pensions (traditional and cash balance)
- 401(k), IRAs, Roth accounts
- Annuities or airline deferred comp plans
- Spouse's income (if applicable)
- **Time Horizon**: How many years until age 65? And how long do you plan to live?

Create a "retirement readiness score" every year. Treat it like your annual recurrent training.

## Step Two: Maximize Retirement Contributions

Pilots often have access to excellent retirement plans—but many don't use them to the fullest.

- Max out 401(k) contributions
- Take advantage of company match and profit-sharing
- If eligible, contribute to a Roth IRA or use a Backdoor Roth strategy
- Use an HSA as a stealth retirement account for medical expenses
- Consider taxable brokerage accounts to build non-qualified savings

Remember, post-retirement income flexibility often depends on having more than one type of account.

**Action Step:** Automate contributions and escalate them by 1-2% every bid cycle until you're maxing out everything.

## Step Three: Protect Your Income on the Way to 65

The biggest risk to your glidepath is losing the ability to work before you hit 65. That's why Loss of License insurance and Long-Term Disability are non-negotiables.

- Review policies annually
- Understand elimination periods, benefit amounts, and exclusions
- Layer private coverage on top of what the airline offers if necessary

Think of it this way: You insure the jet. You should insure your income, too.

## Step Four: Create an Exit Strategy – Not Just a Retirement Plan

Too many pilots treat retirement like an ejection seat. You hit 65 and you're out. But a strategic exit is different.

### *Strategic Exit Includes:*

- A clear retirement date range (not just a single target)
- A phased wind-down if possible
- Understanding how pension elections work (joint vs. single life)
- A rollover plan for retirement accounts
- Evaluating whether to start a side hustle, business, or consulting gig
- Planning health care coverage until Medicare eligibility

Don't just plan for the last flight. Plan for the first year after.

## Step Five: Lifestyle Design After Retirement

Retirement isn't just the absence of work—it's the presence of purpose. What will you do with your time? Who will you spend it with? Where will you live?

- Do you want to travel more or less?
- Will you stay in your current home or downsize?
- Will you volunteer, mentor, or teach aviation safety?

Designing this lifestyle isn't just about fun—it has financial implications. Your spending, taxes, and investment drawdown strategies all depend on what this next chapter looks like.

**Pro Tip:** Create a mock month-in-retirement budget and test-run it for 90 days before you retire.

## Step Six: Build Liquidity Before the Transition

Retirement is a major financial shift, and having liquidity—easily accessible cash—is key.

- Build a cash cushion of 12-24 months of living expenses
- Don't rely on your first pension check arriving like clockwork
- Time market withdrawals carefully to avoid sequence-of-returns risk

Liquidity isn't just peace of mind—it's your buffer from having to make bad financial decisions when you're vulnerable.

## Step Seven: Run Retirement Simulations

Think like a flight instructor. Simulate failures before they happen.

- What happens if the market crashes the year you retire?

- What if your pension is smaller than expected?
- What if inflation spikes?
- What if you or your spouse faces a health crisis?

Run worst-case, average-case, and best-case scenarios. Then build contingency plans.

## Step Eight: Communicate With Your Family

Money silence kills plans. Don't assume your spouse or kids know what your retirement looks like.

- Have regular financial debriefs with your spouse
- Document passwords, accounts, and emergency instructions
- Share your estate plan and legacy goals

You spent your career in a cockpit crew. Carry that same sense of coordination and transparency into your household.

## Step Nine: Review Your Financial Team

Make sure you have the right people in your corner:

- A fiduciary financial advisor who understands pilot pay structures
- A CPA who gets aviation deductions and benefits
- An estate planning attorney to prepare wills, trusts, and directives

This is your cockpit crew for the next phase of life. Choose wisely.

## Step Ten: Give Yourself Permission to Let Go

It's hard to stop flying. No one says that enough. You've lived on adrenaline, checklists, and schedules for decades. And now you're being told to slow down?

That transition is emotional.

But here's the truth: Letting go of flying doesn't mean letting go of purpose. You're not retiring from identity. You're graduating into legacy.

Build a new routine. Mentor young pilots. Travel for fun, not duty. Write your story.

You may be grounded—but your impact doesn't have to be.

## *Final Call to Act:*

Start your FAA Age 65 financial plan today—no matter your age. Download your numbers. Meet with an advisor. Build your timeline. Set your systems on autopilot.

Because when the day comes to hang up your wings, you deserve to do it with peace, power, and pride.

Your retirement shouldn't feel like an emergency landing. It should feel like your best, smoothest landing yet.

Prepare now—and enjoy every mile of the glide path.

# Part V: Final Approach – Transitioning Into Retirement

Retirement isn't the end of the flight—it's the final approach to a new destination. In Part V, we shift from accumulation to deceleration, guiding pilots through the runway lights of retirement planning with precision and clarity. This section is dedicated to helping you prepare mentally, emotionally, and financially for the day your wings are officially clipped by the FAA Age 65 rule.

We explore what retirement means beyond the paycheck—how to structure your days, preserve your identity, and maintain purpose without the cockpit. You'll learn how to turn your savings into a sustainable income stream, when to draw Social Security, how to protect your assets through estate planning, and how to make smart choices about pensions, deferred compensation, and healthcare.

From building a rock-solid glidepath to your last day of flying, to coordinating the financial landing gear that supports your legacy, this section equips you with tools, mindset shifts, and practical frameworks. Whether you plan to retire at 65, take a phased exit, or transition into a second act, *Final Approach* ensures you're not flying blind.

This is where financial literacy meets life design—because what comes after your last flight should feel just as intentional, stable, and rewarding as the career that brought you here.

# Chapter 41: Retirement Timing – Age 65 vs. Personal Goals

You've been flying with the FAA-mandated retirement age of 65 on your horizon for years. It's the built-in final stop on every commercial pilot's flight plan. But what if that number isn't the one that actually defines when *you* should stop flying?

Retirement is not just about regulation. It's about readiness. Financially. Emotionally. Physically. Mentally.

This chapter isn't just a deep dive into the implications of the age 65 rule. It's a runway inspection for your personal goals. We'll explore what it looks like to retire *because you want to,* not just because you have to. We'll help you time the transition, fuel your plan, and touch down into retirement on *your* terms.

## The FAA Age 65 Rule: What It Means (and Doesn't Mean)

Let's start with facts: the FAA mandates that commercial airline pilots must retire from Part 121 operations at age 65.

This is a hard stop for many airline careers. But it's not a full stop for your earning potential, or even your ability to keep flying. What it does is limit your role in the cockpit under certain certifications. What it doesn't do is dictate your financial reality.

The question every pilot must ask is:

*Am I planning my exit based on a* rule, *or based on* readiness?

If you retire *at* 65, will you feel empowered? Or rushed? Will you glide? Or will you panic?

If you want the answer to be: "I felt in control," then you need a strategy that starts long before your final bid cycle.

## Part 1: The Myth of the Magic Number

The problem with rules like the FAA's Age 65 mandate is that they create false comfort. Many pilots subconsciously plan everything around this number. But here's the truth:

- **65 is a regulatory line, not a financial finish line.**
- **Some pilots are financially free at 55. Others are stressed at 67.**
- **Retirement planning is not one-size-fits-all.**

You need to break the myth that the number 65 is your default timeline. Your goals, your health, your spouse, your savings, your stress level—*those* are the real variables.

Let's identify your personal runway.

## Part 2: Building a Timeline Around You (Not Just the FAA)

What's your *ideal* retirement age?

Start here:

1. **If you didn't *have* to work, when would you stop?**
2. **What kind of lifestyle would you want post-cockpit?**
3. **How would you structure your days if you weren't flying anymore?**
4. **Do you want to pursue consulting, instructing, or entrepreneurship afterward?**

5. **Is there another purpose you want to shift toward—family, hobbies, volunteerism, adventure?**

Many pilots who plan for 65 find themselves itching to pivot at 60. Others love flying and want to work until the very last day. There is no right answer. The only wrong answer is *not having one.*

### *Pilot Profile: "The Early Launcher"*

Brian, age 58, realized he had enough in retirement accounts, brokerage savings, and a small side consulting business to comfortably leave flying at 60. His goal? Spend more time at home with his aging parents and take flying lessons with his teenage daughter. He used 65 as a *ceiling,* not a target.

## Part 3: Your Retirement Number, Not Just Your Retirement Age

Timing retirement around your personal goals starts with one question:

> *How much do I need to walk away confidently?*

You don't just need a date. You need a dollar amount. That means calculating:

- **Annual retirement spending goal** (including healthcare, travel, housing, and lifestyle)
- **Social Security projections** (based on your chosen age of claiming)
- **Pension income** (including lump-sum vs. annuity decisions)
- **401(k), IRA, and Roth balances**
- **Taxable brokerage accounts or deferred comp**
- **Any side income or part-time work plans**

Then, simulate:

- Withdrawal rates (can you safely draw 3-4% per year?)
- Market risk and sequence-of-returns danger
- Tax strategies to minimize annual distributions

Once you see your retirement *number,* you can plan around that—not just the FAA deadline.

## Part 4: When Early Retirement Does Make Sense

For some pilots, walking away before 65 is the *better* option. Why?

- **High savings rate has already created freedom**
- **Desire to avoid burnout or declining health**
- **Pursuing a second career or dream**
- **Time-sensitive family or personal goals**
- **Changes in airline policy or contract dissatisfaction**

Retiring early isn't failure. It's a victory if it's intentional.

But it needs to be *funded.*

That means making sure:

- You have sufficient liquid assets (not just illiquid pensions)
- Your healthcare coverage is squared away until Medicare
- You're mentally ready to shift your identity from pilot to civilian
- You've explored bridge strategies like part-time instructing or consulting

## Part 5: When Delaying Retirement Could Be Strategic

If your body, brain, and burnout level are still in a good place, delaying retirement can:

- Maximize pension accrual
- Allow higher Social Security benefits (up to age 70)
- Increase retirement savings
- Shorten the retirement drawdown period

Some pilots enjoy working until 65 because they love the structure, camaraderie, and purpose of flying.

But staying longer needs to be *part of the plan,* not a default out of fear.

Be honest: Are you flying because you love it? Or because you're afraid to let go?

## Part 6: Creating a Multi-Leg Exit Plan

Retirement isn't a single day. It's a process. A series of intentional steps. Here's a suggested outline:

### *Phase 1: Accumulation Optimization (Ages 40-55)*

- Max contributions to all qualified accounts
- Eliminate bad debt
- Begin simulating retirement budgets
- Run pension projections every 2-3 years

### *Phase 2: Glidepath Preparation (Ages 55-62)*

- Pay off mortgage (or have a plan to downsize)
- Nail down your Social Security strategy
- Review your healthcare coverage (especially pre-Medicare)

- Consider part-time opportunities post-retirement

### *Phase 3: Transition Window (Ages 62-65)*

- Run full cash flow projections
- Test your retirement budget for 6-12 months
- Meet with a financial advisor and estate planning attorney
- Prepare your emotional game plan

### *Phase 4: Post-Flight Life Design (Age 65+)*

- Map out what your days, weeks, and seasons will look like
- Define your "mission" beyond the flight deck
- Shift your money strategy to income generation, not accumulation

## Part 7: The Emotional Reality of Leaving the Cockpit

For many pilots, walking away isn't just about the money. It's about the *meaning.*

You spent decades earning respect, commanding crews, mentoring younger pilots, and operating complex machinery with elegance.

Retirement can feel like losing altitude emotionally—even if you're financially fine.

That's why you need a personal runway plan too:

- Join local aviation or veteran groups
- Mentor young aviators
- Volunteer with aviation nonprofits
- Write, teach, or share your experience in creative ways
- Travel for *you,* not for the airline

## Final Call: Retirement Is Not the End of the Flight

It's the start of a new mission. A new vector. A chance to rediscover purpose on the ground. But to do it right, you have to decide:

- When is the *right* time for *you*?
- How will your finances support that timeline?
- What identity will you build next?

### *Call to Act:*

Make one financial move before you go wheels-up tomorrow. Just one. Run your retirement projections. Talk to an advisor. Outline your goals post-65. Then do another next week. The only thing worse than flying blind is staying grounded when you've got the power to soar.

### *Final Note:*

You didn't earn your wings to feel weighed down by money or fear of retirement. You earned them to fly free. So design a glidepath that leads not just to a landing—but to a new lift.

Your legacy is waiting.

So is your next great chapter.

# Chapter: Social Security – Payout Timing, Coordination, and Taxes

You've landed thousands of flights with confidence. Now it's time to prepare for one of the most important landings of all: how, when, and why to take Social Security. If you treat Social Security like an afterthought, you're flying blind into retirement. If you treat it like the powerful income tool it is, you can significantly boost your lifetime income, reduce taxes, and create more breathing room in your post-65 lifestyle.

This chapter walks through everything a pilot needs to know about Social Security—from payout timing strategies to coordination with pensions, to how taxes can sneak up on you in retirement if you don't plan ahead.

## Social Security Is Not Automatic Wealth—It's a Strategic Lever

Many pilots mistakenly believe Social Security is either a minor benefit they shouldn't count on, or that it's a simple switch to flip at age 62 or 67. In reality, Social Security is:

- An inflation-adjusted income stream for life
- One of the few sources of guaranteed income you can't outlive
- A powerful insurance policy against longevity risk
- A key variable in your tax equation and Medicare premiums

Your airline pension, 401(k), IRAs, and investments are only part of the equation. Social Security plays a huge role in how long your money lasts and how flexible your retirement becomes.

## Key Milestones: What Every Pilot Should Know

- **Age 62**: Earliest you can claim. Benefit is reduced by 25-30% compared to full retirement age.
- **Full Retirement Age (FRA)**: Usually 66-67 depending on your birth year. Claiming here gets you 100% of your earned benefit.
- **Age 70**: Maximum payout. For every year you delay after FRA, your benefit grows by 8%.

Delaying from 62 to 70 increases your benefit by 76% or more, depending on inflation and cost-of-living adjustments.

### *Example:*

If your benefit at 62 is $2,000/month, waiting until 70 could yield over $3,500/month. That's a $1,500/month difference—for the rest of your life.

## When Should a Pilot Claim Social Security?

This decision depends on:

- Health status and family longevity
- Spouse's income and benefit history
- Other sources of income (pensions, 401(k), IRAs)
- Desire to continue working in any capacity
- Tax planning and Medicare IRMAA tiers

A one-size-fits-all approach doesn't work. But here are common profiles:

### *1. The Early Exit Pilot (Claims at 62)*

- Wants to preserve retirement savings
- May have health concerns or a family history of short lifespans
- May retire before 65 and need income to bridge the gap

**Trade-Offs:** Lower monthly income for life, higher reliance on savings, possible tax inefficiencies

### *2. The FRA Glidepath Pilot (Claims at 66-67)*

- Retires on schedule, bridges income from 62 to FRA with savings
- Balances longevity risk and opportunity cost
- Reduces reliance on early distributions

**Trade-Offs:** Balanced approach, moderate benefit level, still room for strategic Roth conversions pre-70

### *3. The Delayed Claim Captain (Claims at 70)*

- Excellent health and family longevity
- Has other income sources or continues to work part-time
- Wants to maximize spousal benefits or survivor benefits

**Trade-Offs:** Requires strong savings discipline early in retirement, but provides highest guaranteed income later

## Spousal Coordination and Survivor Benefits

Married? Divorced? Widowed? Your benefit decision affects more than just you.

- Spouses can claim benefits based on their own earnings or up to 50%

of your benefit
- Survivor benefits can be as high as 100% of your benefit if you delay to age 70
- Divorced spouses (married 10+ years) may qualify on your record even if you remarry

**Action Step:** Don't make your decision in isolation. Coordinate with your spouse's timeline and benefits to maximize household income.

## How Social Security Is Taxed (And Why It Matters for Pilots)

Yes, your Social Security benefit can be taxed.

- If your provisional income is over $25,000 (single) or $32,000 (married), up to 50-85% of your benefit is taxable
- Provisional income includes:
- Adjusted gross income
- Tax-exempt interest
- 50% of your Social Security benefit

**Why this matters:**

- Drawing from a 401(k) or IRA in the same year you take Social Security can push more of your benefit into the taxable column
- RMDs (Required Minimum Distributions) after 73 can further spike your taxes

## Strategic Coordination = Tax Efficiency

A tax-smart pilot will look for ways to balance income sources. That could include:

- Delaying Social Security while drawing from taxable brokerage ac-

counts
- Doing Roth conversions before RMDs and Social Security begin
- Tapping HSAs or cash value life insurance as tax-free income bridges

This isn't just about saving a few bucks. The wrong Social Security timing can cost tens of thousands in unnecessary taxes over your retirement.

## Social Security and Medicare IRMAA

Medicare premiums are tied to your income. It's called IRMAA (Income Related Monthly Adjustment Amount).

- If your MAGI (Modified Adjusted Gross Income) exceeds certain thresholds, your Medicare Part B and D premiums go up
- Taking Social Security in a high-income year can cause you to exceed IRMAA thresholds unintentionally

Plan ahead. Keep IRMAA brackets in mind during your income planning years.

## Social Security Isn't Going Away—But It Might Change

Many pilots worry about the program's solvency. While the trust fund may need reform by the 2030s, that doesn't mean benefits will disappear. More likely:

- Higher full retirement age for younger workers
- Higher taxes on higher earners
- Lower benefits for top income tiers

If you're a current or soon-to-be retiree, plan with current rules but remain flexible. For younger pilots, Social Security is likely still a valuable part of your future—just don't build your whole plan around it.

## Your Social Security Preflight Checklist

- Estimate your benefit at SSA.gov/myaccount
- Review spousal or survivor eligibility
- Evaluate claiming ages: 62, FRA, 70
- Consider impact on taxes and Medicare
- Model scenarios with a fiduciary financial planner

## Real-Life Pilot Scenarios

### *Brian, 64, Cargo Captain*

Has $1.5M in 401(k)s, plans to retire at 65, wife is 3 years younger.

- Plan: Delay Social Security until 70
- Bridge income from Roth and taxable accounts
- Wife claims spousal benefit when he turns 70
- Goal: Maximize survivor benefit and lower tax drag

### *Denise, 58, Commercial First Officer*

Early health diagnosis changes her trajectory. She'll retire at 62.

- Claims early Social Security for income bridge
- Preserves pension and investment withdrawals
- Focuses on reducing lifestyle costs and eliminating debt

### *Tom and Maria, 60s, Both Pilots*

- Tom claims at 67 (FRA), Maria at 62
- Coordinate to reduce drawdowns from portfolio
- Maria's lower benefit is boosted by Tom's spousal strategy

## Final Call: Claiming Isn't a Switch, It's a System

Social Security isn't a static payout. It's a dynamic, tax-influencing, income-sequencing system that touches every part of your financial life.

You didn't become a pilot by winging it. You followed a system. You trained, practiced, and adjusted.

Do the same here.

### *Call to Act:*

Make one financial move before you go wheels-up tomorrow. Just one. Log into SSA.gov. Print your earnings history. Book a strategy call. Then do another next week.

### *Final Note:*

This isn't just about getting your check. This is about designing your retirement cockpit—with clarity, power, and peace of mind. You didn't work this hard to guess at glidepath. Chart it with precision. And land your retirement with confidence.

# Chapter 42: Medicare, Retiree Benefits, and Health Insurance Gaps

You've spent decades navigating the skies. But as you approach the final approach of your professional flying career, there's one type of turbulence you can't ignore: healthcare after retirement.

Unlike many professions, where people can gradually scale back and extend employer benefits into their seventies, commercial pilots face a hard stop. The FAA Age 65 rule says you're done. But your body, your financial goals, and—most critically—your healthcare needs aren't retiring at 65.

So, what happens when you hang up your wings and still need to navigate a system of Medicare enrollment deadlines, retiree coverage fine print, and costly health insurance gaps?

This chapter is your checklist for health coverage clarity. Whether you're 35 and want to plan smart, or 60 and approaching the gate, you'll walk away with the tools, timelines, and confidence to ensure your post-cockpit years are covered.

Let's get clear, calm, and coordinated.

## Why Healthcare Becomes the #1 Issue After Retirement

When you lose your ability to fly commercially at age 65, you lose more than a paycheck. You may also lose employer-sponsored healthcare coverage, pilot union retiree benefits, or access to group insurance. If you're not prepared, you could be stuck paying thousands per month out-of-pocket—or worse, be uninsured when you need care most.

Healthcare costs are one of the biggest threats to a pilot's retirement runway. According to Fidelity, the average retired couple will need over $300,000 for medical expenses in retirement. And that doesn't include long-term care.

Now add this complexity:

- Some pilots retire before 65 and need to bridge a healthcare gap
- Some retire right at 65 and don't understand how or when to enroll in Medicare
- Some have a spouse younger than 65 and need to coordinate coverage

Let's break it all down.

## The Timeline: Health Insurance by Age Bracket

### *Age 55–60: Planning Ahead*

- Estimate your annual healthcare costs if you retire early
- Learn if your employer or union offers any retiree health benefits
- Consider a Health Savings Account (HSA) strategy for tax-free medical funds later
- Understand COBRA rules (18–36 months of continuation coverage)

### *Age 61–64: The Gap Years*

- If retiring before 65, you'll need ACA coverage, COBRA, or a private plan
- Estimate monthly premiums and subsidies on the Healthcare.gov marketplace
- Consider short-term insurance only if healthy and understand the limitations

### *Age 65+: Medicare Begins*

- Enroll in Medicare Part A and B during your Initial Enrollment Period (IEP)
- Decide whether to add Medicare Supplement (Medigap) or choose Medicare Advantage
- Enroll in a Part D (prescription drug) plan if needed
- Evaluate retiree coverage coordination with Medicare (some plans become secondary)

## Medicare 101 for Pilots

Let's keep it simple:

- **Part A**: Hospital insurance. Usually premium-free.
- **Part B**: Medical insurance (doctors, outpatient). Monthly premium applies.
- **Part C**: Medicare Advantage. An all-in-one alternative to Original Medicare.
- **Part D**: Prescription drugs. Must be added separately if not included in Part C.

You must enroll in Medicare within 7 months of your 65th birthday month, or you may face lifelong late penalties.

Action Step: Set a calendar reminder for 6 months before you turn 65 to start your Medicare research and paperwork.

## Retiree Health Benefits: Will Your Airline or Union Offer Help?

Every airline is different. Some major carriers offer a limited retiree health plan or allow pilots to buy into a group Medicare Advantage plan. Others offer nothing.

If your airline offers retiree coverage:

- Understand if it's primary or secondary to Medicare
- Know the monthly premium and what's included
- Get a copy of the Summary Plan Description (SPD)

If there's no retiree plan:

- You'll need to build your own healthcare coverage strategy with Medicare, supplements, or private insurance

Pro Tip: Use your union representative or HR benefits coordinator as your first point of contact. Don't just rely on the company website.

## Common Health Insurance Gaps for Pilots

### *1. Retiring Before Medicare*

You'll need to bridge the gap with COBRA, ACA plans, or short-term coverage. Budget $500–$1,000/month or more.

### *2. Medicare Doesn't Cover Everything*

It doesn't cover dental, vision, hearing aids, or long-term care. You may need additional insurance or savings to handle these costs.

### *3. Spouse Isn't Medicare-Eligible*

If you're 65 and your spouse is younger, you'll need a second plan to cover them until they become Medicare-eligible.

### *4. Long-Term Care*

70% of people over 65 will need some form of long-term care. Medicare doesn't cover most of it.

Action Step: Consider a long-term care insurance policy or hybrid plan while you're in your 50s or early 60s.

## HSAs – A Secret Weapon for Retirement Healthcare

If you're eligible for an HSA through a high-deductible health plan, max it out every year. HSAs offer:

- Tax-deductible contributions
- Tax-free growth
- Tax-free withdrawals for qualified medical expenses

Unlike FSAs, the money rolls over and is yours forever. After age 65, you can even use it for non-medical expenses (but they'll be taxed like income).

Max out your HSA while flying, and you could build a six-figure nest egg to cover Medicare premiums, dental work, and more.

## Coordinating With Other Retirement Income

Healthcare and income are connected. The more taxable income you have in retirement, the more you might pay for Medicare.

Medicare premiums are based on Modified Adjusted Gross Income (MAGI). This can increase your Part B and D premiums if you're earning too much from pensions, withdrawals, or rental properties.

Strategies to lower your MAGI:

- Use Roth withdrawals (tax-free)
- Withdraw from brokerage accounts with low capital gains
- Convert traditional IRA to Roth in low-income years

Pro Tip: Coordinate healthcare and income planning with a tax-savvy financial planner.

## Real-Life Scenario: Captain Davis

Captain Davis retired at 62 from a major airline. He took COBRA for 18 months, then bought an ACA marketplace plan until age 65. He used his HSA for premiums, then enrolled in Medicare with a Medigap plan. His spouse, age 59, remained on an ACA plan with a premium subsidy based on household income. They worked with a financial advisor to manage income so they didn't trigger higher Medicare premiums.

## What to Do If You Miss a Deadline

- Late enrollment in Medicare Part B or Part D can lead to permanent penalties.
- Missed Medigap deadlines can result in medical underwriting or denial.

Don't panic. Call Social Security or Medicare. You may qualify for a Special Enrollment Period (SEP) if you had employer coverage past 65.

Action Step: Get everything in writing. Keep documents showing you had other coverage.

## Final Approach: Your Health Coverage Flight Plan

*Age 50–55:*

- Max out your HSA if eligible
- Research employer retiree health options
- Consider long-term care insurance quotes

*Age 55–60:*

- Review COBRA options and ACA costs
- Build cash reserves for early retirement health premiums

*Age 60–64:*

- Get serious about Medicare deadlines
- Budget for gap years if retiring before 65
- Evaluate your spouse's coverage

*Age 65:*

- Enroll in Medicare Parts A & B
- Compare Medigap vs. Medicare Advantage
- Add Part D or ensure drug coverage is included

*Post-Retirement:*

- Reassess coverage annually
- Monitor income for IRMAA (income-related Medicare adjustments)
- Track out-of-pocket expenses using your HSA or tax strategies

## Chapter Close

Health insurance isn't just paperwork. It's your lifeline. It's your freedom to enjoy retirement without fear of financial turbulence from a hospital bill.

Create your healthcare checklist. Know your deadlines. Build the right coverage stack. And make sure your glide path to Medicare isn't filled with surprises.

Because you didn't spend a lifetime flying safely just to crash-land your retirement.

Make one health coverage move this week. Just one. Review your current plan, check a Medicare deadline, or open that HSA.

Your future self will thank you.

So will your family.

So will your bank account.

# Chapter 43: Managing Real Estate in Retirement – Downsizing or Relocating

You've spent decades commuting through turbulence, charting cross-country routes, and juggling jumpseats, crash pads, and layovers. But when the final logbook entry nears and you approach retirement, one question takes center stage:

Where do you land?

Real estate in retirement isn't just about location—it's about lifestyle, liquidity, legacy, and long-term security. For pilots, managing housing in retirement is more than just a change of zip code. It's a shift in identity, rhythm, and responsibility.

This chapter will walk you through the key financial and emotional considerations around keeping, selling, downsizing, or relocating in retirement. Whether you're dreaming of a quiet beach bungalow, a vibrant retirement community, or just a smaller mortgage payment, this is your preflight checklist for making the move.

## Why Real Estate Matters in Retirement

Your home is likely your largest asset—or your largest expense. In retirement, managing housing costs is critical to:

- Protect your cash flow
- Free up equity

- Minimize property tax and insurance burdens
- Reduce physical maintenance and mental bandwidth

But it's also tied to your sense of home, purpose, and stability. It's emotional, and that matters.

For many pilots, the home you bought early in your career may no longer fit your retirement flight plan. That five-bedroom near your hub? It's now too big, too empty, and too costly.

For others, the opposite may be true. Maybe you rented during your flying years to stay flexible—but now you crave a place that's truly yours.

Wherever you stand, the question is the same:

**Is your current real estate setup helping or hurting your retirement readiness?**

Let's walk through your options.

## Option 1: Downsizing – Less House, More Freedom

### *What It Means*

Selling your current home and purchasing a smaller, more manageable property with lower costs (or none, if purchased in cash).

### *Pros*

- Reduces mortgage (or eliminates it entirely)
- Lower maintenance costs, utilities, and insurance
- Potential to cash out home equity for retirement income
- Easier physical upkeep
- Can relocate closer to family or medical care

### *Cons*

- Emotional attachment to your current home
- Cost of selling (realtor fees, moving costs, taxes)
- Smaller space may feel like a downgrade
- Disruption to social or community ties

### *Action Step:*

Run a "Sell vs. Stay" scenario:

- What would you net from selling?
- What does a new home realistically cost?
- What is your break-even point?

Use a real estate agent who understands retiree priorities—not just location and square footage, but tax structure, community, and long-term livability.

## Option 2: Relocating to a Lower-Cost Area

### *What It Means*

Moving to a different city, state, or even country where housing and living costs are lower, and possibly with better tax treatment.

### *Pros*

- Stretch your retirement dollars
- Better weather, slower pace of life, or personal preferences
- May allow you to buy outright with cash
- Opens the door to communities designed for retirees

*Cons*

- Distance from family and friends
- Starting over in a new community
- Healthcare access and insurance coverage concerns
- State tax implications

*Hidden Costs to Evaluate:*

- State income taxes (or lack thereof)
- Property tax rates
- Homeowner association fees
- Insurance premiums (especially in coastal or disaster-prone zones)

*Action Step:*

Narrow down 2-3 possible retirement locations. Spend a week in each. Visit grocery stores, clinics, fitness centers, and local government offices. Don't just vacation—simulate everyday life.

## Option 3: Renting in Retirement

*What It Means*

Selling your home and renting for flexibility, reduced responsibility, or lifestyle preferences.

*Pros*

- No property taxes, maintenance, or repair surprises
- Liquidity from home sale
- Easier to move if your needs change
- Can test out new areas before committing

### *Cons*

- No equity growth
- Subject to rent increases and lease terms
- Lack of permanence or emotional ownership

### *Good Fit For:*

- Pilots retiring solo with minimal need for space
- Couples unsure where they want to settle permanently
- Those who prioritize flexibility over ownership

## Option 4: Keeping the Home and Aging In Place

### *What It Means*

Remaining in your current home and retrofitting it for safety, convenience, and long-term needs.

### *Pros*

- Familiarity and emotional comfort
- Avoids moving costs
- Retain community ties
- No need to sell in a volatile market

### *Cons*

- May require expensive modifications (e.g., ramps, showers, stair lifts)
- Higher utility and maintenance costs
- Property tax and insurance may rise

*Action Step:*

Hire a certified aging-in-place specialist (CAPS) to evaluate your home and develop a retrofit plan.

## The Financial Framework: Questions to Guide Your Decision

1. **What is my mortgage status?**

- Paid off, current, or underwater?

1. **What is my current housing expense (all-in)?**

- Include taxes, insurance, repairs, HOA, and utilities

1. **How does my housing tie into my overall retirement income plan?**

- Does it support or strain my monthly cash flow?

1. **Do I want to leave real estate to my heirs?**

- If so, how does that impact my choices today?

1. **What happens if I or my spouse gets sick or needs care?**

- Can we stay in this home?

1. **What would downsizing or relocating free up?**

- More travel? More giving? More breathing room?

## Real-Life Scenarios: Captain or Copilot?

**Tom, 63, Retired Airline Captain:** Chose to sell his California home and buy a smaller one in Arizona with cash. Freed up $400K in equity and slashed his annual property taxes by 70%.

**Linda and Mike, Both Pilots in Their 60s:** Downsized to a condo near their grandkids. Used the proceeds from their previous home to fund a travel budget and long-term care policy.

**Jordan, 60, Widowed Regional Pilot:** Rented an apartment in a university town after retiring. Enjoys community activities and zero home maintenance.

Each story is different. But each pilot chose their real estate path based on values, goals, and the numbers.

## Psychological Considerations

Downsizing and relocating are emotional. You're not just moving house—you're transitioning identity.

Tips:

- Honor your past, but don't let nostalgia write your financial plan.
- Focus on what you gain, not just what you leave.
- Involve your spouse or family early and often.
- Don't rush. Try before you buy.

## Tax, Legacy, and Liquidity Planning

Housing isn't just shelter. It's also a financial tool.

- **Step-Up in Basis:** Keeping a house until death can eliminate capital gains for heirs.
- **Reverse Mortgages:** May provide income but come with complexity—consult a fiduciary advisor.

- **Gifting or Trusts:** Consider how to pass a property efficiently.
- **Second Homes:** May be turned into rental income or sold to fund long-term care.

## Final Descent Checklist

- Is your home still serving your retirement needs?
- Do you have a plan for taxes, upkeep, and emergencies?
- Can you access the equity if needed?
- Have you considered how housing decisions impact your spouse or heirs?
- Is your real estate aligned with your retirement lifestyle?

### *Call to Act:*

Make one financial move before you go wheels-up tomorrow. Just one. Call a realtor. Run a sell-vs-stay calculation. Have a heart-to-heart with your partner. And do another next week.

The only thing worse than flying blind is staying grounded when you've got the power to soar.

### *Final Note:*

Your real estate strategy in retirement isn't about downsizing dreams—it's about expanding freedom. It's not about square footage—it's about clarity. And it's not about what you're leaving—it's about what you're building next.

Fly smart. Land soft. And remember: your best chapter may still be waiting for you—just a zip code away.

# Chapter 44: Turning Your 401(k), IRAs, and Investments into Income

You've spent decades building a cockpit-ready financial strategy. You've stacked 401(k) contributions, fed your Roth IRA, invested in brokerage accounts, and grown a portfolio with care and discipline. But eventually, every flight plan transitions to final approach. The climb is over. The cruise is done. Now it's time to turn your nest egg into income.

This chapter is about shifting your mindset—and mechanics—from accumulation to distribution. It's about setting up income systems that are reliable, tax-aware, and stress-tested for a long, healthy retirement.

Whether you're a year from mandatory retirement or 20 years out, understanding this transition is mission-critical. Because unlike flying a jet, there's no simulator for running out of money in retirement.

Let's break it all down—clean, calm, and conversational.

## Why Income Planning Is Different from Wealth Building

During your working years, you focused on saving, investing, and growing your assets. You aimed for growth and let compounding do the heavy lifting. Volatility was annoying, but survivable. Down markets were buying opportunities.

But once you retire, everything changes.

- You can't just "ride it out" indefinitely.
- You'll need consistent income.
- Withdrawals become your new "paycheck."
- Sequence of returns risk becomes real.

**Sequence of Returns Risk** means if you retire into a down market and start withdrawing money right away, your portfolio could shrink much faster—even if long-term averages still look good on paper.

That's why retirement income planning is like flight planning with fuel burn, wind direction, and an alternate airport in mind. You need clarity. Cushion. Coordination.

## Know Your Income Needs

Start with your monthly spending. Not the idealized version. The real version.

Break it down:

- Core Expenses: Housing, food, healthcare, transportation
- Lifestyle Expenses: Travel, dining, hobbies, gifts
- Legacy Goals: Giving to family, charities, or causes

Estimate how these will change over time:

- Housing may decrease (if downsizing)
- Travel may spike early and taper later
- Healthcare will rise

Now tally your guaranteed income sources:

- Social Security (at what age?)
- Pension (lump sum or annuity?)
- Rental income or annuities

Then determine your "gap"—what you need to generate from your investments.

## The Income Bucket Strategy

Think of your retirement money in **buckets**:

### *Bucket 1: Cash and Short-Term Needs (1-2 years)*

- Emergency fund
- High-yield savings
- Short-term bond funds
- Bank CDs

This is your paycheck replacement. It should be safe, liquid, and boring.

### *Bucket 2: Intermediate Term (3-7 years)*

- Conservative balanced funds
- Dividend-paying stocks
- Short- to intermediate-term bonds

This bucket replenishes the first one over time. It helps you weather market storms without panic.

### *Bucket 3: Long-Term Growth (8+ years)*

- Stock index funds
- International funds
- REITs or alternatives (if appropriate)

This bucket still works hard while you sleep. It gives your money a chance to grow for the long haul.

Withdraw from Bucket 1. Refill it from Bucket 2. Rebalance annually or during strong markets.

## Required Minimum Distributions (RMDs)

At age 73 (as of current IRS rules), you must start taking withdrawals from traditional IRAs and 401(k)s—whether you need the money or not.

- The amount is based on your account balance and life expectancy
- Failing to take RMDs triggers steep penalties (up to 25%)

Roth IRAs don't have RMDs during your lifetime. Roth 401(k)s now follow similar rules.

**Strategy Tip:** Start planning RMD withdrawals well before 73. Consider "Roth conversions" in low-tax years to reduce future RMD burdens.

## The Withdrawal Rate Question

How much can you safely withdraw?

The old "4% Rule" suggests taking 4% of your portfolio annually, adjusted for inflation. It's a starting point—but not a law of physics.

Factors to consider:

- Your portfolio size
- Age and life expectancy
- Market conditions
- Flexibility in your spending

Some retirees use a **guardrail approach**:

- Withdraw more in good years
- Pull back slightly in bad years
- Reassess annually with a professional

## Tax-Smart Withdrawal Strategies

You don't just want income—you want efficient income. That means thinking about **which accounts to tap and when.**

**Typical Withdrawal Order:**

1. Taxable brokerage accounts (capital gains)
2. Tax-deferred accounts (IRA, 401k)
3. Roth accounts (last to preserve tax-free growth)

**But the best plan depends on:**

- Your marginal tax bracket
- Future RMD size
- Medicare surtax thresholds
- State taxes

**Example:** If you retire at 60 with no income, you might:

- Delay Social Security until 67–70
- Use taxable accounts to cover expenses
- Do partial Roth conversions annually to fill lower tax brackets

## Turning Assets into Paychecks

Consider building "income floors" with these tools:

### *1. Bond Ladders*

- Create a stream of bond maturities that align with annual income needs
- Can include municipal bonds (tax-free)

### *2. Dividend Portfolios*

- Own stocks that pay reliable dividends
- Helps generate income without selling shares

### *3. Systematic Withdrawals*

- Set up monthly withdrawals from your investment account
- Easy, flexible, and predictable

### *4. Immediate Annuities*

- Turn a lump sum into a guaranteed lifetime income
- Less flexible, but removes longevity risk

### *5. Managed Income Portfolios*

- Work with an advisor to customize an income-focused strategy using ETFs, mutual funds, and cash

## Pitfalls to Avoid

### *- Overconcentration in Company Stock*

Don't retire with 60% of your portfolio in your airline's stock. Diversify.

### *- Ignoring Inflation*

Plan for a 2–3% rise in expenses each year—even when markets are flat.

### - *Forgetting About Taxes*

Your 401(k) is pre-tax. That $2 million isn't all spendable.

### - *Spending Too Aggressively*

In early retirement, lifestyle inflation is tempting. Pace yourself.

### - *Failing to Rebalance*

Neglecting your portfolio can expose you to unnecessary risk.

## Life After the Cockpit: More Than Just Income

Your income plan should support your **real life**:

- Do you want to travel more in your 60s?
- Support grandkids through college?
- Leave a legacy?
- Start a hobby business?

Each vision changes the math. Don't let default rules dictate your life. Build it backward—from your dream lifestyle.

## Action Steps to Get Ready

1. Build a year-by-year cash flow projection from age 60–90
2. List all income sources and gaps
3. Organize accounts by tax type (pre-tax, Roth, taxable)
4. Start planning RMD strategy and Roth conversions
5. Choose an income strategy: buckets, guardrails, annuities, or blended
6. Meet with a fiduciary financial advisor to stress test your plan

## Final Call to Act

Make one financial move before you go wheels-up tomorrow:

- Recheck your 401(k) allocations
- Open a Roth IRA
- Run a retirement income calculator
- Schedule that meeting with a financial planner

Just one move. Then do another next week.

The only thing worse than flying blind—is flying into retirement without a plan to land.

## Final Note

You didn't earn your wings just to coast into retirement. You earned the right to live it on your terms—with dignity, clarity, and full control of your financial flight plan.

This isn't about guessing. It's about engineering your freedom.

Fly smart.

Land well.

Sleep soundly.

# Chapter 45: What Happens After the Wings Come Off – Identity and Purpose

You've spent your life navigating the skies, answering callsigns, and trusting checklists. You've woken up in strange cities, flown thousands of souls safely across time zones, and made judgment calls with seconds to spare. But one day, your headset will come off for the last time. No more flight plans. No more jumpseat. No more uniform.

And that's when the real turbulence can hit.

This chapter isn't about Roth IRAs or retirement calculators. It's about something deeper: What happens when flying—the thing you've centered your life around—is no longer on the table?

It's about identity. Purpose. Belonging. Confidence. And how to land that next chapter of your life with grace, strength, and a fresh mission.

## The Emotional Descent: Losing More Than a Job

Pilots are not just employees. You're aviators. You're part of a legacy, a lifestyle, and a language that most people will never fully understand. When that ends—abruptly, at age 65 or sooner—the emotional vacuum can be disorienting.

**Common Emotional Challenges:**

- Loss of structure and routine
- Isolation after leaving a tight-knit crew

- Feeling like your best years are behind you
- Doubt about your value now that you're not flying
- Boredom and lack of direction

If this hits close to home, you're not alone. Retirement can feel like being benched when you still want to play. But here's the truth:

**You're not done. You're just starting a new mission.**

## Deconstructing the Pilot Identity

Let's break down why retirement hits so hard.

Flying is:

- A lifestyle
- A community
- A constant challenge and test of skill
- A source of pride and status
- A rhythm and routine

When that disappears, it can feel like someone turned off the engine without warning. That's why many pilots struggle in early retirement—not because of money, but because of meaning.

**The Mindset Shift:**

You are not just a pilot. You are a person who became a pilot. The same traits that made you great in the cockpit—discipline, communication, technical ability, calm under pressure—are transferable.

You can fly a different kind of mission now.

## Finding Your New Flight Plan: Redefining Purpose

The good news? Pilots are incredibly capable people. You've had to adapt, improvise, and stay calm under pressure. Retirement is just another transition.

**Start Here: Ask Yourself These Questions**

- What gives me joy outside of flying?
- What problem do I still want to help solve?
- Who can benefit from my wisdom and experience?
- How do I want to be remembered?
- What part of my former life do I want to keep alive?

You might:

- Mentor new pilots or aviation students
- Serve on the board of an aviation nonprofit
- Become a financial coach for young professionals
- Volunteer in disaster relief or search and rescue
- Write, teach, or speak about aviation safety
- Dive into a completely unrelated field you've always loved

You don't need a new uniform. Just a new direction.

## The Reality of Time Abundance

During your career, your schedule wasn't your own. Retirement flips that. Suddenly, you'll have time. A lot of it.

**Without a plan, time can become a trap.**

- Days blend together
- Motivation wanes
- You start to feel invisible

**With a plan, time becomes a gift.**

- You can master new skills
- You can deepen relationships

- You can travel by choice, not duty
- You can give back

## Practical Anchors for Your Next Chapter

**1. Create a Weekly Flight Plan (a.k.a. Routine)**
Include:

- Physical movement
- Social time
- Learning something new
- Reflection/journaling
- Volunteer or community engagement

**2. Build a Retirement Crew**

- Stay in touch with former colleagues
- Join pilot retiree groups
- Seek new friends through hobbies and interests

**3. Explore Encore Careers**

- Consultant
- Instructor
- Entrepreneur
- Advocate
- Volunteer leader

**4. Keep Your Mind Sharp**

- Learn new tech
- Take classes
- Teach others

- Stay current on aviation trends even if you're no longer flying

## The Financial Tie-In

This is a financial book—but remember: money is only powerful if it supports the life you want.

Create a purpose-driven spending plan. Ask:

- What experiences do I want to invest in?
- What causes do I care about supporting?
- What relationships do I want to deepen with generosity?

Your nest egg is your fuel tank. Don't just preserve it. Use it wisely to chart meaningful flight paths.

## Common Pitfalls in Post-Retirement Identity

**1. Trying to Relive the Past**

Your best days are not behind you. They're just different now. Don't cling to what was. Honor it, then move forward.

**2. Refusing to Explore**

Retirement is the perfect time to experiment. Try things. Fail at things. Rediscover the thrill of learning.

**3. Letting Isolation Win**

Loneliness is a silent killer in retirement. Stay connected. Invest in friendships. Be part of something.

**4. Overspending Out of Boredom**

Lifestyle inflation often fills an emotional void. Fill the void with purpose instead.

## Your Legacy Flight Plan

In aviation, you leave behind your flight logs, your stories, and your reputation. In life, legacy is broader.

Legacy means:

- The wisdom you share
- The love you give
- The people you lift up
- The example you set

Ask yourself:

- What do I want my grandkids to say about me?
- What kind of elder do I want to become?
- How can I serve even when I'm no longer in command?

## Final Words from the Jumpseat

You didn't become a pilot by accident. You trained. You sacrificed. You studied. You showed up.

That mindset doesn't disappear. It evolves.

You may no longer wear the wings—but everything they stood for still lives inside you:

- Responsibility
- Honor
- Precision
- Calm
- Leadership
- Courage

Bring those traits into this new chapter. Carry them forward into your next mission. And remember:

**You are not retiring. You are redirecting.**

## Call to Act

Make one move today to define your next chapter. Journal. Call someone. Research an opportunity. Book a lunch with someone a few years ahead of you in retirement.

Then do another next week.

The sky may no longer be your office.

But purpose is still your runway.

And your next takeoff is waiting.

# Chapter 46: Teaching Your Kids (or Grandkids) Financial Literacy

You've flown thousands of miles, crossed time zones, braved turbulence, and navigated storms. You've spent your life learning the discipline, focus, and planning required to keep an aircraft and its passengers safe. Now it's time to transfer those same principles to the next generation—not in the cockpit, but in the bank account.

This chapter isn't about creating financial prodigies. It's about planting seeds. It's about using your wisdom to help your children and grandchildren develop the mindset, habits, and skills to handle money with confidence, respect, and purpose. This is your opportunity to pass the baton.

Let's teach them how to fly their own financial planes.

## Why It Matters More Than Ever

The world your kids or grandkids are growing up in is very different from the one you entered as a young adult.

They face:

- Skyrocketing student loan debt
- Instant gratification driven by social media
- Peer pressure to "flex" wealth they don't actually have
- Digital banking and crypto temptations

- A lack of mandatory financial education in schools

You can't control the turbulence. But you *can* teach them how to fly through it.

## Age-Appropriate Money Conversations

### *Ages 3–7: Introducing the Basics*

Keep it simple. This age is about money awareness.
**Teach:**

- Money is earned by working
- You trade money for things you want
- Saving means you don't spend all at once

**How:**

- Use a clear jar for savings
- Role-play "store" with play money
- Let them help you count coins or bills

### *Ages 8–12: Building Habits*

They're old enough to grasp bigger ideas now.
**Teach:**

- The value of saving vs. spending
- Wants vs. needs
- Earning through chores or small jobs

**How:**

- Set up three jars: Spend, Save, Give
- Pay them for completing responsibilities—not just existing
- Let them save for something they want

### *Ages 13–18: Real-World Practice*

Now it's time to let them take the controls—with supervision.

**Teach:**

- Budgeting basics
- Delayed gratification
- How credit works (and why it matters)
- Avoiding financial peer pressure

**How:**

- Open a student checking/savings account
- Co-create a basic budget for their allowance or part-time job
- Introduce debit cards and online banking tools
- Let them experience mistakes (with safety nets)

### *College and Beyond: Launching Financially*

If they're college-bound, financially independent, or early in their careers, the training wheels need to come off—but your guidance stays.

**Teach:**

- Credit score maintenance
- How to use credit cards responsibly
- Student loans: what repayment will actually look like
- Compound interest and investing basics
- Creating an emergency fund

**How:**

- Help them review their financial aid or loan terms
- Talk about the power of a Roth IRA early
- Use your own financial wins (and mistakes) as teaching moments

## Core Money Lessons to Instill (At Any Age)

1. **Money is a tool, not a trophy.**
2. **If you can't afford it in cash, you probably can't afford it at all.**
3. **Delayed gratification is the secret sauce of wealth.**
4. **Budgeting = Freedom.**
5. **Compound interest works best the earlier you start.**
6. **Saving is paying your future self.**
7. **Giving makes you rich in ways money never can.**
8. **Income doesn't equal wealth.**
9. **Everyone makes money mistakes—learn and keep going.**
10. **The more you understand your values, the better your financial decisions will be.**

## Make It a Conversation, Not a Lecture

Pilots are used to giving briefings. But teaching your kids financial literacy isn't about a single talk—it's about hundreds of small, honest conversations.

**Do:**

- Share your financial stories—the good, the bad, and the recoveries
- Ask them what they think money is for
- Involve them in real decisions (like vacation budgeting)

**Don't:**

- Shame their mistakes

- Ignore teachable moments (even if it's awkward)
- Assume school will teach them enough

## Teaching Through Your Example

Kids watch your actions far more than they listen to your words. If they see you:

- Saving consistently
- Avoiding lifestyle inflation
- Talking openly about money
- Giving generously

They're more likely to adopt those behaviors themselves.

**Want them to budget? Show them your budget.**

**Want them to invest early? Let them sit in on your investment meeting.**

**Want them to be generous? Let them help pick the charity.**

## Legacy Conversations

Eventually, the conversation shifts from education to preparation. If you've built wealth, you need to prepare them emotionally and practically.

**Talk About:**

- Your values around money
- What financial independence means to you
- What you hope they do (and don't do) with future inheritance
- Whether you'll help with home down payments, education, etc.

**Prepare Them For:**

- Being good stewards of wealth

- Making financial decisions with long-term thinking
- Being humble about money—not flaunting it

## Use the Cockpit as a Classroom

Flying can be lonely. But it can also be legacy-building.

Leave notes. Share voice memos. Create a family budget debrief at the kitchen table. Take your kids on a "finance flight" where you show them how you track your net worth, update your goals, or pay bills.

If you're a grandparent, schedule monthly calls with your grandkids where you answer their money questions—or ask them to tell you how they're saving. Make it fun. Make it consistent.

## Final Approach Checklist

- Start early, but it's never too late.
- Talk about money with love, not fear.
- Lead by example.
- Celebrate their progress.
- Keep showing up.

## Call to Act:

Make one move today. Set up a savings jar. Start a Roth IRA for your teen. Write your financial story to share with your kids. The best time to teach them was yesterday. The second-best time is right now.

## Final Note:

This chapter isn't just about helping your kids avoid debt or save for a car. It's about legacy. It's about confidence. It's about giving them wings that never expire.

They may not become pilots. But they can still fly financially—because of you.

Your time in the sky changed your life.

Your guidance on the ground will change theirs.

# Chapter 47: Planning Your Legacy – Philanthropy, Endowments, and Heirs

You've spent a lifetime navigating the skies, calculating every move, adjusting for turbulence, and following your flight plan. Now, it's time to think about your legacy—not just what you leave behind, but how it continues to fly without you. This chapter isn't just about writing a will. It's about purpose, impact, and clarity. It's about taking control of what your wealth will do when you're no longer in the cockpit.

We'll explore the mindset, mechanics, and meaning behind leaving a legacy. From charitable giving and endowments to preparing heirs for what they'll inherit, this is your financial debriefing for the next generation.

## Why Legacy Matters to Pilots

Pilots are trained to think beyond themselves—about the crew, passengers, and mission. Financial legacy is no different. It's the final destination in your financial flight plan, and it needs just as much intention and preparation.

Legacy gives your money a mission. It turns a career of earning and saving into something lasting. And it ensures your values don't retire when you do.

## Step One: Define What Legacy Means to You

Before we talk tactics, let's talk about purpose. What kind of legacy do you want to leave?

- Do you want to support your children or grandchildren financially?
- Do you want to endow a scholarship for aspiring pilots?
- Do you want to fund aviation safety initiatives or nonprofits?
- Do you want to ensure your spouse is protected, no matter what?

Legacy isn't one-size-fits-all. Start by writing down your values. Then align those values with actions. This isn't about ego. It's about impact.

## Step Two: Understand the Tools of Legacy

There are several ways to pass on wealth. Some are simple. Some are complex. The key is knowing which fits your situation and goals.

### *1. Wills and Trusts*

A will outlines how your assets are distributed after death. A trust allows for more control, especially if you want to:

- Minimize probate
- Protect heirs from themselves (e.g., spendthrift clauses)
- Support a cause over time (charitable trust)

Action Step:

- If you don't have a will, get one.
- If you do, update it every 3–5 years or after major life events.

## *2. Beneficiary Designations*

Your retirement accounts (401(k), IRA), life insurance, and some investment accounts pass by beneficiary designation—not your will. That means whoever is listed on the form gets the money, no matter what your will says.

Action Step:

- Review all beneficiary forms annually.
- Avoid listing minor children directly.
- Consider naming a trust as beneficiary if complexity is needed.

## *3. Gifting While Alive*

You don't have to wait until you're gone to give.

- You can gift up to $17,000 per person per year (as of 2023) without triggering gift taxes.
- Gifts can reduce your taxable estate and allow you to witness your impact.

Examples:

- Pay for a grandchild's flight school
- Help adult children with a down payment
- Fund a nonprofit you believe in

## *4. Charitable Giving Tools*

If giving back is part of your legacy, structure it intentionally:

- **Donor-Advised Fund (DAF):** Give a lump sum now, distribute over time.

- **Charitable Remainder Trust:** Receive income now, donate the remainder later.
- **Qualified Charitable Distributions (QCDs):** If over 70 ½, you can give directly from an IRA.

### *5. Endowments and Scholarships*

Want to create something lasting? Endow a scholarship at your alma mater or set up a fund through a foundation.

Talk to:

- The university's development office
- A community foundation
- A financial planner with experience in philanthropic strategy

## Step Three: Prepare Your Heirs

Here's the part no one wants to talk about: what happens when your kids or grandkids get the money?

Money doesn't just transfer wealth. It transfers responsibility. If your heirs aren't prepared, your legacy may evaporate.

What to do:

- Start financial conversations early
- Share your values before you share your account balances
- Educate heirs about budgeting, investing, taxes, and charitable giving
- Involve them in your giving decisions if appropriate

## Step Four: Consider Legacy Beyond Family

Legacy isn't limited to bloodline. You can support:

- Your local flight school

- Underrepresented students pursuing aviation
- Air safety, mental health, or veterans' causes

Legacy is also mentorship, time, and testimony. Who can you help fly higher because of what you've learned?

## Step Five: Assemble the Right Team

You don't have to do this alone.

Your legacy planning team may include:

- Financial planner
- Estate attorney
- CPA
- Philanthropy consultant

They work together to ensure your documents, taxes, investments, and intentions align.

Action Step:

- Schedule a "legacy roundtable" once a year to review all parts of your plan.

## The Emotional Side of Legacy

This isn't just math. It's meaning.

Legacy planning often brings up:

- Mortality
- Family tension
- Regret or pride
- Identity shifts

Give yourself time and space to process. This is a continuation of your journey—not the end of it.

## Real-Life Flight Plans: Stories From Pilots

**Captain James, 63:** Created an aviation scholarship for first-gen students at his local university. He funds it with required minimum distributions from his IRA.

**First Officer Anita, 52:** Started a donor-advised fund with her spouse. Each year, they pick one cause to support and include their teenagers in the decision.

**Retired Cargo Pilot Marcus:** Set up a trust to leave 40% to family and 60% to causes he loved—including mental health programs for veterans.

## Final Descent: Your Legacy Checklist

- Write or update your will
- Review and update all beneficiary designations
- Consider trusts for complex goals
- Explore charitable tools (DAFs, CRTs, QCDs)
- Talk with your heirs about values, money, and legacy
- Research scholarships or endowments
- Build your professional team

## Call to Act:

Make one legacy-related move before your next trip. Just one. Schedule a meeting, update a form, write a letter to your kids. Then do one more next month. Your legacy deserves altitude, clarity, and confidence.

## Final Note:

You didn't fly this far to leave it all on the runway.

You built a life of purpose. Now make sure your wealth keeps flying with purpose, too.

Legacy isn't about being remembered. It's about making a difference long after the cockpit door closes.

Fly well. Finish well. Leave a trail that others can follow.

# Chapter 48: Lifestyle Design – Living Well Without Overspending

You've earned your wings. You've flown through storms, clocked thousands of hours, managed schedules across time zones, and balanced a career that demands both precision and endurance. But here's the question most pilots never get trained to answer:

What does "living well" actually look like—and how do you do it without constantly overspending?

This chapter is about building a lifestyle that reflects your values, brings you joy, and honors your work—without letting lifestyle creep sabotage your financial altitude. Whether you're a 28-year-old first officer or a 58-year-old senior captain, lifestyle design is about one thing:

**Intentional living with financial clarity.**

## The Myth of "I Deserve It"

You've probably heard it. You might have said it yourself.

"I deserve the car."

"I deserve the watch."

"I work hard, I deserve this vacation."

Of course you deserve nice things. You've sacrificed time with family, missed holidays, battled fatigue, and carried the responsibility of hundreds of lives at 38,000 feet. But here's the truth:

You don't need to *prove* your hard work with purchases.

A meaningful, joyful life is not the same thing as an expensive one.

Lifestyle design starts with separating identity from spending—because if your identity is tied to what you can buy, then you'll always need to buy more to feel worthy.

## Defining "Living Well" On Your Terms

Let's get clear: what does "living well" mean to you?

Is it:

- A house that feels calm, not cluttered?
- Travel that feels enriching, not draining?
- A schedule with white space for hobbies and rest?
- A budget that lets you be generous—without guilt?
- A financial foundation that makes work optional sooner?

You get to define the answers.

**The goal is not to spend less. It's to spend better.**

## The Silent Saboteur: Lifestyle Inflation

Lifestyle inflation is what happens when your expenses rise to match your income—or exceed it. The moment your salary increases, you:

- Upgrade your car
- Take longer vacations
- Move into a bigger home
- Add premium cable, luxury services, tech toys

Before you know it, you're making $200K and still living paycheck to paycheck.

Why?

Because your lifestyle took every raise and bonus hostage.

**Solution:**

- Keep a percentage-based savings strategy (e.g., save 50% of all raises)
- Delay major upgrades by 6 months after promotions or bonuses
- Celebrate milestones with experiences or time, not just spending

## Budgeting That Fits Your Schedule

Pilots don't have 9-to-5 schedules. So traditional monthly budgets don't always work. Try this instead:

- **Base Budget on Pay Periods:** Align your budget with your bid cycles or paychecks.
- **Use the 3-Account System:**
- Fixed expenses account
- Variable spending account
- Automated savings/investing account
- **Use Apps That Work for Mobile Lifestyles:** Tools like YNAB, Monarch, or Rocket Money
- **Build a Travel Buffer:** Account for airport meals, Uber rides, and hotel incidentals without guilt—just plan for them

## Smart Spending While Traveling

It's easy to overspend when you're constantly on the go. Here are a few high-impact rules:

- **Set a Per-Diem Limit:** Even if your airline reimburses, cap your daily personal spending
- **Travel-Friendly Rewards Cards:** Use cards with no foreign transaction fees, high travel points, and lounge access
- **Meal Planning:** Keep healthy, packable snacks. Avoid relying only on airport restaurants.

- **Entertainment Budget:** Download audiobooks or shows for layovers—avoid impulse airport purchases

## The "Enough" Equation

Here's a radical idea:

What if you already have enough?

Enough income.

Enough gadgets.

Enough square footage.

Lifestyle design means *consciously capping* your consumption so you can expand your time, energy, and wealth.

Ask yourself:

- Would more really make me happier?
- Would I trade peace of mind for another upgrade?
- If I had less, what would I gain?

## Building a Budget That Honors Joy

Don't build a bare-bones budget. Build a *value-aligned* budget.

Ask:

- What do I love?
- What adds energy to my life?
- What do I want to remember 10 years from now?

Spend lavishly on those.

Then ruthlessly cut or cap everything else.

## Relatable Pilot Profiles

**Jordan, 29 – Regional First Officer**

- Lives on 65% of income
- Uses rest to pay debt and invest
- Vacations with friends using points and rewards

**Melissa & Andre, 43 – Dual-Pilot Household**

- Downsized to one car
- Created a shared "dream fund"
- Still travel first class, but only once a year—on miles

**Derrick, 61 – Retired Captain**

- Says no to new tech every year
- Focused on coaching young pilots
- "Peace over prestige" became his motto after retirement

## What to Say No To

Sometimes, living well means saying no to:

- One more credit card
- The upgraded lease
- The pressure to compete with peers
- Gifts that cost more than you can afford
- "Treating yourself" when it blows your budget

## Final Thought: Design With the End in Mind

You didn't fly all these years to retire broke or burned out.

You're building something: A life with structure, meaning, and *enough.*

When you design your lifestyle with clarity, you'll find that:

- Less clutter brings more calm
- Less spending brings more freedom
- Less pressure brings more joy

### *Call to Act:*

Make one financial move before you go wheels-up tomorrow. Just one. Trim a subscription. Increase a savings percentage. Name your "enough."

Then do another next week. The only thing worse than flying blind is staying grounded when you've got the power to soar.

### *Final Note:*

This isn't just about cutting back. It's about choosing boldly.

Choosing dignity.

Choosing freedom.

Choosing the kind of life that lets you show up—grounded, grateful, and truly wealthy.

You didn't earn your wings to feel weighed down by debt, burnout, or pressure.

Design the life you want.

Then go live it—on purpose, not autopilot.

# Chapter 49: Final Words from the Cockpit – Fly Your Financial Life With Intention

You've checked every instrument. You've flown through turbulence, weathered storms, and navigated long-haul routes. You've hit V1, rotated, climbed, cruised, descended, and landed. Now it's time for something that doesn't come with a checklist or a flight computer.

Flying your financial life with intention.

This chapter isn't about a specific financial strategy. It's not about Roth IRAs, tax loss harvesting, or estate planning. This chapter is about mindset, meaning, and mission. This is the cockpit conversation you never had in flight school. This is the one that matters most.

## You Were Never Just a Pilot

Maybe flying was your dream since you were six. Maybe it was the career that gave you purpose and identity. Maybe it was just a job that paid well and gave you structure. Whatever your relationship with the yoke and throttle, here's the truth:

You are more than your profession.

You are more than your call sign.

You are more than your wings.

Financial planning isn't just about retiring. It's about defining who you are when the headset comes off. Because money without meaning is just noise. But money with intention? That's clarity. That's freedom. That's lift.

## The New Flight Plan

In aviation, everything comes down to intent. What is your flight path? What are your fuel reserves? What are your alternates? Your financial life needs that same approach.

Here are the core components of an intentional financial life:

### *1. Purpose Over Pressure*

Most pilots live under pressure—schedule pressure, fuel pressure, financial pressure. The temptation is to react. To jump into a house because your peers did. To upgrade the car. To say yes when your gut says wait.

**Intentional living starts with slowing down.**

Take a breath. Step back. Ask:

- What kind of life do I actually want?
- What brings me fulfillment, not just status?
- Who do I want to help, teach, impact, support?

Then aim your financial resources in that direction.

### *2. Systems, Not Willpower*

You don't fly by gut. You fly by systems. Checklists. Protocol. Procedures.

Your financial life should be the same. Don't rely on memory or motivation. Rely on:

- Automated savings
- Pre-set investing schedules
- Quarterly money reviews

- Boundaries and policies for big purchases

**Systems protect you from future-you.**

### *3. Simplicity Is Safety*

The more complex your financial life gets, the easier it is to miss a warning light.

That real estate syndicate in another state? That crypto fund run by a guy from flight school? That startup you don't really understand?

These can be distractions. Or worse, financial engine failures.

Simplicity doesn't mean small. It means understandable. Predictable. Transparent.

### *4. Time as a Currency*

Pilots understand better than most: time is not renewable.

Don't build a life where you have all the money but no time.

What do you want time for?

- More with your kids before they're grown
- More with your spouse before the years slip away
- More adventure, service, or rest

Use money to buy back time. Not just things.

### *5. Alignment > Optimization*

Financial advice often obsesses over optimization:

- Max the tax deferral
- Harvest the loss
- Time the market

But optimization without alignment is just tinkering.

Ask instead:

- Does this financial choice align with my values?
- Will this decision get me closer to peace, purpose, and people I love?

If it does, it's probably a smart move. Even if it's not "optimal."

## Lessons From the Left Seat

Every senior captain has stories. Here are a few lessons passed down from pilots who flew before you:

- **Never upgrade your lifestyle faster than you upgrade your plan.** A new bid doesn't mean a new car.
- **Don't confuse being busy with being effective.** Make your money work, even when you're resting.
- **Retirement isn't the goal. Meaning is.** Don't retire from something. Retire *to* something.
- **Start the conversation early.** With your spouse. With your kids. With your advisor. Financial silence breeds stress.
- **Play the long game.** Legacy, not leverage. Wealth, not flash. Security, not speed.

## What Intention Looks Like in Practice

Let's get real. Here's what flying with intention might look like:

- You skip the second home and fund your niece's college tuition instead.
- You downsize your house and use the freed-up equity to travel with your spouse.
- You set up a donor-advised fund and support scholarships for young pilots.

- You switch from accumulation to contribution: mentoring, teaching, volunteering.
- You schedule regular, peaceful money meetings instead of reactionary panic reviews.

None of this is about deprivation. It's about **intention.**

## Your Legacy Begins Now

Most people think legacy begins after they die. Pilots know better.

Legacy begins with your choices today. With:

- The example you set
- The boundaries you enforce
- The generosity you show
- The wisdom you pass on

What do you want to be remembered for? What lessons do you want to echo long after your last flight?

Write that story now. In your words. In your money. In your life.

## Final Call to Action

You don't need to overhaul everything overnight. But you do need to start.

- Pick one financial ritual to build (weekly review, monthly check-in)
- Write down your top three values, and compare them to last month's spending
- Have a money conversation you've been avoiding
- Set one "legacy goal" for the year
- Choose peace over pressure

Then keep flying. With purpose. With clarity. With swagger.

## Final Note

You didn't spend your career defying gravity to be grounded by financial confusion.

You learned how to command a 200,000-pound jet through the sky. You can absolutely learn how to command your money.

And not just for you. For your family. Your community. Your legacy.

This isn't about perfection. It's about direction.

So fly intentionally. Live wisely. And never forget: financial literacy is not about restriction. It's about freedom.

That's your final clearance. Wheels up.

Let's fly.

# Disclaimer

**Important Notice About This Book**

This book, *Financial Literacy For Pilots,* was written with the intention to educate, empower, and encourage pilots—from student aviators and regional first officers to senior captains and commercial flight veterans—to take control of their financial lives with clarity and confidence. The insights shared throughout these pages reflect the author's personal experience, professional background, and decades spent advising high-performing professionals in aviation, retirement planning, and wealth education.

That said, it is important to understand the following:

## *Educational Purpose Only*

The content in this book is provided for general educational purposes. Its goal is to help pilots understand core financial principles, recognize industry-specific financial pitfalls, and begin to design a flight plan for long-term financial health—whether you're managing per diem and crash-pad expenses in your 20s or evaluating a pension lump sum at 64.

However, this book does **not** provide personal advice. It is **not** tailored to your unique circumstances. Your income, taxes, career stage, family situation, risk tolerance, and financial goals all matter—and this book cannot account for those differences.

What works for one pilot may be completely inappropriate—or even risky—for another.

Before making any significant financial decisions—especially those related to investments, retirement accounts, legal structures, or insurance—it is strongly advised that you consult a licensed financial advisor, CPA, attorney, or insurance professional who understands your full situation.

### *No Legal Advice*

This book does **not** provide legal advice and should not be used as a substitute for professional counsel. Whether you are:

- Creating a will or trust
- Starting a side business or aviation-related LLC
- Reviewing your contract or negotiating compensation
- Planning your estate or power of attorney documents

...you should speak with a qualified attorney in your state.

Every legal situation carries nuances. You deserve insight that fits your life—not a one-size-fits-all checklist.

### *No Investment or Financial Advice*

While this book explores investing, retirement planning, budgeting, 401(k)s, and other money management strategies, it does so from a general and educational perspective. It is **not** personalized investment advice. It does **not** recommend specific securities, asset allocations, or financial products.

You should never act on investment decisions based solely on the content of this book. Always speak with a Certified Financial Planner™, licensed fiduciary, or investment advisor who can help you align your portfolio with your goals, timeline, and tax profile.

Your financial plan deserves the same precision and attention to detail as a flight plan. Don't improvise it.

### *No Tax or Accounting Advice*

This book is not written by a CPA or tax attorney. It does not provide tax or accounting advice.

While we reference common pilot-relevant topics such as:

- Taxable vs. tax-deferred accounts
- Backdoor Roth IRAs
- HSA and FSA strategies
- Multi-state income from different domiciles or contract work

…this information is educational only. Tax law changes frequently, and your personal filing status, income, state of residence, and benefits package can affect your decisions.

Consult a licensed tax professional or enrolled agent before filing or restructuring anything with tax consequences.

### *No Guarantees*

There are no guarantees in aviation—and there are no guarantees in personal finance.

Reading this book will not guarantee wealth, retirement readiness, or peace of mind. Financial outcomes depend on your behavior, habits, decisions, timing, income, expenses, and sometimes even sheer luck.

This book offers mindset, structure, and frameworks—but not a magic formula. Use it as a co-pilot. Not an autopilot.

### *Limitation of Liability*

By reading this book, you agree that the author, Pat Brown, MBA, and affiliated platforms such as *FinancialLiteracyForPilots.com*, *FinancialLiteracyForNIL.com*, and other associated educational brands, are not liable for any financial, legal, tax, or investment actions you take based on the content within.

We are not responsible for losses, penalties, missed opportunities, or financial outcomes resulting from your interpretation or application of this material.

## *A Reminder to Build Your Financial Team*

One of the key messages in this book is this:

**You don't have to fly solo.**

If you don't yet have a trusted financial advisor, estate planning attorney, insurance specialist, or CPA—start building your crew. Interview professionals. Ask questions. Get referrals. Look for those who serve with integrity and act in your best interest.

Pilots are known for their skill, calm under pressure, and ability to manage complexity. You deserve financial advice that reflects that same level of precision and trust.

Let this book be a foundation for asking better questions, having smarter conversations, and acting with intention—not reaction.

Because when you understand the financial controls in front of you, you stop flying blind. And when you stop flying blind, you give yourself the best possible approach—not just for retirement, but for your entire financial runway.

So read on, take notes, reflect deeply, and fly your financial life with confidence. You've earned it.

# A Month-by-Month Guide to Staying Ahead Financially

This calendar isn't just about taxes—it's about staying ahead of the turbulence. Whether you're a first-year regional pilot still adjusting to per diem income, a mid-career airline officer juggling 401(k) contributions and college savings, or a senior captain preparing for that final approach at age 65, knowing when to act financially can make all the difference.

Pilots live and breathe by checklists and flight plans—why should your money be any different?

Here's your month-by-month guide to help keep your financial systems calibrated and your flight path to wealth smooth all year long.

## *January – Start the Year Like a Pre-Flight Walkaround*

- **New Tax Year Begins** – Time to start fresh. New budget. New goals.
- Set up or refresh your household budget, tracking fixed costs (mortgage, insurance), variable costs (travel, dining), and savings goals (401(k), Roth IRA, HSA).
- Review W-4 withholding if your life has changed (new base, marriage, kids, side income).
- **Rule of Thumb**: Save 25%–30% of any 1099/self-employed income for taxes.
- **Jan 15** – 4th Quarter Estimated Tax Payment Due (if you flew contract or fractional work in Q4)
- **Jan 31** – Deadline for Receiving Tax Docs (W-2, 1099, 1098, investment statements)

- **Pro Tip**: Start a digital folder named "2024 Taxes – Pilot" and upload documents as they arrive.

*February – Organize and Prepare*

- Start gathering your documents, especially if you had non-W-2 income (charter, sim training, part-time instructing).
- Know Your Forms:
- **Schedule C** – Contract/side flying income
- **Schedule E** – Rental property income
- **Schedule SE** – Self-employment tax
- Finalize bookkeeping for your aviation side hustle, if applicable.

*March – Business Owner Deadline Zone*

- **March 15** – Tax filing deadline for S-Corps and partnerships.
- If you run a flight school, LLC for public speaking, or rent out a hangar under a business entity—this one's for you.
- **Form to Know**: IRS Form 1120-S

*April – Final Countdown to File*

- **April 15** – Federal Tax Day
- File your taxes or request an extension using Form 4868.
- Make your 1st quarter estimated tax payment if needed.
- Last day to contribute to:
- **Traditional IRA / Roth IRA (for previous year)**
- **Health Savings Account (HSA)** for prior-year tax benefit
- **Tip**: Even if you can't pay your tax bill yet—**file**. The penalty for not filing is worse than the penalty for not paying.

### *May – Mid-Year Money Checkup*

- Review your spending YTD. Are you overspending on lifestyle creep?
- Check progress toward:
- Roth IRA maxing
- 401(k) contributions
- HSA savings (if eligible)
- Set or reset financial goals for the remainder of the year.
- Schedule a meeting with your advisor or sit down for a solo cockpit-style money check-in.

### *June – Second Quarter & Summer Flying Season*

- **June 15** – Estimated Tax Payment Due
- Required if you've earned 1099 or consulting income and didn't withhold properly.
- Review how much you're withholding/saving for taxes.
- Plan ahead for summer travel expenses without sabotaging savings goals.

### *July – Reset and Rebalance*

- Mid-year review of your overall financial plan:
- Are your savings automated?
- Is your investment allocation aligned with your risk tolerance?
- Do you need to rebalance your 401(k), IRA, or brokerage account?
- Check insurance coverage:
- Long-term disability
- Loss of license insurance
- Life insurance (term vs. whole)
- Umbrella liability

### *August – Credit, Debt, and Loans*

- Pull your **free credit report** from AnnualCreditReport.com
- Review mortgage, real estate holdings, or investment property performance
- Reassess student loan or refinancing options (especially if retiring soon or paying off aggressively)
- Look into travel reward cards or professional expense tracking apps

### *September – Strategic Year-End Planning Begins*

- **September 15** – 3rd Quarter Estimated Tax Payment Due
- Look at:
- Year-to-date income from flying, bonuses, and side gigs
- Deductions available (business, education, charity)
- Roth conversions, especially in low-income years
- Adjust income, contributions, or distributions if necessary

### *October – File That Extension*

- **October 1** – FAFSA Opens (if helping your kids/grandkids through college)
- **October 15** – Final Tax Return Filing Date (if you filed an extension)
- Review health coverage and plan for **Open Enrollment**
- Compare plans, HSAs, FSAs, and retirement benefits

### *November – Year-End Tax Strategy Session*

- Meet with your advisor or CPA to cover:
- Required Minimum Distributions (RMDs) if 73+
- Roth conversions
- Real estate depreciation
- Charitable giving and donor-advised funds

- Tax-loss harvesting for brokerage accounts
- Check Section 179 deductions if you've made business equipment or vehicle purchases

### *December – Land the Plane Smoothly*

- **December 31** – Deadline for many tax-smart moves
- Max contributions to Solo 401(k), SEP IRA, or employer plans
- Use FSA funds before they expire
- Make final charitable donations for the year
- Run your net worth snapshot and track year-over-year progress
- Set 1–3 financial goals for the coming year

## Bonus: Best Practices for Pilots

- **Always Save 25%–30% of 1099/Contract Income for Taxes**
- **Separate Business and Personal Accounts**
- **Track Deductions**: Uniforms, training, hotels, crash pads, mileage, licenses
- **Use Tools**: MileIQ, Keeper Tax, QuickBooks Self-Employed, or even a Google Sheet
- **Review Benefits Annually**: Max your 401(k), HSA, FSA, and check pension vesting
- **Build Your Flight Crew**: Advisor, CPA, insurance broker, estate attorney
- **Do a Sunday Money Preflight Check**: 15 minutes to check cash flow, accounts, and goals

You wouldn't enter a holding pattern without a fuel check, and you shouldn't navigate your financial year without a strategy. Let this calendar serve as your co-pilot—reminding you to stay ahead, stay organized, and stay intentional.

# Financial Terms Every Pilot Should Know

**Asset** – Anything you own that holds value, such as cash, stocks, aircraft, property, or investments. Assets are your fuel tanks—they power your financial journey.

**Liability** – Money you owe to others, including loans, mortgages, and credit card debt. Think of liabilities as drag on your aircraft—manageable, but they'll slow you down if left unchecked.

**Net Worth** – The difference between what you own (assets) and what you owe (liabilities). This is your personal altitude indicator—it tells you how high you're flying financially.

**Budget** – A monthly or weekly plan for how you spend, save, and invest. This is your flight plan for money—without it, you're flying blind.

**Emergency Fund** – Savings set aside specifically for financial turbulence—such as job loss, medical expenses, or aircraft grounding. Aim for at least 3–6 months of expenses.

**Compound Interest** – Interest that earns interest over time. It's the autopilot of wealth building—slow and steady growth that gains momentum.

**Diversification** – The practice of spreading investments across different asset classes (stocks, bonds, real estate) to reduce risk. Think of it as flying with multiple navigation systems in case one fails.

**Roth IRA** – A retirement account funded with after-tax dollars. Withdrawals in retirement are tax-free, making it ideal for younger pilots expecting higher tax brackets later.

**Brokerage Account** – A flexible investment account where you can buy and sell stocks, ETFs, bonds, and other securities. Great for mid- to long-term wealth growth.

**ETF (Exchange-Traded Fund)** – A bundle of investments that trades like a stock, offering diversification and low fees. Like owning a fleet instead of a single plane.

**Inflation** – The general rise in prices over time, which reduces the purchasing power of your money. Your $1 today may only buy $0.90 worth in a few years.

**Credit Score** – A number that measures how responsible you are with credit. It affects your ability to borrow money and the interest rates you're offered.

**Interest Rate** – The cost of borrowing or the earnings on your savings/investments, expressed as a percentage.

**Risk Tolerance** – Your emotional and financial ability to endure market fluctuations. Important when building a portfolio.

**Stock** – A share in the ownership of a company. Stockholders benefit from appreciation and sometimes dividends.

**Bond** – A fixed income investment where you lend money to a company or government in exchange for regular interest payments and eventual repayment.

**Capital Gain** – The profit from selling an asset for more than you paid. Long-term gains (held over a year) are taxed more favorably than short-term.

**Liability Insurance** – Protects you if you're legally responsible for damages to another person or their property.

**Term Life Insurance** – Insurance that covers you for a set period (like 20 or 30 years). Ideal for income protection while you have dependents.

**Financial Literacy** – The ability to understand and effectively use financial tools and knowledge to make sound decisions.

## Accounting Terms for Pilots and Their Side Ventures

**Income** – Any money earned through salary, flight hours, consulting, speaking, rental properties, or investments.

**Expenses** – All costs related to your daily living or side businesses: rent, mortgage, fuel, lodging, etc.

**Profit** – What's left after subtracting expenses from income. Profit is the goal of every flight plan.

**Loss** – When your expenses are greater than your income. Common in early business ventures, but something to monitor closely.

**Cash Flow** – The movement of money in and out of your accounts. Positive cash flow keeps your financial engines running.

**Invoice** – A document requesting payment for services rendered—common for charter flights, training, or freelance aviation work.

**Receipts** – Records of purchases. Keep these organized for tax deductions and audit defense.

**Write-Off** – Expenses you can subtract from your taxable income, such as travel costs or training material if you're self-employed.

**Deduction** – A reduction in taxable income based on qualifying expenses, including retirement contributions and mortgage interest.

**Depreciation** – A non-cash expense that represents the reduction in value of an asset over time, like your aviation headset or laptop.

**Revenue** – Your total income before expenses.

**Net Income** – Your take-home after subtracting all expenses and taxes. This is the number that matters most.

**Gross Income** – All earnings before deductions or taxes.

**Audit** – An examination of your financial records, typically by the IRS, to verify accuracy and compliance.

**Chart of Accounts** – A structured list of financial categories used to organize your income and expenses.

**Bookkeeping** – Recording financial transactions. You can DIY or outsource this—just don't ignore it.

**Taxable Income** – The portion of your income that you owe taxes on after deductions and adjustments.

**Form 1099** – A tax form for non-employment income (e.g., independent contract flying).

**Form W-9** – A form you give to clients so they can legally report payments made to you.

**Schedule C** – IRS form for reporting income and expenses from sole proprietorships or side hustles.

## Questions to Ask a Financial Advisor

- Do you work with pilots or those in aviation?
- Are you a fiduciary 100% of the time?
- How do you charge (fee-only, commission, hourly)?
- Can you help me plan for irregular income or bid cycles?
- How do you handle retirement distribution strategies and tax minimization?
- Will you collaborate with my CPA and estate attorney?

## Questions to Ask a CPA

- Are you familiar with pilot pay structures and travel deductions?
- Can you help me maximize write-offs if I do contract work?
- Do you provide proactive tax planning, or just file returns?
- What software or tools do you recommend for tracking receipts and mileage?
- Do you help with multi-state income issues or aviation-specific per diem rules?

## Questions to Ask an Attorney

- Can you review employment, non-compete, or aircraft lease contracts?
- Do you offer estate planning services (will, trust, POA)?
- Can you help set up an LLC or S-Corp for aviation or speaking side gigs?
- What legal coverage do I need for mentoring, coaching, or content creation?

## Questions to Ask Business Partners

- What are your long-term goals and expectations for the project?
- What role will each of us play—and how will we make decisions?
- Are we both investing capital or just time?
- How do we split profits or losses?
- What's our exit plan if one person wants out?

## Aviation-Specific Financial Terms

**Per Diem** – Daily allowance for food and incidental expenses during travel, sometimes tax-free.

**Crash Pad** – Low-cost temporary housing used by commuting pilots. May be deductible if not near your tax home.

**Loss of License Insurance** – Replaces income if you lose your FAA medical and can't fly.

**Bid Cycle** – The monthly schedule process where pilots select their flying schedule—impacts income and quality of life.

**Reserve Duty** – Time spent on standby. Can influence monthly earnings significantly.

**Deadhead** – Non-revenue travel to position a pilot for a trip. Know whether this counts toward duty or flight time.

**Profit Sharing** – Bonus based on your airline's profitability—often deposited into a 401(k) or deferred comp plan.

**Non-Qualified Deferred Compensation (NQDC)** – Optional deferral of part of your salary to save for retirement. Carries risk if the company goes bankrupt.

**Vesting** – The process of gaining full ownership of employer contributions to retirement or stock plans.

**W-2 vs. 1099 Income** – W-2 is traditional employment with withholding. 1099 is self-employment—great flexibility but requires tax diligence.

**Hub** – Your official airline base. Not always where you live—impacts commuting, taxes, and quality of life.

**Jumpseat** – Extra cockpit or cabin seat used by commuting or off-duty crew. Travel benefit that can save thousands yearly.

**Furlough** – Temporary leave without pay—have a cash cushion ready.

**Medical Certificate** – Required to fly professionally. Losing it can be financially devastating—insure against it.

**CASS (Cockpit Access Security System)** – Program allowing jumpseat access across airlines. Saves money and makes commuting viable.

**CDOs (Continuous Duty Overnights)** – Overnight stays with early return flights. Can disrupt sleep and finances if not accounted for.

# Final Word: Use This. Don't Shelf It.

This book exists because financial education is a powerful tool—especially for pilots.

It can unlock freedom, protect your legacy, and give you the confidence to take control of your future both in and out of the cockpit. But just like in aviation—and in life—long-term success isn't about luck. It's about discipline, precision, planning, and knowing when to call for backup.

Use this book as a guide—not a rule book. Let it spark your curiosity and your next financial move. But don't let it replace the value of licensed, professional advice when it matters most.

You wouldn't fly into weather without checking your systems, reading your charts, and calling dispatch. Why would you treat your money any differently?

Be proactive. Stay informed. Ask questions before making important financial decisions. And know this: You're not alone.

## Need Help? Start Here.

Connect with a team that understands what it means to fly for a living—and how to build wealth with altitude, not attitude.

**Contact:**

**Pat Brown, MBA**

Financial literacy advocate and advisor to pilots nationwide

info@financialliteracyforpilots.com

www.financialliteracyforpilots.com

Subscribe to the newsletter for cockpit-to-retirement financial guidance, straight to your inbox—flight-tested, pilot-approved.

## Final Word

These tools weren't meant to gather dust.

They were meant to help you make confident, informed decisions from your first paycheck to your final landing.

Revisit this book. Highlight it. Dog-ear it. Share it with your fellow aviators. Use it as your preflight financial checklist.

Because the best flight plans are made on the ground.

And your financial journey deserves just as much planning as your next departure.

Your future self—the one with freedom, options, and peace of mind—will thank you.

Wheels up.

# Choosing the Right Professionals: 30 Questions Every Pilot Should Ask a Financial Advisor or CPA

You've trained for thousands of hours. You trust checklists. You rely on co-pilots, dispatch, and mechanics to keep every mission safe and smooth.

Your financial life deserves the same level of support and diligence.

Choosing the right financial professionals can make a massive difference in your trajectory. The wrong fit could cost you years of progress, hidden fees, or missed opportunities. The right team? It can save you thousands, provide clarity under pressure, and help you fly with confidence—no matter what turbulence life throws at you.

Whether you're evaluating a financial advisor, CPA, or both, these 30 questions will help you vet their credentials, philosophy, and how they fit into your flight plan.

## Questions to Ask a Financial Advisor

### General Fit and Philosophy

1. Are you a fiduciary 100% of the time—and can you put that in writing?
2. How are you compensated—fee-only, commission-based, or fee-based?
3. Do you specialize in working with pilots or other high-income professionals?
4. What licenses and certifications do you hold (CFP®, CFA, MBA, ChFC,

etc.)?

5. What is your core investment philosophy?
6. How do you approach risk management for someone in their 30s or 40s with a volatile schedule?
7. How will you personalize my financial plan based on my airline, pension, and travel lifestyle?
8. What types of clients do you typically serve—individuals, dual-income couples, entrepreneurs?
9. Do you have an asset minimum to work with you?
10. Can we work together virtually, or do you only offer in-person meetings?

**Services and Ongoing Support**

1. What services are included beyond investment management—do you advise on tax, estate, or insurance issues?
2. Will you help me evaluate my benefits package, 401(k), and deferred comp options at my airline?
3. How often will we meet to review progress and adjust the plan?
4. What financial planning software or tools do you use to track and project my finances?
5. Do you offer help with budgeting, lifestyle spending, or cash flow planning?
6. Can you help me understand my student loan repayment options or refinancing choices?
7. Do you collaborate with my CPA or estate planning attorney if I have one?
8. How do you measure success for your clients? What benchmarks do you use?
9. If I decide to end our relationship, are there termination fees or transfer costs?
10. Will I work directly with you, or will I be passed to junior staff or a call center?

## Questions to Ask a CPA or Tax Advisor

**Tax Planning and Filing**

1. Do you have experience working with pilots or professionals who have complex pay structures (W-2, 1099, per diem, bonus)?
2. Do you provide both tax preparation and year-round strategic tax planning?
3. How are your fees structured—flat rate, hourly, or retainer-based?
4. Can you help me optimize tax strategies across salary, freelance income, investments, and real estate?
5. Will you advise me on how much to save for estimated quarterly tax payments on consulting or side gigs?
6. Are you familiar with pilot-specific tax concerns like per diem deductions, multiple state filings, or foreign earned income?
7. Can you help me maximize charitable giving strategies, including donor-advised funds?
8. Do you offer audit support or representation if I'm ever contacted by the IRS?
9. Can you advise on tax-efficient withdrawal strategies in retirement (401(k), Roth, HSA, brokerage)?
10. How do you stay up to date on new tax laws that affect high-income professionals and retirees?

## A Few Reminders From the Jumpseat:

- Don't be afraid to ask these questions directly. You're hiring someone to help protect your financial life.
- A great financial advisor or CPA will welcome transparency and curiosity—they're not here to sell. They're here to serve.
- Ask for a discovery call before committing. Take notes. And remember: you're not just choosing someone for today. You're choosing a partner to help navigate the decades ahead.

## One More Thing

Every pilot knows that systems fail when assumptions go unchecked.

Don't assume that just because someone is licensed, they're the right fit.

Don't assume that just because someone sounds confident, they understand your industry.

And don't assume that "professional" always means "personalized."

**Ask. Vet. Verify.** Then decide.

This is your money. Your future. Your family's well-being.

Treat it with the same intentionality and discipline you bring to every flight.

# Pros and Cons of Working with a Financial Advisor

As a pilot, you're trained to follow checklists, interpret data, and stay composed under pressure. Your job demands precision, structure, and situational awareness—and you bring those same qualities to your personal life.

So when it comes to managing your money, the question often becomes: *Should I fly solo, or bring in a co-pilot?*

The truth? Working with a financial advisor can offer tremendous value—especially for high-income professionals like pilots who face a unique mix of volatility, career transitions, and time constraints. But just like evaluating a flight plan or upgrading to a new aircraft, it's important to weigh the pros and cons before making the commitment.

## Pros of Working with a Financial Advisor

### *1. Cross-Functional Expertise*

A qualified financial advisor brings deep knowledge across multiple areas: investing, taxes, insurance, estate planning, college savings, long-term care, and retirement distribution strategies. That's especially helpful for pilots navigating airline pensions, variable income, union contracts, loss-of-license risks, or career shifts in their 50s or 60s.

### *2. Time-Saving and Stress-Reducing*

You're already managing a demanding schedule, rotating layovers, and limited time at home. Reviewing Roth conversion strategies or mapping out estate plans isn't always a priority between flights. A good advisor helps you stay organized and focused—freeing you up to focus on family, health, and flying, while they manage the financial navigation.

### *3. Rational, Objective Guidance*

Even the most disciplined pilots are human. When the markets tank, your schedule changes, or a loved one gets sick, emotions creep in. A financial advisor is like your financial ATC—offering calm, rational input when your instincts might be fighting the data. They help you zoom out and stick to your flight path, even in turbulence.

### *4. Accountability and Follow-Through*

Just like keeping up with recurrent training, financial tasks require structure and consistency. A financial advisor doesn't just give you a plan—they help make sure it gets implemented. That includes adjusting your beneficiaries, securing umbrella insurance, rebalancing investments, funding trusts, or building your tax strategy before retirement.

### *5. Customized Planning for the Pilot Life*

Pilots don't live on 9-to-5 schedules. You deal with per diem, union pensions, airline mergers, early retirement mandates, and rotating home bases. A quality advisor builds your financial strategy around your career timeline, lifestyle goals, and long-term vision—not just a generic portfolio model.

Whether you're a 30-year-old FO climbing the seniority list or a 62-year-old captain preparing for the FAA Age 65 cutoff, the right advisor helps you optimize the journey.

## Cons of Working with a Financial Advisor

### *1. The Cost*

Most advisors charge a percentage of assets (often 0.5% to 1%), a flat annual fee, or hourly rates. For early-career pilots still building savings, the cost might feel steep. Be clear on what you're getting in return—and whether the value justifies the fee.

### *2. Not All Advisors Are Created Equal*

Some advisors are true fiduciaries—legally required to put your best interests first. Others are brokers or insurance agents who earn commissions on products they sell. It's up to you to vet them. Ask questions, understand how they're paid, and don't settle for vague answers.

### *3. You Still Need to Stay Involved*

A financial advisor can steer, but you're still the captain. You'll need to participate in major decisions—especially around retirement timing, real estate, risk tolerance, and legacy planning. Delegating is smart. Disengaging entirely is not.

### *4. Risk of Templated Advice*

If your advisor isn't asking about your seniority number, your company's pension system, your loss-of-license coverage, or your post-65 goals, they're not customizing the plan. Pilots expect detail and accuracy—and your financial plan should reflect that.

### *5. You Might Not Need One—Yet*

If you're financially literate, enjoy managing your own accounts, and have relatively simple needs (401(k), Roth IRA, low debt, no dependents), you might be fine flying solo for now. But as your career—and your finances—get more complex, professional guidance can become invaluable.

## So… Should You Hire a Financial Advisor?

Start by asking yourself a few honest questions:

- Do I have the time, tools, and discipline to manage my money effectively—year after year?
- Am I confident in my tax, investing, and retirement strategies?
- Do I know how my airline benefits, union rules, and pension options work together?
- Do I have a system for handling loss-of-license risk, estate planning, or market downturns?
- Would having a knowledgeable, trustworthy advisor reduce stress and help me avoid expensive mistakes?

If you answered *no* to one or more of those, it might be time to bring a co-pilot onboard.

## Final Thought

The best advisors don't just tell you what to do—they help you think better. They bring clarity to the fog, structure to the chaos, and alignment to your ambitions. Most importantly, they help you fly with confidence.

You've worked hard to earn your wings. Don't fly your financial life on autopilot.

Hire with intention. Plan with discipline. Adjust your course when needed. And always know where you're headed.

Because a smooth financial landing doesn't happen by chance. It happens by design.

Made in United States
Orlando, FL
04 November 2026

90201053R00226